# SUPPLY CHAIN

# Transformation

## *Building and Executing an Intregrated Supply Chain Strategy*

## J. PAUL DITTMANN, PhD

New York   Chicago   San Francisco   Lisbon   London
Madrid   Mexico City   Milan   New Delhi   San Juan
Seoul   Singapore   Sydney   Toronto

1 2 3 4 5 6 7 8 9 10   DOC/DOC   1 8 7 6 5 4 3 2


ISBN      978-0-07-179830-3
MHID        0-07-179830-7

e-ISBN   978-0-07-179831-0
e-MHID      0-07-179831-5



**Library of Congress Cataloging-in-Publication Data**

Dittmann, J. Paul
   Supply chain transformation : building and executing an integrated supply chain strategy / by J. Paul Dittmann.
     p. cm.
   ISBN 978-0-07-179830-3 (alk. paper)—ISBN 0-07-179830-7 (alk. paper)
   1. Business logistics.   2. Strategic planning.   I. Title.
   HD38.5.D58 2013
   658.7—dc23                                                        2012017098

# Contents

CHAPTER 1   Transforming Your Supply Chain                                           1

CHAPTER 2   Start with Your Customers                                               25

CHAPTER 3   Assess Your Internal Supply Chain Capabilities Relative to
            Best in Class                                                           43

CHAPTER 4   Evaluate the Supply Chain Game Changers                                 65

CHAPTER 5   Analyze Your Competition's Supply Chain                                 89

CHAPTER 6   Survey Supply Chain Technology                                         109

CHAPTER 7   Manage Risk in the Global Supply Chain                                 125

CHAPTER 8   Determine the New Supply Chain Capabilities and
            Develop a Project Plan                                                 145

CHAPTER 9   Evaluate the Organization, People, and Metrics                         175

CHAPTER 10  Develop a Business Case and Get Buy-In                                 191

CHAPTER 11  Case Study: Developing a Supply Chain Strategy                         209

            Notes                                                                  239

            Index                                                                  243

# CHAPTER 1

# Transforming Your Supply Chain

Perhaps you picked up this book because your supply chain strategy is not generating the results you expect and need, or perhaps you did so because you know that you need to completely transform your supply chain. Perhaps your supply chain routinely fails to deliver products on time and to manage inventory and cost to the right levels. Perhaps you realize that your firm's lack of a good supply chain strategy is a major problem that is causing your supply chain to flounder without real direction. This book is for all those who need a transformational supply chain strategy.

As I define it, a supply chain strategy is a multiyear road map that starts with the needs of your customers. It must honestly evaluate the strengths, weaknesses, opportunities, and threats faced by the firm relative to best practices. It must recognize the most likely megatrends and their implications. It must comprehend the challenges generated by foreign and domestic competition, and it must account for the evolving technology that will be available. It must satisfy the financial goals of the company, and it must assess the organization and its people and metrics. It must be accepted fully across the company, and finally, it must do something! Namely, it must generate a set of actions that creates the supply chain capabilities the firm will need in the future.

I often see companies without a supply chain strategy chasing the latest hot trend or flavor of the month. In January, it might be cost savings, and by May, it's lower inventories. Like a ship without a rudder, it sees any wind as favorable. People in these companies complain that there are too many initiatives. As one executive said, "All we do is launch and then leave initiatives. We rarely focus on the critical few and complete them. We have no strategy."

1

# WHY DOES YOUR COMPANY NEED A SUPPLY CHAIN STRATEGY?

A few years ago, I coauthored a book called *The New Supply Chain Agenda*,[1] in which my coauthors and I argued that supply chain excellence creates economic profit, and that economic profit is tied directly to shareholder value in public companies and to owners' equity in private companies. Economic profit, very simply, is *profit less the cost of the capital needed to generate that profit.* Economic profit is a big deal because it shows that the company is delivering returns greater than the cost of the capital invested in it.

When economic profit increases over time, shareholder value increases. Stern Stewart, a global management consulting firm, has done extensive research on this concept, which it calls EVA (economic value added). It has demonstrated through extensive analysis of many companies that the relationship is very strong, especially over time.[2] As we demonstrated in *The New Supply Chain Agenda*, supply chain excellence, driven by a clear and compelling supply chain strategy, is one of the most underutilized tools for creating economic profit. The supply chain of a firm often manages 60 to 70 percent of the cost, controls 100 percent of the inventory, and provides the foundation for all of the revenue generation. It is the lifeblood of the firm, and as such must be guided by a robust strategy.

Unlike other areas of the firm, the supply chain process is a horizontal end-to-end process that guides the seamless flow of product across the extended enterprise. Products flow from suppliers to customers through the firm. But this flow must in effect pass smoothly through vertical functional barriers. In addition, the customers' requirements must guide the flow, and those requirements must flow smoothly back through the functional barriers. Because of this highly complex, cross-functional, cross-company challenge, a supply chain strategy represents a different set of challenges in its scope, its development, and especially getting buy-in to do it.

## DEVELOPING THE SUPPLY CHAIN STRATEGY MODEL

During my industry career at Whirlpool Corporation, I led the development of several major supply chain strategies. After doing plenty of things wrong there, my team and I created, I felt, a good process for supply chain strategy development. When I came to the University of Tennessee in 2005, where I now serve as executive director of the Global Supply Chain Institute, I was exposed to a vast database of documented supply chain best practices from hundreds of firms. The supply chain programs at the University of Tennessee include the traditional education of graduate and undergraduate students, but we also maintain an extensive network of partnerships with many companies, including the more than 50 member firms that participate in our semiannual Supply Chain Forum. Our faculty ranks among the world leaders in supply chain research, and it is that faculty I am referring to when I use the pronoun *we* in this book.

In all the data on hundreds of companies kept by the university, I was surprised to see very little material on supply chain strategies in a collection that exceeds 400 firms of all sizes and types. Most companies were all about execution and lacked a real multiyear road map for achieving competitive advantage. I have personally experienced the same situation. In working directly with well over 100 firms through our Supply Chain Forum, as well as through the supply chain assessments we do for companies, I continue to be surprised at the paucity of real strategy work. In a range of companies that includes manufacturers and retailers of all sizes in many industries, we see up-to-date, multiyear supply chain strategies in less than one in five companies.

The lack of comprehensive supply chain strategies in industry compelled me to write this book. Few would debate the principle that a company's supply chain is critical. I am fully convinced that supply chain excellence drives shareholder value and controls the heartbeat of the firm, that is, the fundamental flow of materials and information from suppliers through the firm to its customers. Unfortunately, too many companies have a supply chain that is crippled by the lack of a comprehensive strategy.

Yet it would be inaccurate to say that no company has a strong supply chain strategy. Some excellent practices definitely exist. The supply chain assessments we do for scores of firms have produced more than 700 interviews and uncovered some best practices that offer excellent revisions to the strategy process I had used at Whirlpool. Evidence from those more than 700 interviews is the basis for the strategy model and many of the examples I use in this book. In addition, in the last two years, my colleagues and I have applied this strategy model successfully in two major companies, building confidence in its effectiveness. A detailed case study in Chapter 11 shows how a major corporation recently implemented this best practices model. Using all of this as a foundation, this book will guide you through the process of developing a breakthrough supply chain strategy, and will help you avoid some of the mistakes others have made in the process.

## THE STATE OF SUPPLY CHAIN STRATEGY DEVELOPMENT TODAY

My colleagues and I recently conducted a survey on the state of supply chain strategy at our Supply Chain Forum meeting. Forty companies responded directly. These firms ranged in size from close to $1 billion to more than $50 billion in sales. They included retailers, heavy manufacturers, consumer packaged goods (CPG) companies, and others. Overall, 62 percent of the respondents said that they have a supply chain strategy, but, upon further probing, only 30 percent of those respondents confirmed that their strategy was a *documented, multiyear strategy*. Thus only 18 percent of companies (30 percent of 62 percent) can produce an up-to-date supply chain strategy document with a detailed project road map that goes out at least three years.

The addendum at the end of the chapter includes the details of this survey, but some highlights of it are included here:

- Of those companies that do *not* have a supply chain strategy, the main reason given was lack of resources to develop one. However, virtually all firms indicate that they hope to develop a strategy in the future.
- Of the strategies that exist, 78 percent go three to five years into the future. However, 22 percent cover only the short term (a one- to two-year period), putting them those more in the operating plan category, as opposed to a strategic plan.
- In only 45 percent of cases did companies with strategies believe that the consultants they hired were crucial. The others said that, while the consultants were somewhat helpful, they could have developed the strategy without the extensive assistance of consultants.

- Cross-functional buy-in to the supply chain strategy was good or excellent in only 24 percent of the cases. Only 8 percent reported excellent buy-in! Buy-in was average to poor in the remaining 76 percent of respondents, indicating that cross-functional acceptance of a supply chain strategy is a huge challenge, requiring a major change management effort. (Chapter 10 addresses this critical issue.)

I have personally interviewed hundreds of businesspeople over the past five years. When I ask them about their supply chain strategy, I hear a range of answers. A supply chain executive from a large manufacturing company gave an all-too-common answer when asked the question: what is your supply chain strategy? "Well, we don't have a supply chain strategy, but we desperately need one." In interview after interview, there was significant alignment around the need to have an enterprisewide supply chain strategy. What is going on here? If these executives realize that they need a supply chain strategy, why don't they have one? Part of the answer lies in the fact that there is a great deal of confusion about what this thing called "supply chain" really is.

## WHAT IS A SUPPLY CHAIN? THE SURPRISING NEED TO ANSWER THE QUESTION

In discussions with professionals at a very well known and profitable Fortune 100 firm, an executive told me, "We don't have a supply chain strategy. Heck, we don't even have a supply chain leader, and frankly, we don't even know what supply chain really means!" Consistent understanding of what the term *supply chain* means is obviously necessary for developing a strategy.

So what is the supply chain? The Council of Supply Chain Management Professionals (CSCMP) defines supply chain management as follows:

> Supply Chain Management encompasses the planning and management of all activities involved in sourcing and procurement, conversion, and all logistics management activities. Importantly, it also includes coordination and collaboration with channel partners, which can be suppliers,

intermediaries, third-party service providers, and customers. In essence, Supply Chain Management integrates supply and demand management within and across companies.

This expansive view of the supply chain includes all of the material and information flow across the entire end-to-end chain, even extending outside the firm, backward to the suppliers, and forward to the customers. In addition to material and information flow, it is important not to forget the third leg: cash flow. The ability to sequence information flow, material flow, and cash flow creates competitive advantage.

## Some Definitions of Supply Chain Are on Target

When we interview managers, we sometimes get responses that are perhaps limited, but are still consistent with this expansive view of the supply chain. For example, the following are some definitions from interviews we have conducted:

- "It's ultimately getting the product to the customers where and when they need it, and all the things upstream that make that happen. All the functional groups."
- "To me, it is end to end. It is suppliers to customers."
- "Supply chain management deals with every aspect of bringing a project to market, from the very beginning to market."
- "Supply chain deals with everything from raw materials to final goods to the customer."
- A retail executive defined supply chain as "everything from the vendor to the customer's trunk."

## But Many Definitions of Supply Chain Fall Short

In about 20 percent of firms (some of which were quite large), the basic definition of supply chain management clearly lacked full comprehension of its vast scope. The following comments were taken from interviews in major corporations.

- "I think of it as getting the products into the distribution centers (DCs) more than what happens from the DCs out. I look at the supply chain as 'manufacturing in.' One side of the coin is inbound, and then outbound is the other side. Supply chain is one group, and logistics is considered a different group."

- "Supply chain management means logistical aspects of two parts: vendor management and then logistics warehousing and transportation. We talk purchasing and manufacturing here. I do think we need someone who understands the flow of goods throughout the whole process/supply chain."

## Is Supply Chain a Process or an Organizational Function?

Maybe this is the source of some of the confusion. As described in the CSCMP definition, the supply chain is a broad end-to-end process that ties together the firm's functional areas, and also its customers and its suppliers. Unlike other areas of the firm, like sales or manufacturing, which typically are organized vertically, the supply chain process is a *horizontal* end-to-end process guiding the seamless flow of product, information, and cash across the extended enterprise. In other words, although product flows forward, from suppliers through the firm to the customers, the strategic and information requirements (and cash) should move backward, starting with the customers' requirements (see Figure 1-1).

Some executives lack clarity regarding how the horizontal *process* of the supply chain relates to the *vertical* organizational functions across which the supply chain passes, such as logistics, manufacturing, procurement, product design, and so on. Of course, no one department or function can encompass all of the activities involved

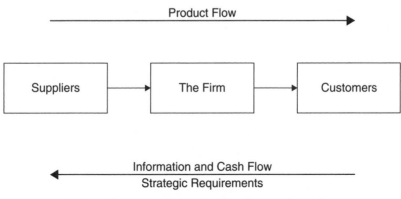

FIGURE 1-1 Product, Information, and Cash Flow in a Supply Chain

in the supply chain *process*, and hence the confusion. Therefore, the first step in preparing to develop a supply chain strategy is to educate management across all business functions on a consistent expansive definition of the supply chain and the difference between the supply chain *process* and a supply chain *function.*

## MISCONCEPTIONS ABOUT SUPPLY CHAIN STRATEGY

Clearly, Step 1 in developing a supply chain strategy involves defining the term. But, even among those participants who have the correct view of a supply chain, there was often confusion about the existence of a supply chain strategy. Some people we interviewed perceived the strategy as being very short term in nature. For example, one executive in a large medical products company said that the supply chain strategy was to "increase unit throughput per shift." Another executive in the same firm said that the supply chain strategy was to meet this year's corporate objectives for growth and profitability. Such short-term goals, of course, are not the same as a comprehensive supply chain strategy.

Other typical interview comments were:

- "There is not a real solid supply chain strategy in our firm."
- "It's hard for me to answer. Each functional area has a strategy, but I'm not sure if they fall under a general corporate supply chain strategy."
- "I would imagine there is, but I don't have it."
- "We need more communication about clear strategy and clear priorities. We need to know how the organization should work together. Parts of the organization that don't get broad exposure . . . they need to know what to do."
- "There's no strategy that I'm aware of. We want to eliminate cost and waste. We want to integrate our material acquisition process with manufacturing. Some pockets fit together, but there is not an overriding vision."
- "I don't think we have something that would address the whole value stream from customers to raw materials. We need a comprehensive customer service policy and explode it out to everyone so we are all rowing the boat in the right direction."

- "Supply chain strategy? Not that I am aware of. Not that is communicated well enough. I don't think one exists."

In one company that makes a major component for the automotive industry, almost all the interview participants told us the same thing when asked about the firm's supply chain strategy: each of them described it as a goal of achieving a 98 percent service level. Although this was definitely a well-communicated, consistent supply chain *goal*, none of those interviewed could articulate a real strategy that was in place to reach that goal.

A similar situation occurred in a retail company. When asked about the strategy, we heard about a goal to reduce inventory by $70 million. Again, there was no clearly defined project strategy to achieve that goal. The $70 million goal was simply split up and passed along to individual product categories. For example, the Product A business unit was required to cut inventory by $7 million, Product B to cut inventory by $12 million, and so on.

When pressed further, interviewees in these firms agreed that their companies desperately needed a solid multiyear supply chain strategy that everybody could support, and one that would serve as an umbrella under which decisions would be made. Interviewees universally acknowledged that more alignment should exist between strategic goals and execution in the company.

## WE NEED A STRATEGY!

As indicated previously, virtually all business professionals we talk with confirm that they either need a supply chain strategy or need a better one. They know that the supply chain is essential to driving shareholder value, and so do their bosses. In a 2011 survey by the Chief Supply Chain Officer Summit, 85 percent of senior executives said that their supply chain was a real source of business value and competitive advantage, not simply an operational function, and 70 percent of those same respondents said that strategic excellence is at least as important as operational excellence.[3] How then can we explain our findings that the majority of firms have no comprehensive multiyear supply chain strategy in place? If business executives universally acknowledge that a supply chain strategy is needed and that strategic excellence is so important, why do so few have one?

# WHY DO SO FEW COMPANIES HAVE A SUPPLY CHAIN STRATEGY?

Our surveys say that the main reason is "lack of time and resources," but further probing reveals other reasons as well. In a number of cases, firms strongly acknowledge that they need a strategy and even approach the CEO with a proposal to develop one. In one instance, the CEO, sensing a political problem with the sales organization, nixed the idea. Instead, he said that they would discuss it in one of his future staff meetings.

Another supply chain executive told us that companies don't have a supply chain strategy because the senior executives in the firm don't really understand the scope of the supply chain and its potential impact. He stated, "A lot of people just don't know how to develop a vision, a strategy, a plan, metrics, and in general lead improvement." He added that many firms have multiple supply chains and one strategy does not fit all of them, which makes the strategy process complex and daunting.

In another case, a logistics VP at a major manufacturer reported to a CEO who had spent his career in sales. This CEO's functional experience did not give him the context to understand the full scope and possibilities for the company's supply chain. The logistics VP knew that his group had "picked all the low-hanging fruit" by greatly reducing transportation and warehousing costs within the logistics function with a multitude of initiatives. To go further, he needed a cross-functional, integrated strategy. He approached the CEO and tried to convince him that the time was right for this effort. After a long discussion, the CEO objected on four grounds. The four reasons cited by this particular CEO align very well with the reasons, highlighted here, that we most commonly hear when we ask why a company does not have a supply chain strategy.

## Major Resources Will Be Needed for Supply Chain Strategy Planning

We see two prevailing attitudes when it comes to the creation of a supply chain strategy. The first attitude is that it is a simple matter, accomplished with a limited number of hours and resources. The second is that it is a huge, even overwhelming effort, for which the company cannot spare the resources.

In the first camp, many companies think they can develop a supply chain strategy during a one-day off-site brainstorming session. In one firm I worked with, I was asked to present the results of a supply chain assessment during the morning session, then the management team spent the afternoon brainstorming projects for the next year. While this one-day approach is certainly better than nothing, it falls far short of what's required in today's complex global business environment.

Creating a comprehensive supply chain strategy requires far more than such firms dedicate to it. The amount of time needed is in the range of months, not days. As you will learn in more detail in the following chapters, you need this much time to gather the information and do the analysis necessary to understand the customers' needs, conduct the firm's internal best practices analysis, identify the upcoming trends and emerging technologies, and so on. Yet when compared with the huge and lasting impact such a strategy will have on the performance of the firm, the strategy model advocated in this book takes a relatively modest amount of resources.

Realistically, a supply chain strategic planning process typically consumes three to five months of time for several of the best performers in the company. I recognize that many firms will resist investing that level of resources, or feel that they can wait until "later." Shorter, less thorough efforts are always an option and may be better than nothing. However, shortcuts mean that firms don't leave enough time to collect the needed content for effective planning and, more important, don't leave enough time to generate a good level of cross-functional buy-in.

Time notwithstanding, an effective supply chain strategy needs a strong leader, someone who could be a future senior leader of the firm's supply chain function. It requires a core team, consisting of cross-functional representatives who can spend up to 50 percent of their time on the effort. This team should include participants from logistics, merchandising/sales/marketing, finance/sourcing, IT, and operations. And it may be helpful, for reasons I'll explain shortly, to use a modest amount of outside consulting resources.

Companies need to select high-potential, valuable people to serve on the strategy team. These people will be the key players who execute the strategy. By being deeply involved in its development, they will own it and better drive a successful implementation. In fact, one forward-thinking firm asked a very high potential person to lead the development of the supply chain strategy, then promoted him to VP of the supply chain. It was not his job to do it! People like this are not easy to free up. In one company, we unfortunately heard: "Well, let's put Joe on the strategy team. He's between assignments and doesn't have much to do." It's tough to find the organizational capacity to use an A team for this effort, but it's absolutely essential for success.

## It Requires Using Expensive Consultants

Some firms we surveyed delayed the strategy work because they thought they would need to hire expensive consultants. While consultants can provide some useful insights into best practices, about half (55 percent) of the companies that used consultants believed that, while the consultants were somewhat helpful, they could have developed the strategy without the extensive assistance of consultants. When considering whether to use consultants, there are pros and cons to consider.

### Pros of Using Consultants
- Everyone else is too busy to take the time to do strategy work.
- The right consultants bring best practices expertise.
- Hiring consultants can energize an organization as a result of the sudden presence of energetic and expensive outsiders, as well as the launch and communication events they initiate.
- Consultants feed back the ideas that are already in the organization, but they do it in a way that consolidates knowledge and makes it actionable in a way that it didn't seem to be before.
- Many executives accept the advice of outside experts more readily than they do advice from their own employees. Since consultants are "more than 100 miles from home," they create an aura of outside expertise, which can be useful in selling a plan.

### Cons of Using Consultants
- Consultants need to be trained about the business and pushed up the learning curve, which requires a significant investment of time.

- The final strategy may become "the consultant's plan," not a plan that is owned by the organization. This could be devastating and is likely to cause the implementation effort to fail.
- The company may need to fend off the consultant's efforts to push for the next assignment. Generating the next hunk of revenues from existing projects is the lifeblood of consulting.

In reality, most successful strategy efforts involve a modest amount of time from an outside consultant. Consultants bring an energy level that is useful, and also some outside credibility, whether deserved or not. Just be aware of the consultant's limitations. As most consultants will admit in rare moments of candor, "We don't actually *do* anything." In the end, ownership of any supply chain strategy must lie with the employees, who must stay behind and actually do the real work of implementation.

## Planning Runs Counter to the Company Culture

Some companies have a culture of action. A cynic might say that they have a "ready-fire-aim" culture. In these firms, there is little appetite for planning or strategy development. People are just too busy. It brings to mind the story of a woodsman whose job it was to cut four trees per day. The first day, he was finished by noon. The second exhausting day ended at 5:00 p.m. as the axe got duller. On the third day, when he was still swinging the dull axe on the first tree after five hours, a passerby asked, "Why don't you stop and sharpen your axe?" The woodsman replied, "I can't! I don't have time. I'm falling behind." Sometimes a company should just pause and sharpen its axe.

Supply chain people often have a bias for action. In rising through operations, many of them have been rewarded for "shooting the engineer" and getting things done. Planning and strategy development just aren't on their radar screen. The total focus becomes delivering this year's objectives. But, as one executive observed, "Often the arsonist is the best firefighter." He knew that in many cases, people are promoted because of the heroic intensity they bring to a crisis, when in fact it would have been far better if they had prevented the crisis from occurring in the first place.

In other firms, priorities blow with the wind. This month, it's inventory; next month, it's cost; and the month after, it will be product availability. This "whack-a-mole" approach to management confuses the organization, resulting in little real progress. A supply chain strategy helps a company deliver on all three goals simultaneously. Priorities need not shift, because progress occurs on all dimensions.

## It Will Set a Political Firestorm in Motion

Many executives who have been schooled in the tough school of corporate politics sometimes see the launch of a supply chain strategy as a way for some executives to gain advantage. Since the supply chain process is so broad, there is often concern that strategy development could lead to a consolidation of responsibilities away from their area and into a new broad supply chain department. The DNA of the corporate executive evolves in a crucible of aggressively craving additional responsibility. The threat of giving up authority is anathema to the political corporate animal.

For example, another logistics VP strongly felt that her company, a retailer, needed an expansive supply chain function to achieve breakthrough goals in cost, inventory, and fill rates. She proposed to the CEO that the company launch a strategy effort to define this opportunity clearly. When the SVP of merchandising heard of her proposal, he resisted the effort out of fear that he would eventually lose a part of his organization, and that it would diminish his power base in the company. He struggled to find a logical way to approach the CEO. Finally he settled on the argument that the company had more important priorities right now. He told the CEO that any new supply chain strategy should be developed only after a merchandising strategy was developed. After all, he said, "Shouldn't our supply chain strategy complement our efforts to expand market share and drive higher revenue?" The CEO had been a merchant in the past, and so identified with the SVP's argument. He told the logistics VP that we should "wait until next year" to start a supply chain strategy effort, effectively killing this idea for the foreseeable future.

Only 8 percent of the companies in our survey said there is excellent cross-functional buy-in to a supply chain strategy. This dismal statistic strongly suggests that political issues may well be the biggest impediment to developing a supply chain strategy.

# OBTAINING APPROVAL TO START A SUPPLY CHAIN STRATEGY

In many companies, the four issues just discussed have prevented a supply chain strategy effort from being launched. How do you make sure that your efforts get the support they need? Sometimes the best approach to obtaining approval to initiate a strategy effort is to commit to the specific benefits that it will yield. For example, I worked with a VP of supply chain in a midsized firm who faced a potential political problem in starting a strategy effort. If it were to happen, he would need to take the risk of promising significant results. He began his argument by telling the CEO, "We have to develop a strategy because a lot of money is on the table, and we're losing ground to our competitors." With his interest piqued, the CEO asked what he meant by "a lot of money on the table." This VP of supply chain then had the courage to say that he believed that the results in Table 1-1 were achievable.

Would it have been safer to be vague about the possible benefits? Unless the VP was specific, forceful, and confident, the CEO would not have been interested. Furthermore, the VP felt very confident that he could achieve these benefits; in fact, he believed that, in reality, his efforts would deliver much more. Once the CEO understood the VP's commitment to achieving these benefits, he had no problem sponsoring the strategy effort.

TABLE 1-1 Benefits of a Supply Chain Strategy

| Benefit | One-Year Potential | Three-Year Potential |
|---|---|---|
| Cost of goods sold (COGS) savings | 1% of COGS, or $70 million | 4–5% of COGS, or $250–350 million |
| Inventory reduction | $180 million | $300 million |
| Fill rate improvement | 95–96% | 99% |
| Store support Faster/more efficient | 10% cost reduction; 20% cycle time reduction | Best in class, based on benchmark data: 30% cost reduction; 45% cycle time reduction |

## WHAT DOES A SUPPLY CHAIN STRATEGY ENCOMPASS?

Most people we interview intuitively know that either they don't have a supply chain strategy or the one they have is significantly lacking. So what are the necessary elements of a supply chain strategy? As depicted in Figure 1-2, the supply chain strategy starts with the customers' current and future needs. It honestly evaluates the strengths, weaknesses, opportunities, and threats faced by the firm relative to best practices. It considers all supply chain megatrends. It comprehends the threats generated by foreign and domestic competition, and the opportunities presented by new technologies.

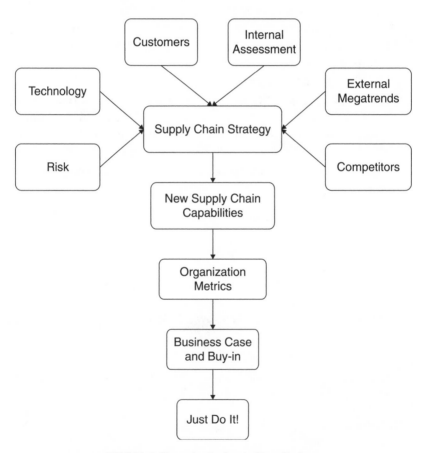

FIGURE 1-2 Elements of a Supply Chain Strategy

It recognizes the risks facing the supply chain. It identifies the needed new supply chain capabilities, and then develops an organization and metrics framework to execute the strategy. It must then create a business case and achieve pan-organizational buy-in. And finally, it must achieve results! Like any strategy, a supply chain strategy must analyze all of these inputs, determine the critical issues to address, define a strategy to deal with these critical issues, and then identify a set of action plans to develop new and enhanced capabilities. A strategy guides the firm's supply chain evolution for three to five years. Beyond that time frame, and possibly even sooner, a major strategy refresh will be necessary because of the incredibly volatile environment that most businesses face.

The remainder of this chapter follows the outline of the book and summarizes at a high level each of the steps involved in developing a supply chain strategy. A short synopsis of each chapter is included. Also, at the end of this and the other chapters, I include key action steps and takeaways.

## Start with Your Customers

Chapter 2 argues that a supply chain strategy absolutely must begin with the customers' current and future needs. I had to learn this the hard way. When I was with Whirlpool, I developed several supply chain strategies, always starting with our suppliers and moving forward to the customers. In the mid 1980s and the late 1990s, this approach seemed the most logical to follow. After all, material physically flows in this direction. I suppose the real reason I started on the supply side involved staying in my comfort zone. The strategy team back then always consisted of career-long supply-side people. The problem was that when the team finally got to the real point, the customers, it was out of time, energy, and resources, so the customers became an afterthought.

## Assess Your Internal Capabilities Relative to Best in Class

Chapter 3 includes real examples of how some firms did a comprehensive SWOT (strengths, weaknesses, opportunities, and threats) analysis as a first step in an internal assessment. The best way to complete a supply chain SWOT analysis is to first do a supply chain assessment. Strengths and weaknesses exist only when compared to best in class. Opportunities and threats matter only if a company knows where it stands relative to a model of supply chain excellence. When we use the term *best in class* or *best practices* in this book, we are referring to our database of best practices at the University of Tennessee, consisting of data from more than 400 companies. The term refers to best practices that we have observed to work successfully and produce outstanding, measurable results relative to those achieved by other firms. In Chapter 3, we discuss a proven approach to a supply chain assessment of your firm.

## Evaluate the Supply Chain Game Changers

Chapter 4 serves as a bridge from the internal to the external environment by considering the supply chain game changers that should be addressed in any supply chain strategy. What important trends should firms embrace as they face the future? I chose the seven game-changing trends discussed in this chapter from among a range of options because our data show, and industry executives tell me, that these seven trends have the most strategic impact, as well as being the most challenging to fully implement.

## Analyze Your Competition

Chapter 5 describes a process for analyzing your competitors' supply chains. The essence of strategy often lies in choosing what not to do. Most companies must place their bets carefully. Walmart can make a mistake and recover, but some companies cannot. Firms make good strategic choices only if they have good insight into what their competition is doing vis-à-vis what their customers need.

## Survey Technology

Chapter 6 turns to the role of technology in the supply chain strategy process. Most supply chain strategies will have to be supported with new tools. The tools serve as an essential component of a plan to move to a new process and institutionalize it. Technology should be viewed as an enabler of the new processes demanded by the strategy. Therefore, a technology assessment needs to be an essential part of a supply chain strategy development.

## Deal with Supply Chain Risk

Chapter 7 discusses the place of risk assessment in a supply chain strategy. One of the greatest impediments to sustaining successful supply chain implementation is the lack of any process to identify, prioritize, manage, and mitigate risks. In our database, it is rare to find such a process in place. Frankly, most firms ignore risks, sometimes with dire consequences.

## Determine New Supply Chain Capabilities and Develop a Project Plan

Chapter 8 shows how to take all of this information and determine the new supply chain capabilities that need to be developed. This chapter also includes a section on developing a project plan to implement the strategy. At this stage, you have analyzed the needs of your customers, and you have done a brutally honest internal SWOT assessment and considered the supply chain megatrends. You have assessed the landscape of supply chain technology and best practices. You have done an analysis of your competitors as best you can. How do you bring all of this together? How do you determine what new supply chain capabilities your firm needs? And, equally important, how do you prioritize these capabilities so that you get the right things done first? These topics are covered in Chapter 8.

## Evaluate the Organization, People, and Metrics

The new strategy is very likely to imply the need for a new supply chain organization. Along with that, new metrics will undoubtedly be required. As Eli Goldratt said, "Tell me how you will measure me, and then I will tell you how I will behave. If you measure me in an illogical way, don't complain about illogical behavior." Successful implementation of the supply chain strategy is very likely to require you to reevaluate your organization and metrics, and this is the subject of Chapter 9.

## Develop a Business Case and Get Buy-In

Chapter 10 deals with probably the most important part of strategy development: how to get the extended organization to accept the strategy. Without cross-functional buy-in, a brilliant supply chain strategy becomes simply another frustrating exercise in the corporate world that delivers no significant results. A firm's supply chain process is the ultimate cross-functional entity. Most supply chain initiatives of any consequence cross functional boundaries. As one executive said, "Getting buy-in is tough. Someone's ox is being gored with everything we try to do." Although this chapter comes toward the end of the book, the process of getting buy-in in fact starts at the very beginning of the strategy process through the engagement of key decision makers, and culminates near the end with a great business case. A tight business case is not a sufficient condition for buy-in, but it is absolutely a necessary one. Chapter 10 describes how to use the business case and other tools to achieve cross-functional buy-in for your strategy.

## Case Study: Developing a Supply Chain Strategy

Chapter 11 discusses in detail the development of a supply chain strategy in one company I worked closely with. This brings together everything from the prior chapters and shows how one firm did it. This case gives a clear, real-world example of how to develop a supply chain strategy.

# HOW GOOD IS YOUR SUPPLY CHAIN STRATEGY? A SELF-TEST

The supply chain strategy self test in Table 1-2 can help firms assess the quality of their supply chain strategy.

## Scoring

If you scored 100 to 120 points, congratulations. You have the groundwork in place for a good to excellent strategic planning process. If you scored 85 to 100 points, you have a reasonable foundation to begin developing a true supply chain strategy. If you scored below 85 points, you have a great deal of work to do to develop the necessary background to implement a supply chain strategy process.

TABLE 1-2  Supply Chain Strategy Evaluation

| Question | Rating |
|---|---|
| | 1 = Not Done<br>10 = World Class<br>(Note: If you do not know what "world class" is, the maximum rating should be 5.) |
| 1. Do you know what your customers will need in the future, and have you translated the future needs of your customers into supply chain requirements? | _____ |
| 2. Have you completed a SWOT assessment of your supply chain, comparing your capabilities to the best in class? | _____ |
| 3. Have you assessed the external environment, including the supply chain megatrends and how they may affect you? | _____ |
| 4. Have you analyzed the supply chains of your major competitors? | _____ |
| 5. Have you evaluated the future technology environment for your supply chain? | _____ |
| 6. Have you prioritized the risks associated with your supply chain, and do you have a risk mitigation plan in place to deal with the highest-priority risks? | _____ |
| 7. Have you assessed the global requirements of your supply chain? Have you identified the supply chain issues in each country you will do business in? | _____ |
| 8. Have you reevaluated your supply chain organization and metrics to make sure you are making progress rapidly in the right direction? | _____ |
| 9. Do you have in place a three-year or longer road map of supply chain initiatives driven by a strategic plan? | _____ |
| 10. Are the initiatives prioritized, and is each project managed in a disciplined way so that these initiatives are delivered on time, on budget, and on benefit? | _____ |
| 11. Do you completely update the strategy at least every three years? | _____ |
| 12. Are you delivering world-class results in cost reduction, working capital, and product availability that are best in class? | _____ |
| Total | _____ |

## CHAPTER 1 ACTION STEPS _____

1. Take the test in Table 1-2 to assess the state of your supply chain strategy.
2. Using the results, develop an argument to convince the organization to update or create a supply chain strategy.
3. Quantify the potential impact by estimating possible benefits in cost reduction, inventory reduction, and revenue enhancement as a result of an availability improvement.

## ADDENDUM: SUPPLY CHAIN STRATEGY SURVEY RESULTS _____

1. In those companies that do *not* have a supply chain strategy, the main reason given was lack of resources to develop one. However, virtually all firms indicate that they hope to develop a strategy in the future.
2. Topics that those companies with existing strategies considered in developing their strategy include:
   a. Best practices in supply chain analysis: 83 percent
   b. Interface with corporate strategy: 80 percent
   c. Technology assessment: 67 percent
   d. Competitive analysis: 55 percent
   e. Customer needs assessment: 50 percent
   f. Internal SWOT analysis: 50 percent
   g. Social/demographic trends: 5 percent
3. Overall, 78 percent of the strategies go three to five years into the future. However, 22 percent cover only the short-term (a one- to two-year period), putting them more in the operating plan category as opposed to a strategic plan.
4. Resources used to develop the strategy were:
   a. Consultants: 55 percent
   b. Corporate staff: 40 percent
   c. Supply chain staff: 38 percent
   d. Supply chain line: 38 percent
   e. Customers: 8 percent
   f. Logistics providers: 8 percent

5. Areas addressed by the strategy were:
   a. Transportation: 90 percent
   b. Inventory management: 76 percent
   c. Fill rates/product availability: 75 percent
   d. Warehousing: 75 percent
   e. IT decision support systems: 66 percent
   f. Suppliers: 56 percent
   g. Procurement: 52 percent
   h. Manufacturing: 55 percent
   i. Customers: 38 percent
   j. Environmental: 42 percent
6. Cross-functional buy-in to the supply chain strategy was good or excellent in only 24 percent of the cases. Only 8 percent reported excellent buy-in! Buy-in was average to poor in the remaining 76 percent of respondents, indicating that cross-functional acceptance of a supply chain strategy is a huge challenge and requires a major change management effort.

## CHAPTER 2

# Start with Your Customers

Where should supply chain strategy development start? Should you start with your *suppliers* and work logically forward through the supply chain, just as material physically flows through it? Or should you start with your *customers*' needs and work backward? The question may seem trivial, but in fact it is extremely important. Where you start drives everything in the strategy development process. It sets the tone and creates the focus for the supply chain strategy. To illustrate, let's review the two basic approaches to the flow of strategy development.

## TWO BASIC APPROACHES

### Approach A

In Approach A, the supplier forward approach, start with your suppliers' capabilities and move forward following the five steps listed below (see Figure 2-1):

1. Assess your suppliers' capabilities.
2. Analyze the inbound flow to your facilities.
3. Study and benchmark your internal operations.
4. Analyze the flow from your facilities to your customers.
5. Determine how well you are meeting your customers' needs.

FIGURE 2-1 The Supplier Forward Approach

## Approach B

In Approach B, the customer focus approach, start with your customers' needs and work backward (see Figure 2-2):

1. Assess your customers' supply chain needs.
2. Design the flow to meet those needs.
3. Design your internal operations to meet customers' requirements.
4. Manage the inbound flow from suppliers to support the operations requirements.
5. Manage suppliers to support those requirements.

FIGURE 2-2  The Customer Focus Approach

In my career in industry, I developed supply chain strategies using both Approach A, the supplier forward approach, starting on the supply side, and Approach B, the customer focus approach, starting on the demand side. In my experience, the two approaches yield very different results. Approach A focuses strategy teams initially on determining supply chain best practices and developing a strategy to employ those best practices appropriately from the vendor base to the firm and finally out to the customer. Approach B, in contrast, concentrates the supply chain strategy on responding to the needs of the customers and determining how best to satisfy those needs all the way back to the vendor base.

## Most Supply Chain Strategies in Industry Are Supplier Forward

Based on our data, 85 to 90 percent of supply chain strategies use Approach A, supplier forward. These strategies start with an analysis of best practices on the supply side and work forward to the customer. When we surveyed the 40 supply chain executives I mentioned in Chapter 1, whose firms range from retailers to manufacturers and vary in size from nearly $1 billion in annual sales to more than $50 billion, we asked them to indicate the *main drivers* of their supply chain strategy work. Their answers are as follows (see Figure 2.3):

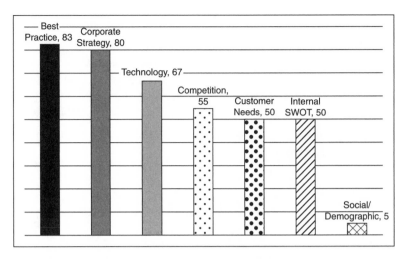

FIGURE 2-3  Supply Chain Strategy Drivers

- Best practices in the supply chain: 83 percent
- Corporate strategy: 80 percent
- Technology: 67 percent
- Competition: 55 percent
- Customer needs: 50 percent
- Internal SWOT assessment: 50 percent
- Social, demographic, or economic trends: 5 percent

These results indicate that understanding best practices on the supply side of the supply chain is the biggest driver of supply chain strategy work. Customer needs, as a strategy driver, is in fifth place. It makes a lot of sense to me that Approach A would be more popular. Launching a study of best supply practices is "supply chain stuff," and we supply chain professionals love digging into and learning more about our own area of expertise. It's our comfort zone, and we feel at home when we're nestled in this cocoon. Unfortunately, that's where many of us stay, or get stuck. Often we simply run out of steam before the strategy reaches the real point, *serving the customer*. The customer unfortunately becomes an afterthought.

When the customers come last, two dangerous possibilities emerge: either the internal view fails to meet the customers' requirements, or companies overengineer as they shoot to meet generalized best practices without taking the time to find out what is necessary and what is overkill.

While understanding the customer helps companies avoid missing their target in either direction, it requires a shift in mindset for many supply chain professionals. In a supply chain assessment we did for a manufacturer of a product used in residential housing and sold commercially, we almost never heard the customer mentioned. When we specifically asked one supply chain executive about the needs of the customer, he shrugged and said, "The sales folks are watching out for that." His perspective was not unique.

## Starting with the Customer Is Better

But who is the customer? Leading companies answer this question by looking not only at the next upstream step in their supply chain, but also at the end consumers of their products. For example, when I was at Whirlpool, we saw retailers like Lowe's and Sears as customers, and we viewed their customers, the general public, as our end consumers. We considered the needs of each equally vital, but somewhat different from a supply chain viewpoint.

Approach B starts with the needs of the customer. It is hard to argue against such an approach. Starting with the customer gives a company a clear sense of the needs it is serving and how those needs may be changing, and some insight into what will be needed to continue to serve them over the planning horizon. However, those requirements then need to be considered and balanced with the other key metrics that most companies use to assess supply chain performance. After all, supply chain professionals tend to be evaluated on a scorecard consisting of more than customer service. Specifically, supply chain executives have at least two other major metrics, namely cost and working capital (inventory). Leading companies look for ways to balance these three factors and meet their goals in each area. Sure they want to serve the customer well, but they generally must also meet very aggressive operating cost and inventory goals.

In a recent supply chain assessment, we reviewed a company's North American supply chain strategy and noted that this company, like many, considered the customer to be a secondary thought. The strategy focused on best practices in supply chain systems and processes. The senior supply chain executive responded with an interesting and probably rhetorical question, "Does starting the supply chain strategy with the customer mean that cost and working capital goals take a backseat?" He quickly added, "Of course, the reality of business today demands that we address all three simultaneously. We constantly react to aggressive demands by sales to take care of specific customer needs. Sales watches out for the customer. Sure, we in supply chain need to react, but at the lowest possible cost and inventory."

Fulfilling customer needs with the lowest possible costs and inventory levels may sound impossible, sort of like the customer who wants best-in-class quality at lowest-in-class prices. Yet our experience with many companies makes us confident that such performance is in fact quite possible, especially with a comprehensive supply chain strategy that is supported by a solid business case and grounded in the enhanced customer-first approach described next.

## AN ENHANCED CUSTOMER-FIRST APPROACH

Approach A drives the supply chain strategy based on best practices in supply chain processes and systems. Approach B focuses on the customers' needs first as the strategy driver. We believe that the strategy development effort should absolutely start with the customers' needs. But that doesn't mean that best practices considerations go out the window. Nor does it mean that the strategy ignores the company's and shareholders' needs to also achieve world-class levels of cost and working capital. Addressing customers' needs at low cost with low working capital is best achieved by following an enhanced customer-first process, labeled Approach C. The steps in Approach C mirror the strategy process in this book:

1. Assess your customers' supply chain needs, with the objective of designing a supply chain flow that meets those needs.
2. Study and benchmark your internal operations and your suppliers' operations and identify the gap to best in class.
3. Comprehend the supply chain megatrends that are affecting the industry, as well as competitive trends and technology trends. Also consider the risk to your supply chain.
4. Determine the new supply chain capabilities that you need to develop to satisfy your customers' needs while meeting your cost and working capital targets.
5. Finally close the loop and determine how well you are meeting your customers' needs.

The customer absolutely drives this strategy process, but in addition, Approach C and the strategy process in this book emphasize using supply chain best practices to also achieve aggressive cost and working capital targets.

Starting with the customer may be unfamiliar ground for you, as it was for me. The remainder of this chapter offers a number of examples to help you jump-start your thinking about how to bring your customers to the forefront of your supply chain strategy process.

## HOW A CPG COMPANY STARTED WITH THE CUSTOMER

Customers' needs are often thought to be product- and service-based, not supply chain–based. But one consumer packaged goods (CPG) company we audited found through its own surveys that some consumers who bought its products in retail stores found hidden damage once they opened the package. The supply chain folks knew that this damage did not occur within their logistics system, because they randomly conducted damage audits at every stage in their logistics system, from the point where the product left the factory until the time it arrived at the retail store. The company concluded that the retailers were causing the damage. How could this be? After studying this situation, CPG Co. found that in some retail stores, employees removed the product from its outer case in the backroom before putting it on the store shelf. The product package was not designed to be stacked and roughly handled—only the case carton was designed to be treated in that way. The company asked itself whether this was a logistics issue or a packaging design issue, but in the end it didn't matter. This situation made the supply chain organization aware that it needed to worry about handling damage *after* it turned the product over to the customer's retail store. It was the organization's problem to solve, which it did by training the local personnel in its customers' stores to avoid this damage.

Encouraged by this small victory, CPG Co. decided to do a comprehensive survey of its retail partners (its first-tier customers), and it identified *nine* supply chain requirements that would be needed in the future. Those requirements were:

1. *Reduce replenishment lead time.* The average time from submission of an order to delivery was 4.8 days. A number of customers wanted this reduced to a 48 to 72 hour range so that they could reduce the amount of inventory carried.

2. *Provide expedited deliveries when needed.*
3. *Offer a reverse logistics service to pick up returns.* A number of customers wanted merchandise to be returned to be placed on delivery trucks once they are unloaded.
4. *Provide real-time order tracking.* This capability existed in this firm on an ad hoc special request basis, but the turnaround time for an answer often exceeded 24 hours.
5. *Do VMI (vendor-managed inventory) for selected items.* Some customers wanted to experiment with VMI, where CPG Co. decides how much should be ordered and placed in the customer's distribution centers (DCs). CPG Co. would then be responsible for the inventory until it sold at retail.
6. *Provide a home delivery service for certain dot-com orders.* CPG Co. carried products that could be shipped to a customer via FedEx or UPS. But it also had some big-box merchandise that has to be delivered by common carrier.
7. *Participate in a collaborative forecasting process.* This means holding weekly meetings with the retailer and discussing those stock-keeping units (SKUs) where CPG Co.'s forecast and the retailer's forecast differ significantly.
8. *Put in place a single point of contact for all availability and delivery issues.* CPG Co. currently had different points of contact for each product line.
9. *Deliver damage free.* More of its customers were asking for a Six Sigma of damage, that is, a maximum of only 3.4 defects per million.

These nine *customer* requirements, plus the initial damage situation, became the starting point for a supply chain strategy for this firm. (Past strategy efforts in this company had focused on supply chain operations, with the needs of the customer having been only an afterthought.)

## CHANGING CUSTOMER NEEDS

Customers should be assessed regularly to identify both their present and their future supply chain requirements. For example, a large retail customer supplied by a manufacturing company planned in two years to reduce the number of distribution centers it maintained and instead require its suppliers to deliver directly to many of its retail stores. The manufacturer's supply chain VP told us that his company found out about the coming change when he interviewed the retailer as part of the strategic planning process, and that the company probably found out at least a year before the official announcement. The change would require his company to increase the number of delivery locations from 8 DCs to 4 DCs and 386 store locations. This clearly represented a massive change in distribution requirements, and required an aggressive and strategic response. As the supply chain VP said, "Better to find out about something like this sooner rather than later!"

In another case, a firm found that one of its large customers was close to launching a major dot-com initiative and would expect the firm to provide delivery support directly to the consumer's home. The manager of logistics told us, "We were blindsided by this request. We did not see it coming. We have no experience doing home deliveries. That's a whole new ball game." Only by conducting an ongoing dialogue with your customers will you have the lead time you need to respond to changes like this.

Other companies have found that the inventory sensitivity of customer firms should be closely monitored for changes. Some retailers are hypersensitive to working capital and cash flow considerations, and some are not. Some require their vendors to carry inventory for them and serve them quickly. Others believe that they need their own DCs in order to control the fill rates to their customers, and can tolerate less frequent deliveries.

One manufacturer found that the SKU strategy of its customers needed to be closely surveyed when one of its customers abruptly communicated its plan to greatly expand its SKU offerings beyond the limited set carried in a nearby warehouse. Will customers continue to expand SKUs, or will they hold the line? If a major SKU expansion is in your future, you will need a strategy to deal with that.

A few of the questions that manufacturing firms should routinely ask about their customers are:

- Will your customers expect you to hit very narrow delivery windows in the future?
- What will be their future policy regarding returns?
- What are their plans regarding packaging and damage?
- Will they want special labeling or other customization of their product?

- Will they require special delivery services for their emerging dot-com business?
- Will they radically change their network, such as reducing the number of DCs and increasing the direct-to-store deliveries?
- Will they change their inventory policy and expect their suppliers to carry much more of the inventory?
- Will they want an expansion in SKUs?

These questions may seem tactical, but they could lead to the development of costly and complex new supply chain capabilities. Questions like these will be critical to your supply chain strategy as you strategically plan for dealing with changing customer needs.

## UNDERSTAND CONSUMER TRENDS

End consumers are a completely different challenge. Retailers need to understand the needs of their end consumers, and many manufacturers could benefit from understanding consumer supply chain needs as well. Firms need to anticipate how end consumers will behave in the future, and use that as critical input in determining what new supply chain capabilities they will need to create in light of those trends.

One large retailer surveyed its consumers and used that information to identify seven major consumer trends that would have an impact on its supply chain strategy. They were:

1. The *time-pressured* customer who wants a faster shopping experience in a smaller format
2. The *aging* customer who wants a friendlier shopping experience that is not physically challenging
3. Customers who are *technologically savvy* and want to combine store purchases with online supplements
4. *The dot.com era*, with more shopping taking place online
5. *Social networking*, with its impacts not yet fully understood
6. *Green sensitivity* in customers who increasingly prefer products that are made, packaged, transported, used, and disposed of in an environmentally friendly way
7. *Greater responsiveness to exciting in-store marketing, such as "shopper marketing," described later in this chapter*

These trends suggest a number of major implications for the supply chain strategy. For example, Trend 5, social networks, could have major consequences for the supply chain. Social networks and social communication tools allow consumers to share good and bad shopping experiences immediately. Depending on the size of the individual's network, such news can spread virally and affect local stock levels. If a customer feels that she got a good deal, she might share the news and encourage more people than anticipated to buy the item, perhaps leading to a surprise spike in demand. Few customer experiences are worse than not being able to find promoted merchandise in stock, but all stock-outs hurt customer trust and loyalty. The ease and scale with which people can share their dissatisfaction will increase the pressure on retailers to make sure that out-of-stocks are minimized. In addition, retailers will need an accurate measure of out-of-stocks on the retail shelf. It will no longer be sufficient to simply impute the fill rate metric based on inventory levels. (Many retailers assume that if the system shows inventory at the store level, it must be available to consumers, which ignores problems like inaccurate inventory records or failure to move product from the backroom to the retail shelf in a timely manner.) Fill rates will need to be reported accurately as seen through the eyes of consumers.

Trend 3 in the previous list, technology, could have far-reaching and unknown implications. There is the growing phenomenon of in-store price and availability comparisons using mobile devices with bar code scanning apps, which could lead to more dynamic and unforecastable demand patterns. Supply chains of the future will have to contend with orders that are placed through a range of personal devices used in a myriad of different ways, and are delivered in widely varying ways. Many supply chain organizations have responsibility for order processing. In the future, consumers will order products directly, using devices ranging from PCs to iPhones to other devices that have not yet been invented. Retailers will need new fulfillment capability to deal with the wave of dot-com business coming at them. Furthermore, the supply chain organization will have to devise a strategy to deliver products ordered in this manner directly to the end consumer's home. Retailers will increasingly offer two options: pickup at the store or, for a higher price, delivery to the consumer's home.

For example, Walmart's Site to Store is a free service that lets you ship your online order to any Walmart store in the contiguous United States, giving convenient in-store access to tens of thousands of items, many of which are not available in the local stores. The program gets shoppers into stores more frequently and creates a more convenient way to buy from Walmart. Home delivery is the next step, as customers order merchandize such as groceries, health and beauty items, over-the-counter medicines, and household supplies like paper towels and laundry detergent from the company's website. The local store will then drive the goods over to customers' homes at their time of choice.

Trend 6, increasing green sensitivity, will create an emphasis on reverse logistics and disposal of waste, especially electronic waste. The emphasis on green will continue to spread throughout society as environmental topics expand in the curriculum of the school systems, along with the heavy emphasis on green by the news media. This trend will affect packaging, making the management of supply chain damage more challenging. When the product reaches the end of its life, supply chains of the future will have to contend with disassembly and disposal of sometimes hazardous material. And as online sales expand, so will returned merchandise, placing a great emphasis on the reverse logistics strategy of the firm.

In total, these consumer trends suggest that managing the supply chain is only going to get more complex. If your supply chain is struggling now, it's not going to operate more smoothly in a rapidly changing future world driven by these trends and others that have not yet been imagined. Without a robust supply chain strategic planning process, your firm will be in jeopardy. This environment demands a strategic planning process far beyond the one-day brainstorming sessions employed in some organizations.

## HOW FAR DOWN THE CHAIN SHOULD YOU GO?

Many manufacturers are blind to consumer trends, since they are at least one step removed. A company that makes, for example, the glass used in residential windows might find it hard to be sensitive to what the consumer wants, since it has no direct contact with end consumers. Supply chain line operating people especially struggle, since they are focused intensely on meeting incredibly challenging cost and inventory targets.

I worked recently with a company whose CEO felt strongly that supply chain personnel needed to better understand the consumer, even though they interfaced only with the retail stores' DCs and were a long way from the actual consumer. The CEO did this not as a strategic planning exercise, but simply out of an intuitive sense that consumer contact needed to be a normal business practice. He formed a team, and it devised a series of ingenious exercises to accomplish that.

For example, supply chain management personnel were asked to work a retail sales floor for a couple of days. One manager told us that he learned a lot, but that he had never felt more out of place and incompetent in his life. A second exercise involved riding the retailer's truck to deliver and install the product. A variation on this theme involved riding with a service technician for a day. Next, the supply chain team donned headsets and listened in on consumer calls to the customer service center. This placed them in direct contact with the intense emotion of consumers who were having problems with the product. And finally, they gave each supply chain employee a list of consumers to call to discuss a problem he or she had reported in the past. The employees were instructed to ask each of those consumers if in fact the problem had been resolved, and many were shocked by the blunt comments they received.

These activities truly helped the members of the supply chain management group at this firm feel closer to the end consumer. And, it helped them incorporate consumer trend implications into their supply chain strategy. One executive in the company creatively dubbed this whole exercise the "prepositional imperative." The supply chain people were not simply focusing *on* the consumer, but seeing the situation *as* the consumer would see it.

## DETERMINE FUTURE OPERATING MODELS NEEDED TO SERVE THE CUSTOMER

After surveying and determining its customers' needs, another progressive firm I worked with took an impressive next step in anticipating what future operating models the firm would need in order to serve its customers. Of course the firm knew that it must continue to support the current base operating model, shown in Figure 2-4.

FIGURE 2-4  Base Model: Factory to the Company's DCs to the Retailer's DCs to the Store

In addition to this model, the firm felt that there were three other operating models that would emerge in the future. In fact, they saw some elements of each beginning to emerge already. The other three operating models were:

*Shared supply chain.* In this model (see Figure 2-5), the retailers' and the company's distribution networks were considered as one entity. This model looked for synergies among the combined network locations.

FIGURE 2-5  Shared Supply Chain

*Consumer direct through retailer.* In this model (see Figure 2-6), the retailer captures the order and then immediately passes it on to its supplier for delivery directly to the consumer. Two versions of this model were later identified. One version was for retailers that had distribution assets, like warehouses and truck fleets. A second version was for those that did not have distribution assets, at least for all of their products, such as eBay, or Amazon for some products; these retailers expected their suppliers to deliver directly to the end consumer.

FIGURE 2-6  Consumer Direct Through Retailer

*Consumer direct.* This operating model (see Figure 2-7) bypasses the retailer totally. The company captures the consumer's order directly on its website and ships it directly to the consumer.

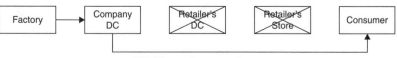

FIGURE 2-7  Consumer Direct

Next, the company estimated the future size of each operating model. For example, it felt that the base model would dominate 80 percent of the business for the three-year planning horizon, but that consumer direct through retailer would double over the three years after that.

## SEGMENTING THE CUSTOMERS

Best-in-class companies segment their customer base and develop a different logistics approach for each class of customer. Failure to do so can lead to dramatic missteps. For example, an executive in a large manufacturing company was shocked when her boss came to her at midyear with a directive that she deliver a $17 million cost reduction from her $300 million base cost by the end of the year. The following year, he told her, the cost reduction target would be $30 million! Panicked, she and her team decided to reduce customer deliveries from three per week to two per week, praying that there would not be a revolt. That was exactly the wrong thing to do. Sales dipped almost immediately, and she faced the wrath of customers, as well as the ire of sales management inside her own company.

A far better tactic would have been to segment the customers by their delivery needs. For example, some retail customers carried a lot of inventory and did not mind infrequent deliveries, whereas others kept stocks so low that major and immediate availability problems occurred when deliveries were cut. In addition, she could have worked with sales management to change delivery terms. The company required that a customer order only $100 worth of merchandise to enjoy prepaid freight. This resulted in many highly expensive LTL (less than truckload) shipments to small dealers. When the company later fully analyzed this situation, it found that such small-volume dealers were only 6 percent of sales, yet generated 23 percent of freight costs!

The supply chain executive in the example just given did not understand the needs of each *class* of customer. She didn't bother with advance planning. She simply rushed into battle and found that she was unarmed. A little segmentation could have made a big difference.

When I was with Whirlpool, we segmented customers as:

- Large mass retailers (e.g., Sears or Lowe's)
- Regional powers (e.g., hhgregg or P.C. Richard)
- Small independent retailers
- Large national builders (e.g., KB Home or Ryan Homes)
- Small and medium builders

Once we had segmented the customer base, we could design a unique supply chain strategy to serve each market. But we soon found that this was not good enough. After much discussion and analysis, we decided that we could better segment our customers using a grid with two variables: the level of service needed by the customer, and the number of locations we had to serve. At one extreme, we had customers who required 24- to 36-hour response to hundreds of store locations. At the other extreme, one customer had only one warehouse location, and was comfortable waiting 5 to 7 days. We put all customers in the nine-cell grid pictured in Table 2-1.

TABLE 2-1 Level of Service Required: A Nine Cell Segmentation

| Sales Volume Divided by the Number of Locations to Serve | | |
|---|---|---|
| Low service<br><br>High volume per location<br><br>OK to wait to fill trucks | High sales volume | High service<br><br>High volume per location<br><br>High-cost model<br><br>Look for consolidation and backhaul opportunities. Try to charge for high service |
| Low level of service | Medium level of service | High level of service |
| Low service<br><br>Low volume per location<br><br>OK to wait to fill trucks. Look for milk run opportunities (i.e., starting as a full load and dropping goods at several locations using optimal routing) | Low sales volume | High service<br><br>Low volume per location<br><br>May have to ship some LTL. Try to charge for premium service |

Then we developed a supply chain strategy for each cell in the grid. Essentially, we had nine supply chain strategies, not one. Some of these strategies are shown in Table 2-1.

This customer segmentation model pointed to some cross-functional opportunities as well. The customers on the right side of the grid were high-cost customers to serve. For these customers, we had to know the exact cost of serving them, and communicate that to sales. The salespeople could hopefully use this information in pricing negotiations to attempt to recover some of the cost premium.

## THE EMERGING SHOPPER MARKETING WAVE

The emerging shopper marketing wave, mentioned previously in the discussion of retail trends, bears more explanation. This trend will force more supply chain professionals to focus on the end consumer. Shopper marketing is a hot topic among marketing professionals. At its simplest level, it means marketing to the consumer while he or she is in the store, that is, in the last "three feet" of the buying experience. Will this new wave have supply chain implications? The answer is absolutely yes. In effect, this new trend in marketing will lead to a much more challenging and complex supply chain environment. In the world of shopper marketing, the retail environment will hold the following new requirements:

- Multiple stores each requiring unique SKUs, assortments, and support, even if they are located near each other
- Customized retail programs by store
- Delivery at specific retailers for precisely timed in-store shopper marketing programs
- Customized packaging solutions
- More supply chain partner coordination involved in multiple complex initiatives
- Returns management
- Extreme agility and visibility to support short-lead-time and short-run initiatives
- Forecasting at the SKU and the store level to support more, unique shopper marketing programs

This new environment will require that collaboration between a retailer and its suppliers be taken to an entirely new level. It will necessitate a supply chain strategy that can bring supply chain agility to a new level while finding ways to minimize cost and inventory. Supply chain professionals do not have all the answers here, but clearly they must consider this new trend as they put in place supply chain strategies for the future.

## WHERE DO WE GO FROM HERE?

Companies should begin their supply chain strategy by understanding the needs of their customers, as described in this chapter. But much more work remains to be done before a strategy takes shape. The supply chain strategy ultimately determines the new supply chain capabilities that are needed. Many companies make a mistake in the strategy development process by leaping to a project plan too quickly. On the one hand, paralysis by analysis is unacceptable, but just a little more patience and due diligence will yield great benefits in the end. There are more steps to take in the strategy development process. The next chapter focuses on assessing the firm's supply chain as it is today relative to best in class.

## CHAPTER 2 ACTION STEPS

1. Survey your key customers and rank-order their supply chain requirements.
2. If possible, survey your customers' customers to gain a better understanding of supply chain needs further down the chain.
3. Define the future distribution models that could be used to serve your customers, and especially define a future distribution model involving the web.
4. Segment your customers according to supply chain service criteria.
5. Understand the supply chain implications of the nascent retail trends that are sweeping across industry, especially the new shopper marketing wave.

CHAPTER 3

# Assess Your Internal Supply Chain Capabilities Relative to Best in Class

You've started with the customer, and you are now grounded in what your customers needs now and will need in the future. Customer requirements are actually the *minimum* requirement for a supply chain strategy. Customers often don't know what they want until you or a competitor exceeds their expectations and delivers a capability that amazes and delights them. How do you do that? I would argue that you should follow the process described in this book and fully analyze supply chain megatrends, your competition, and technology trends. But, before doing that, you should step back and assess your internal supply chain capabilities relative to those that are best in class. And, by best in class, I don't mean "best in your industry," but "best period." In fact, we have found that supply chain best practices transfer amazingly well across disparate industries and even between retailers and manufacturers.

Many supply chain executives who moved up as line executives in operations are tempted to dispense with analyzing their internal supply chain capabilities so that they can start "doing something" as soon as possible. As one executive told us, "I'm impatient. ... I just like to get things done. I don't waste time with analysis paralysis." In fact, successful supply chain executives feel that they were promoted precisely because of their impatience and their ability to drive hard every day. One such executive became legendary in his firm when he admitted that he read his staff's activity reports during a root canal!

But organizations that lack a clear strategic direction waste a lot of time. Lack of clear strategic goals makes it very tempting to abandon in-process initiatives in favor of the next flavor of the month. These constant shifts in priorities may in fact represent the largest waste of time in industry today. Investing a short amount of time to conduct an up-front assessment of your supply chain capabilities saves a huge amount of time later.

## DON'T GET BOILED LIKE A FROG

You need to assess your internal supply chain capabilities relative to the best in class so that you won't get "boiled like a frog." With apologies to frog lovers everywhere, there is a powerful and well-known fable that involves frog boiling, and it provides an apt analogy for business. The myth goes something like this: if you throw a frog into a pot of cold water, it floats contentedly, and if you bring the water to a boil before tossing the frog in, it jumps out immediately upon contact. But if you put the frog in a pot of cold water and raise the temperature one degree a minute, our hapless frog will eventually let himself be boiled. Businesspeople do this, too. We all are smart enough to jump out of boiling water, but many times, we are oblivious to the competitive temperature slowly rising until it is fatal.

How does one avoid being boiled like a frog? Commit to lifelong, aggressive learning. Repeatedly benchmark your competition and best-in-class companies. Attend industry forums, and participate in executive education programs. Do more of what you are doing now: read, read, read! But by far the most aggressive way to avoid the fate of the frog is to do an assessment of your supply chain capabilities relative to the best in class. Doing so will challenge you; you'll probably be uncomfortable with the gap between your company's performance and that of best-in-class performers, and that will keep you from being lulled to sleep with internal rationalizations.

Change occurs constantly, as depicted in Figure 3-1, especially in the extended supply chain. In fact, the rate of increase is probably exponential, not linear. The longer the organization ignores external change, the more pain it will have to endure in order to catch up. Like being in a hospital bed, the longer one stays horizontal, the tougher it is to get vertical.

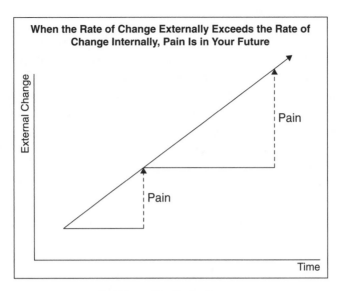

FIGURE 3-1 The Change Process

How can you avoid falling behind an accelerating change curve? You must constantly assess your internal supply chain environment relative to the best in class, and that requires doing a supply chain assessment.

## DO A SUPPLY CHAIN ASSESSMENT

It is best to have a supply chain assessment done by an outside, unbiased organization that has a database of best practices built through years of interaction with hundreds of companies. This is a service that we offer at the University of Tennessee. Of course, we aren't the only ones who do supply chain assessments. But, after conducting more than 50 of them, we believe that we have refined a very good process that I openly share in the following material. Whether you use inside or outside resources, this gives you a template for an assessment process that has proven to work well. The assessment process determines where the firm stands today compared to a best practices model, and it leads to a series of implementable recommendations for improvement. Because of the extensive reach of the supply chain, the first step in doing a supply chain assessment is to scope it carefully.

## Establish a Scope for the Assessment

An assessment of the supply chain can easily become quite broad in scope because of the vast expanse of the modern supply chain. Some firms focus the assessment only on their immediate pain points. Most executives believe that they already know where the problems in their supply chain are, so they narrow their focus to address those areas, whether they involve the organization structure, or exploring how to cut inventory, or how to achieve a cost breakthrough, or the best way to improve transportation or warehousing processes, or approaches to improve product availability. They scope the audit so that it deals only with pain points and thereby miss other opportunities.

One consumer packaged goods (CPG) company took a broad view and told the assessment team: "We want you to focus on the whole supply chain. We think we're pretty good, and we want to be motivated to move to the next level." This challenge generated a target-rich environment. The assessment shocked the executive by offering 73 separate recommendations in the final report. No company is quite as good as it thinks it is when compared to best practices across industries. We recommend a broadly scoped supply chain assessment to avoid missing opportunities.

## Gather Data

After scoping the assessment, the outside assessment team begins its work with a request to the company for the following types of information:

- A description of the current supply chain management organization
- A description of the current supply chain management process
- A description of the current supply chain management systems
- Examples of available forms and reports concerning inputs to the process
- Examples of available reports concerning outputs from the process
- Examples of performance documentation (reports, graphs, and so on)
- Total stock-keeping unit (SKU) count and description
- General company background

## Conduct Interviews

After analyzing this information to establish a base understanding of the firm's supply chain, the team schedules interviews. Interviews should cover a diagonal slice of the organization, meaning that the assessment team should interview both high-ranking executives and frontline workers in the organization. Interviewees should include representatives from multiple functions and multiple organizational levels, including employees in the functions of logistics, inventory management, forecasting/demand management, purchasing, information systems, product management/merchandising, finance, sales, marketing, and human resources, and also customers and suppliers. It is important that the interviews be as free-flowing as possible. Interview techniques should be designed to elicit frank and open descriptions of the organization and its processes, systems, and metrics and should be tailored to the company and to the individual interviewed. (See the sample interview guide in the addendum to this chapter.)

We believe it's important to interview only one person at a time and to guarantee absolute confidentiality. When we do supply chain assessments, we tell interviewees that they absolutely will not be quoted by name or position in the final report. We simply aggregate all of the responses to construct an accurate description of the company's current situation. Does this result in complete honesty? We believe it helps tremendously, especially in face-to-face interviews. In telephone interviews, the confidentiality guarantee carries less weight, but nonetheless seems to be reasonably effective. Even suppliers are more candid than one would think.

On balance, it is better to bias the interview population a bit toward more senior executives. Their broader span of control and greater experience tend to generate the best strategic insights. But even senior executives themselves admit that they do not understand how the frontline work is done. As one vice president wryly observed, "When you are promoted to the executive level, you have heard the truth for the last time." To capture the "true" view, we make sure to interview managers lower in the organization.

### Interviews Can Have a Hidden Agenda

Interviews can also serve another agenda. One electronics firm we assessed wanted to focus on inventory management best practices, and how to cut inventory significantly while simultaneously improving product availability. Surprisingly, this firm had a culture of caring very little about inventory and working capital. The senior executives were "bonused" on EBITDA (earnings before interest, taxes, depreciation, and amortization), and none of them except the CFO saw any connection between inventory and EBITDA. Focusing the assessment on inventory management helped to sensitize management to the importance of inventory.

It's a good thing that happened. Shortly thereafter, stock market analysts pointed out that this firm's earnings per share multiple was being depressed by poor cash flow performance caused by excessive inventory levels. These high inventory levels had been building for some time as a result of a poor inventory management process and a lack of attention. The outside stock analysts focused much of the quarterly discussion on inventory management practices, sending a strong message that inventory was critically important. We still smile when we recall an earlier response from the SVP of sales. When asked if he felt that inventory was important, he responded, "My CFO tells me it is." But later, we heard that when he finally saw the relationship between inventory and the value of his stock options, he was transformed into an inventory zealot.

### Supply Chain Assessment Interviews Are a Two-Person Job

Standard assessment interviews last for about one hour. Outside assessors often schedule interviews back to back to capture as much knowledge as possible, but doing too many can reduce the quality of the results. One day, I had just finished nine one-hour interviews in a row at Lockheed Martin. Exhausted, I heard a roar and looked out the window just in time to see a Lockheed jet fighter come roaring low, belly up, over the parking lot before it ascended again. Now that's one way to clear your head! But, most companies don't have products that appear just in time to wake up an exhausted interviewer.

More common is the experience of one of our fatigued interviewers, who sheepishly admitted that he once asked the same question twice in a row, confusing the interviewee, who responded, "Didn't I just answer that?"

Interviewing is exhausting. Interviewers have to listen to the respondent's answer, while simultaneously taking notes and thinking of the next question. It is impossible to use a standard questionnaire, since each person's experience determines the next question. Because of the grueling nature of the assessment interview process, interview teams should consist of two highly experienced people. In our case, we often pair an experienced doctoral student with a faculty member. Also, firms should insist that their outside assessors take an extra day or two and do the interviews when they are fresh. The supply chain assessment interview guide, found in the addendum at the end of the chapter, covers the expanse of the supply chain, including questions on organization, metrics, logistics operations, inventory management, and customer service, and concluding with a "wish list" question.

### The Wish List

One of the most powerful questions asked in assessment interviews is the "wish list" question: if you were king of the world and could have anything you wanted, how would you change things in your company? Interviewees often give surprising responses. Rather than ask for tangible items like more capital for new systems or facilities, we hear people pine for a company in which functions work together seamlessly, in which there are no functional silos and everyone strives for the good of the company as a whole. People seem to know instinctively how effective integrated cross-functional processes would be. They also yearn for the right organization and metrics, two topics that are covered in a later chapter.

### Compare the Results to a Database of Best Practices, Identify Issues, and Write Recommendations

Given the vast nature of global supply chains, the assessment team needs to have a framework to organize the assessment report, including its final recommendations. In our assessments, we use a framework like the one shown in Figure 3-2.

## WHAT COMMON SUPPLY CHAIN PROBLEMS DO FIRMS FACE? _____

In the many supply chain assessments we have conducted over the years, we have identified six supply chain problems that are consistently faced by nearly all the firms we have assessed. These issues arise independent of company size, industry, or position in the supply chain. They are difficult issues to address, but leading companies

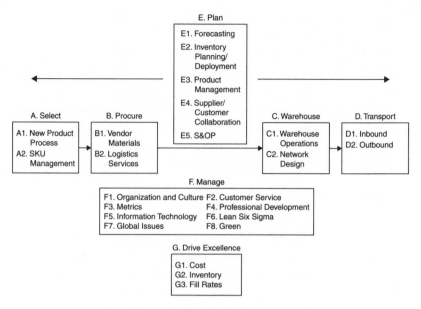

FIGURE 3-2  Assessment Framework

have a unique opportunity to address these challenges and build competitive advantage. The time will never be better to address the following strategic issues:

1. *Too much product complexity.* All firms admit that they carry too many SKUs, and further concede that they don't have a good process for eliminating underperforming products. Yet a very few have broken the code on this intractable issue and have a disciplined process in place to manage SKU growth, proving that it is possible to manage SKUs effectively. These firms challenge SKUs at both the beginning and the end of life with a process that demands that SKUs be justified.

2. *Too much slow-moving and obsolete inventory.* Companies struggle to step up to the problem of disposing of obsolete products in a timely manner. They always resist reducing price. Unfortunately, obsolete products never get more valuable. They sit there month after month, consuming cash and incurring inventory holding costs, until they are finally scrapped or sold at a steep discount, sometimes literally years later. It's a classic case of pay me now or pay me more later.

3. *Supply chain considerations are not part of the product design process.* When product design engineers develop a new product, they rarely consider inventory, transportation, or warehousing issues. Sometimes small changes in a product configuration can yield big logistics savings, such as the "square milk carton" employed by Walmart to better fill the cube in trailers. This applies to retailers as well as manufacturers. Retailers ignore the new product development process at their suppliers at great peril to their supply chain performance.

4. *Ineffective matching of supply with demand.* This problem stems from the classic struggle among functional silos in most companies. On an overly simplistic level, sales endeavors to generate revenue, while operations strives to cut cost. Often these goals conflict with each other. Leading firms address this issue by establishing a sales and operations planning (S&OP) process to align the various corporate functions around a plan that matches supply capabilities with demand requirements. Many firms attempt such a process, but most of them will acknowledge that they still have a long way to go.

5. *Physical network problems.* Where should warehouses, factories, suppliers, and stores be best located in this era of incredibly volatile transportation costs? This question is very prominent today. Currently, transportation costs are being driven up rapidly by the cost of fuel, driver shortages, infrastructure issues, environmental constraints, and other such problems. Logisticians facing this plethora of issues are confused, to say the least, and the old answers don't work anymore. One thing is certain: all firms should question their physical network configuration under a wide range of future scenarios as a key lever in keeping these costs under control.

6. *Global issues and outsourcing problems.* The global arena offers an even more confusing picture. Many firms are rethinking the mad rush to outsource outside the United States. The long supply lines, incredibly volatile fuel costs, exchange-rate volatility, and geopolitical risks have all come home to roost. Few firms consider the total cost of an outsourcing decision, and even fewer incorporate the additional risk of a global source in their analysis. A Boston Consulting Group analysis

found that manufacturing outsourced to China has begun to return to the United States as economic advantages shift, with Chinese wages rising 15 to 20 percent per year and the Chinese currency appreciating against the dollar.[1]

Since almost all companies face some combination of these six issues, we and others have a rich database of best practices that can be transferred across highly diverse industries. All firms should engage in outreach activities such as industry forum participation and especially assessment benchmarking as just described to make sure that they understand these best practices. Once they see how other companies are addressing the same issues that they face, they have a good portion of the foundation needed to assess their current supply chain capabilities relative to the best in class.

## INTERNAL ENVIRONMENT ASSESSMENT

After an in-depth examination of your supply chain by an outside, unbiased group, and after considering some of the common problems just described, the next step should be taken by your internal team as a group. This step should consist of a thorough examination of your internal supply chain strengths and weaknesses. Many companies do this with a classical SWOT analysis (strengths, weaknesses, opportunities, and threats).

To give you a specific example, a very prominent retailer, after extensive discussion in a one-day off-site meeting, completed the following SWOT analysis:

### Strengths
- A comprehensive supply chain organization is in place with both inventory management and logistics operations in the supply chain function. (Many retailers mistakenly put inventory management in the merchandising function.)
- Collaboration capabilities with suppliers are leading-edge compared to many other retailers.
- Leading technologies like profiling and voice picking are well advanced in the regional distribution centers.
- Advanced Lean capabilities exist to reduce waste and shorten cycle times in the logistics operations.

- Cube utilization for the outbound trailers has improved by nearly 20 percent in the past two years.
- Inventory management strategies are very sophisticated.

### Weaknesses/Opportunities

- Very little cross-docking is done.
- There is an inflexible warehousing network, with each warehouse being able to serve only one type of customer.
- Inbound delivery from the vendors is totally controlled by the vendors.
- A process to manage and control SKUs is lacking.
- Sales volumes are lower than those of other competitors, limiting the resources available to reengineer the supply chain, and creating scale problems not faced by competitors.

### Threats

- Competitors' supply chain capability is able to advance rapidly because of their superior resources.
- There are no second chances. Priorities and strategy must be right on target. There are only limited resources to invest; the bets must be placed on a winning strategy.

## A Five Pillar Analysis

Another company performed the internal evaluation slightly differently. Rather than do a SWOT analysis, the group based its discussion on the five pillars of excellence discussed in *The New Supply Chain Agenda*.[2] We assisted the group members as they worked through this analysis to order to bring in an outside perspective.

A Five Pillar analysis involves comparing your internal supply chain capabilities with the five pillars of excellence. The first pillar, *talent,* entails having a process to hire the very best supply chain talent, and then, just as important, a process that provides the opportunities to develop that talent. Supply chain is a complex profession, and supply chain managers need both extensive training and experience in the field if they are to be effective.

This company found that it was especially deficient in providing opportunities for professional development. With business today moving at the speed of light, everyone needs to engage in aggressive professional development, or quickly become irrelevant. To address this deficiency, this firm partnered with us to design a customized education program for its supply chain managers.

This firm next turned to the second pillar of supply chain excellence, *technology*. It did a complete technology assessment and identified the gaps, the highlights of which are depicted in Table 3-1.

TABLE 3-1 Technology Assessment

| Software | An excellent in-house capability for network cost simulation. |
|---|---|
| | The transportation management system is JDA-Manugistics, and it is considered a good system as long as the firm keeps up with the newer releases. An upgrade is planned for the near future. |
| | The warehouse management system is an SAP hybrid. It is considered acceptable, but the firm may benefit from looking at other applications such as Red Prairie or Manhattan. These could include good slotting capability and labor-management engineered standards. |
| | JDA-Manugistics is used for distribution requirements planning, forecasting, and replenishment planning. |
| | Collaborative forecasting occurs for the top 25–30 suppliers. This is a weekly call supported to compare forecasts in both companies. |
| | The biggest issue is the disconnect between the non-SAP internal systems and SAP. |
| E-business technologies | Automatic shipment notices are received from most vendors. They are not always complete, but the company is above average in this area. |
| Visibility and productivity | The company has automated conveyor systems in its warehouses. However, these conveyor systems do not extend into the receiving area for the inbound trucks from the vendors. Some companies cross-dock by loading vendor boxes into the automated conveyor system, which then flow directly to outbound trucks. |
| | The company has voice picking in place. The technology continues to advance. A leading firm is working on a second generation that is even faster. |
| Process advances | The company's Lean initiative is well advanced. |
| | The company is not using Six Sigma tools. |

The firm then addressed the third pillar, *internal collaboration*. We stressed to the company that successful internal collaboration occurs when sales, marketing, and the supply chain function are able to align and focus on serving the customer in a way that maximizes product availability while minimizing cost and asset investment. The supply chain team agreed, but unfortunately each organizational function marched to the beat of its unique performance metrics. This company did not have an S&OP process in place, but at our urging, it resolved to implement S&OP as the first major step down the long road toward a more effective internal collaboration capability.

*External collaboration* with vendors came next as the fourth pillar. This company was actually quite advanced already in this area, with several examples of win/win collaborations with its vendors. It committed to continuing to build on this strength.

The team assessed the fifth and last pillar, *effectively getting things done,* as a problem area. The supply chain team conceded that the company definitely lacked disciplined project management and change management processes. Although turnover was slowed temporarily by the Great Recession, people don't stay in their jobs long in today's the dynamic business environment. All the constant turnover and turmoil raises tremendous barriers to getting things done, and this firm was no exception. This means that successful execution of a supply chain excellence strategy requires more than just a competent supply chain executive—it requires a disciplined project and change management process.

With supply chain projects especially, it is important to make sure that the root cause issues are addressed, that project size (scope) is contained properly, and that risk is addressed more rigorously than many senior executives may assume necessary. After some research, this firm decided to team up with the Project Management Institute (PMI) to implement more disciplined project management processes. It further committed to getting all people who managed projects certified by PMI as PMPs (Project Management Professionals).

Whatever approach is used in the internal assessment, whether a SWOT or a Five Pillar analysis, one fact is indisputable: a supply chain strategy must build on existing strengths and address weaknesses, opportunities, and threats. However, companies need to deal with internal assessments in a way that fits their corporate culture.

## DIFFERENT INTERNAL ASSESSMENT CULTURES _____

Some companies see the positive and others focus on the negatives. Companies in many cultures around the world are much less willing to admit weaknesses than American companies are. In my career at Whirlpool, the culture almost exclusively saw the negatives. One of our executives astutely observed that we had a "pathological fear of inducing complacency." Other firms see the world differently. They have a need to feel proud of their accomplishments and seem to get very uncomfortable when they are criticized. Whirlpool loved flagellation, but other firms want to be stroked.

In one supply chain assessment review, I found myself in front of the firm's senior executives telling them bluntly about the weaknesses we had seen in the assessment. We followed the philosophy that they weren't paying us to lie to them. As the review progressed, we began to see a growing horror spreading across the faces of the executives as we described problem after problem in their supply chain. Subconsciously we found ourselves softening the blows and pulling our punches as the review progressed.

Healthy firms have a hybrid culture that is somewhere between these two extremes. In fact, a firm would be well served by following the advice of Admiral Jim Stockdale in his famous Stockdale paradox, explained so well by Jim Collins in *Good to Great*.[3] Admiral Stockdale was a U.S. military officer who was held captive for eight years during the Vietnam War. Stockdale was tortured more than 20 times by his captors, and never had much reason to believe he would survive the prison camp and someday get to see his wife again. And yet, as Stockdale told Collins, he never lost faith during his ordeal: "I never doubted not only that I would get out, but also that I would prevail in the end and turn the experience into the defining event of my life, which, in retrospect, I would not trade." Stockdale approached adversity with a very different mindset. He accepted the reality of his situation. He knew he was in hell, but rather than bury his head in the sand, he stepped up and did everything he could to lift the morale and prolong the lives of his fellow prisoners. He created a tapping code so that they could communicate with each other. He developed a milestone system that helped them deal with torture. And he sent intelligence information to his wife, hidden in the seemingly innocent letters he wrote.

When supply chain organizations assess their strengths and weaknesses, they would be well served by doing it in the same manner as Admiral Stockdale: with brutal realism coupled with a strong dose of optimism. For example, in the 1980s, Harley-Davidson faced a huge threat from Japanese imports that nearly capsized the company. When I visited there in the 1990s, people told me how they initially were blinded by what seemed to be an unfair playing field. But soon they stopped making excuses and openly acknowledged that they faced a real threat that was not going away. Rather than wring their hands, they believed that they could win; they became one of the first American companies to pursue Lean manufacturing, and eventually they prevailed.

## ASSESSING THE SUPPLY CHAIN IN BAD ECONOMIC TIMES

Tough times really are an opportunity to get things right across the entire business. The Great Recession of 2008–2010 and the economic malaise that followed were incredibly painful for most firms. It would be a shame to miss the window of opportunity that comes with a crisis such as that. But bad business conditions can overwhelm the strategy process, and the reflex reaction is to stop anything new and cut everything. The management team in such a situation focuses on what it can do right now to take out cost. Everyone asks, "What are the quick hits, the 'low-hanging fruit'?" There are obviously no easy answers. We often hear, "If it were easy, we would have already done it." Budget reductions may be necessary, but they certainly shouldn't be spread evenly. Now is the time for careful surgical cuts that avoid crippling a firm for the future. Only by assessing the supply chain relative to the best in class or, better yet, by having a complete supply chain strategy in place is it possible to do that in an intelligent way. Management may not have the patience to do a complete supply chain strategy, but an assessment at least provides some guidance.

One firm was doing a supply chain assessment as the Great Recession of 2008–2010 struck. The supply chain leader told us that the process led him to make some very good decisions. As he told us, "I came to realize this was the time to make sure the best employees feel valued. Best-in-class companies have outstanding people. So, even in the face of the forced layoffs, I knew that there would never be a better time to retain and hire talent for the future. As everyone else retrenched, there was an incredible opportunity for us to find the star performers for the next 20 years, and I actually convinced my boss to hire a couple of them." He continued, "This was the perfect time to address those tough cross-functional issues that are nearly impossible to deal with in good times. It was time to finally cut SKUs and get rid of that obsolete inventory. It was time to really bring the supply chain folks into the planning of new products. And it was time to forget organizational politics and get rid of waste, such as an underperforming, but politically connected distribution center (DC). It was the time to rise above the sacred cows and make the organizational changes that needed to be made. I just don't think I would have approached things that way without the supply chain assessment results."

In another similar example, one of our Supply Chain Forum member firms told us how his firm was on the verge of bankruptcy. In desperation, the firm decided to push decision making down, eliminate the red tape, and transfer approval power from corporate to the local operations. It gave its people a budget and goals, and that was about it. It essentially eliminated the multilayer approval process for spending. The teams in several of the company's locations had recently completed a supply chain assessment and knew exactly what to do. In this case, the corporate bureaucracy got out of the way, and the results were spectacular, with a cost reduction of 21 percent in the first year. Unfortunately, once the company started to recover, the approval controls immediately went back into effect.

An eerily similar example involved the Whirlpool Corporation. In 2001, a recession year, the company faced a profitability crisis. The top mount refrigeration business and the factory in Evansville, Indiana, had big losses and were hemorrhaging money. The company knew from prior analyses that it carried too many SKUs, but organizational politics had prevented any action prior to this time. In desperation, the firm cut the number of SKUs in half, from around 350 to less than 170. This action, along with others, produced an almost magical return to profitability. However, as the economy improved, SKUs found their way back into the refrigeration line. By 2003, all the previous SKUs and a few more had been added to the line. The profitability of top mount refrigerators suffered again, and finally, in 2010, the Evansville, Indiana, plant closed, and Whirlpool exited the manufacturing of top mount refrigerators in the United States forever. When a crisis forces tough action to be taken, it is tragic if that decision gets reversed when better times return.

In yet another example, a firm in the auto parts retail business had a network of more than 60 warehouse locations. A recent supply chain assessment supported by a network optimization analysis had found that the optimal number was closer to half that—around 30 warehouses at a savings of more than $50 million! But this firm had historically had a decentralized organization. A general manager ran both a warehouse and the sales function for the geographic area served by that warehouse. This firm had based its entire system of accountability and rewards on this feudal approach for its 57-year history. In effect, the general managers were little monarchs of their geographic areas, and most of them had a long history with the firm. When the general managers learned that the assessment and network analysis indicated that nearly half of the branches should be closed, they revolted. They told the CEO that if he closed branches, sales would plummet. This argument paralyzed the firm into inaction. But then the Great Recession hit and the firm faced a survival situation: either take action or perish. In that environment, the leadership made the difficult decision to close more than 20 branches. The act saved the firm, but only because it had first done the supply chain assessment and network analysis, and knew the right thing to do.

## START WITH YOUR CUSTOMERS AND THEN ASSESS THE INTERNAL ENVIRONMENT

At this point in the supply chain strategy development process, you have determined the needs of your customers, and you have assessed your supply chain relative to the best in class. Congratulations. These are critical building blocks on which to construct a supply chain strategy. But much more work remains. Next in the strategy development process, you will need to bridge from the internal to the external environment. The next chapter begins that process of looking outward by introducing seven supply chain game changers that should be considered in your supply chain strategy process.

## CHAPTER 3 ACTION STEPS

1. Using outside assistance, assess your supply chain relative to best-in-class practices.
   a. Precisely scope the assessment.
   b. Gather performance data.
   c. Conduct interviews.
   d. Compare the results to a database of best practices.
   e. Identify and document the gap to best in class.
2. With your internal team, complete an in-depth SWOT or Five Pillar analysis for your supply chain.
3. Take advantage of business crises to make the tough decisions to strengthen your supply chain.

## ADDENDUM: A SAMPLE SUPPLY CHAIN ASSESSMENT INTERVIEW GUIDE

1. Role in your company:
   a. Describe your current role within the company.
2. Scope of supply chain activities:
   a. What does the term *supply chain* mean?
   b. Do you have a supply chain strategy?
3. Metrics and reports:
   a. What are the key metrics and reports that you use?
   b. How could your key performance indicators be improved?
4. Organization alignment issues:
   a. Are goals aligned?
   b. Are roles and responsibilities clearly defined?
   c. What are your biggest organization issues?
   d. Describe the interface of logistics with production planning and inventory management.
5. S&OP (sales and operations planning):
   a. Describe the S&OP process here.
   b. Which functions are involved? Who leads it?
   c. Is the process strategic or tactical?
   d. What metrics and reports are used? Are they shared cross-functionally?
   e. What opportunities are there to improve the S&OP process?

6. Inbound transportation:
   a. Describe the inbound transportation process.
   b. Does the company manage it, or do the vendors?
   c. What are the pros and cons of this arrangement?
   d. What are the opportunities to improve inbound transportation?
   e. What are the global challenges currently?
   f. What opportunities exist across business units?
7. Outbound transportation:
   a. Describe the physical network for outbound transportation.
   b. How are carriers selected and loads tendered?
   c. How are trucks routed?
   d. Describe the global issues.
   e. What are the opportunities across business units?
   f. What initiatives to reduce transportation cost are underway or planned?
      - Maximize cube utilization.
      - Streamline the physical network.
      - New systems . . . TMS (transportation management system).
      - Increase backhaul opportunities.
      - Coordinate with inbound.
      - Outsource.
      - Green initiatives.
      - Use of rail or intermodal.
8. Warehousing:
   a. Describe the warehouse operations.
   b. What initiatives to reduce warehouse cost are underway or planned?
      - New systems: WMS (warehouse management system).
      - RF, RFID, sophisticated bar codes.
      - Use of ASNs.
      - Yard management.
      - Warehouse layout, or use of warehouse cube.
      - Picking and material movement.
      - Profiling.
      - Receiving and put-away.
      - Warehouse physical network.
      - Use of Lean and Six Sigma tools.

- Returns processing.
- Truck loading optimization.
- Opportunities across business units.

9. Physical infrastructure:
    a. Do we have the right number of warehouses in the right places?
    b. What opportunities exist across business units?
    c. Are warehouses serving the right customers?
    d. Is the network optimized for $5/gallon diesel?

10. Customer service:
    a. How does the company measure customer service?
    b. What metrics are in place for customer service? Are they visible to the entire organization?
    c. How good are your customer service results?
    d. What feedback do you receive from your customers? Describe some of this feedback.

11. Inventory:
    a. What does inventory mean to you?
    b. What is your role in the inventory management process?
    c. What is the current inventory management strategy?
    d. What inventory management metrics are in place? Are they visible to all employees?
    e. How many SKUs does the firm have? How many of them are active?
    f. What are the long-term requirements for repair and service of equipment sold?
    g. Can you describe your global supply network structure and lead times?
    h. How accurate are your product forecasts? Describe your forecast accuracy problems.
    i. Does the firm have much slow-moving inventory? If so, why?
    j. How effective is your S&OP process? Is this process coordinated among functions? Is there in-person representation from all functions involved in the process? Are you present at these sessions?
    k. How does inventory affect your bonus?
    l. Does the firm have quarter-end and year-end spikes in demand?

m. What is the best way to optimize inventory without affecting customer service?

n. What initiatives are ongoing to optimize your inventory levels, days on hand, and inventory turns results? Are you a part of these initiatives?

o. What do you specifically think needs to be done to optimize inventory?

12. Information technology:
   a. How effective are the IT systems for managing supply chain activities?
   b. Do systems provide adequate visibility?
   c. What new initiatives are underway or planned?

13. Opportunities:
   a. What do you see as the greatest short-term supply chain opportunities?
   b. What do you see as the greatest long-term supply chain opportunities?

14. Barriers:
   a. What are the biggest challenges or barriers to overcome to address these supply chain challenges?

15. Wish list:
   a. If you could wave your magic wand and change one thing about the supply chain, what would it be and why?

## CHAPTER 4

# Evaluate the Supply Chain Game Changers

The previous two chapters stressed the importance of starting your supply chain strategy creation process by understanding your consumers' needs and following that by an internal assessment of your supply chain relative to the best in class. This chapter bridges from the internal to the external environment by considering the supply chain game changers that should be addressed in any supply chain strategy. What important trends should firms embrace as they face the future? I chose the seven game-changing trends discussed in this chapter from among a range of options because our data show, and industry executives tell me, that these seven have the most strategic impact, and are also the most challenging to fully implement. I recommend that your supply chain strategy team discuss these trends and determine how each of them can help you strategically serve your customers while meeting your aggressive strategic goals for cost and working capital.

## TREND 1: COLLABORATION

Collaboration deserves a prominent position in your supply chain strategy. There has been a lot more talk than action regarding both collaboration across functional silos within the firm and collaboration with trading partners outside your organizational walls. As one supply chain executive noted about collaboration in his firm, "When all was said and done, there was a lot more said than done." However, we have seen examples of more and more leading companies that are changing this dismal track record. We now hear success stories frequently, some of which are described in the 2010 book *The New Supply Chain Agenda.*[1]

Research overwhelmingly shows that collaboration is on the rise. In a recent Accenture study, 78 percent of executives said that "developing collaborative relationships in supply chain planning and execution operations with your trading partners" is very or extremely important. Four years earlier, only 54 percent of executives felt that way.[2]

### Collaborative Planning, Forecasting, and Replenishment

A growing number of companies that we work with are practicing an advanced form of supply chain collaboration known as CPFR (Collaborative Planning, Forecasting, and Replenishment). With CPFR, a supplier and a customer collaborate on a shared forecast, which then drives replenishment to better satisfy demand. The VICS (Voluntary Interindustry Commerce Solutions Association)[3] maintains updated standards for CPFR, and a growing number of VICS members have implemented advanced collaboration processes. Successful CPFR implementations can reap rewards such as reductions in stock-outs, lower lead times, stronger relationships between trading partners, shorter cycle times, increases in sales revenues, improved inventory management, better overall system visibility and customer service, and improved cost structures. Even those who have managed to implement only collaborative *forecasting* report that this process alone yields great benefits.

When two firms decide to implement CPFR, they often progress together through the following steps:

- *Strategy and planning.* Defining the relationship in terms of goal, scope, roles, and responsibilities
- *Demand and supply management.* Joint sales forecasting, market data analysis, and order/replenishment/demand planning
- *Execution.* Order generation and fulfillment
- *Analysis.* Exception management, execution monitoring, and joint performance assestments with the use of scorecards

One company we assessed (a consumer durables manufacturer) worked with its customer, a major retailer, on a collaborative forecasting model. The model they produced improved forecast accuracy at the stock-keeping unit (SKU) level from a 60 percent forecast error to a 36 percent error—a reasonable level of accuracy at the

SKU level. The two companies followed a simple process. Each did a forecast. Then, on a weekly basis, they held a conference call to compare the two forecasts. They discussed any differences of more than 15 percent between the respective SKU forecasts and resolved the difference. For example, in one such meeting, they noted that the forecast for SKU X was more than 100 percent greater in the retailer's forecast than in the supplier's. In the ensuing discussion, they quickly learned that the retailer planned a promotion that had not been communicated to the supplier. This short conversation not only translated into a major improvement in forecast accuracy, but also avoided expediting costs for the supplier and provided a much better level of availability for the retailer.

## S&OP

CPFR is a good example of *external* collaboration betweeen a supplier and a customer. S&OP (sales and operations planning) is the best practice for *internal* collaboration between in-house functional silos. S&OP processes normally consist of a series of analytical activities and meetings at both the operating and the executive level. The purpose of these activities is to achieve cross-functional alignment on a demand plan, a supply plan, and a financial plan. S&OP provides a framework for marketing, sales, merchandising, logistics, manufacturing, finance, and procurement to come together and communicate, plan, and identify opportunities to improve and align the business.

Companies that implement S&OP successfully have an integrated supply plan that matches the demand plan and is consistent with the company's financial plan. Furthermore, companies with successful S&OP processes deal with risks and uncertainties more effectively by developing contingency planning–based strategies. For example, managers of a $35 billion company that manufactures a diverse range of products for homes and businesses told me that they always discuss opportunities and risks in their S&OP meetings. They gave an example involving a new security product that they were going to introduce in three months. They said that history proves that forecasts for new products like this are no more than educated guesses. In the S&OP meeting, they discussed the action they would take if sales were double or triple the forecasted volume, and how they would react if the sales of this new product fell flat. Considering issues like these in a cross-functional setting is the power of S&OP.

Manufacturing companies have been implementing and reimplementing S&OP for at least 20 years. The task often requires a good deal of time and effort to yield a successful S&OP process. One consumer packaged goods (CPG) company, for example, told us that it was in its third attempt to implement S&OP successfully. The prior failures were caused, it said, by a "functional silo problem" (misaligned objectives between sales and operations) and lack of support from senior management. Manufacturing leadership and sales leadership could not get on the same page because of the classic problem of being driven by totally different metrics. It finally took support from a new CEO to give S&OP new life in this company.

Even though S&OP has been around at manufacturers for decades, it is still relatively new among retailers. Manufacturers naturally see the need to balance supply with demand. Retailers, which usually don't have internal supply sources, don't grasp this need as readily. Retailers need S&OP just as much as manufacturers, and some are just now beginning to discover its power. Though the need is the same, differences exist, as outlined in Table 4-1.

## The Challenge of Collaboration

Collaboration is a long, yet necessary journey that is both challenging and rewarding. Designing the process and implementing the technology are only half the battle. Culture plays a vital role in the success of any collaboration initiative. Companies that intend to implement enhanced collaborative relationships must accept the idea that true success depends on the culture of the company more than on any other factor. That culture must support a foundation of trust between partners, along with the eradication of long-entrenched fiefdoms, turfs, and silo mindsets.

Not every company can make these changes. However, if a company can make them, the payoff can be huge. When I was at Whirlpool, one of the earliest successes in the turnaround of the supply chain in 2001, after a difficult SAP implementation, was the rollout of a new S&OP process. We soon pushed forecasting capability further by launching a CPFR pilot. Within 30 days of launch, forecast error at Whirlpool fell by one-half. Each one-point improvement in the SKU/location forecast accuracy yielded $3 million in inventory reduction, as well as product availability improvements that improved customer satisfaction and competitiveness.

TABLE 4-1  The Difference Between S&OP at a Manufacturer and at a Retailer

| Dimension | Retailer | Manufacturer |
|---|---|---|
| Supplier contact point | Merchandising Buyers | Procurement Manufacturing |
| Bull-whip effect: larger swings in demand the further back a firm is in the supply chain | Controls the end of the bull whip | Gets bull-whipped |
| Operations (the "O" in S&OP) | Most see operations as logistics, warehouses, and transportation | Views operations as logistics and manufacturing |
| Forecasting | By touching the end consumer, should have an advantage in understanding consumer behavior and using point-of-sale data | Is at least one layer removed from the end customer, with fewer opportunities to understand customer behavior |
| Understanding of suppliers' capabilities | Limited because manufacturing is usually a more distant concept, which reduces the opportunities for joint improvement initiatives | More sophisticated understanding of the suppliers' manufacturing capabilities, which should generate more opportunities for joint improvement initiatives |
| Understanding of lead time and flexibility | Generally accepts what is given by the supplier | In a better position to challenge the supplier to compress lead time, since the manufacturer should understand the process better, yet many don't manage lead time effectively or aggressively |
| Inventory | Hard to control in the retail stores, given hundreds or thousands of locations | Better able to manage inventory in a limited number of DC locations |
| SKU management | Say suppliers push them to carry SKUs<br><br>Slotting allowances, in which suppliers pay retailers to put their products on the shelves, become an addiction<br><br>Most retailers do a poor job of managing SKUs | Should have more control over SKUs, but claim that retailers push them to produce more (Note that the retailers believe it is the suppliers who push them.).<br><br>Like retailers, they do a poor job of managing SKUs |
| Slow-moving inventory | Should be good at managing inventory, since they control pricing at the end of the supply chain, but in practice they rarely are | Generally do a poor job because of misaligned metrics and no end-of-life processes |
| Supplier collaboration | Some best practices exist, but true supplier collaboration is rare | A bit more appreciation of the power of collaboration, but still more talk than action |

### Benefits of Collaboration

Does collaboration live up to the hype? The answer we hear from companies that have tried it is a resounding yes. As reported by the Aberdeen Group, best-in-class companies collaborate with supply chain suppliers more frequently than other companies, and are 50 percent more likely to collaborate with their third-party logistics providers. This has a positive impact on their ability to meet their launch dates, hit target revenues, and cut costs, as well as increase life-cycle quality and value.[4]

As supply chains compete against each other for customer loyalty, collaboration is no longer optional. External collaboration involves trust between companies and the ability to overcome the barriers that hindered that trust in the past. Internal collaboration means the same thing, namely, overcoming the barriers that cause functional silos to pull against each other. Barriers include siloed organizational structures, resistance to change, lack of managerial support, lack of process transparency, and poor information sharing. When companies overcome the obstacles to both external and internal collaboration and put that in the framework of a comprehensive supply chain strategy, they enjoy lower costs, achieve higher levels of inventory turnover, improve customer satisfaction, enhance visibility, and see greater levels of responsiveness in their supply chains.

## TREND 2: LEAN AND SIX SIGMA APPLIED TO THE SUPPLY CHAIN

In your strategic planning process, you'll need to decide whether to adopt (or enhance) Lean and Six Sigma techniques aggressively and apply them to the entire end-to-end supply chain. Lean concepts were invented by Toyota more than 60 years ago, and Toyota has pursued *kaizen* (continuous improvement) ever since. U.S. manufacturing companies discovered Lean in the early 1980s and started widely adopting it in the 1990s. Many manufacturing companies tried to do an initial Lean implementation in the early 1990s, lost momentum, and then reimplemented it aggressively five to ten years later with much better results.

Six Sigma had widespread success in manufacturing companies in the 1990s and also continues to grow in popularity. (The term *Six Sigma* refers to a level of good quality encompassing plus or minus six standard deviations from a normal distribution mean, implying a very small level of process defects—only 3.4 defective parts per million units produced.) Six Sigma consists of a set of tools used to reduce variation and thereby defects in any process. Lean and Six Sigma are closely associated with each other in many firms. More than a few companies call their improvement program "Lean-Sigma" or something similar.

Lean and Six Sigma concepts are no longer just for manufacturing operations. Retailers are now discovering these tools in a major way. Supply chain organizations currently apply them to transportation and warehousing operations, with many success stories. Now that they see that the benefits from Lean and Six Sigma extend well beyond the manufacturing floor, companies are adapting their key principles to build efficient, fast, flexible, and collaborative operations across the extended supply chain.

## Lean Logistics

Manufacturers and retailers now implement Lean in their logistics operations, both in transportation and in warehousing operations. For example, I recently interviewed an executive in a consumer durables company that applied Lean and Six Sigma concepts in the organization's major transportation corridors, or "lanes." The company dubbed the project "Lean Lanes." The results of this effort are impressive and are depicted in Figure 4-1.

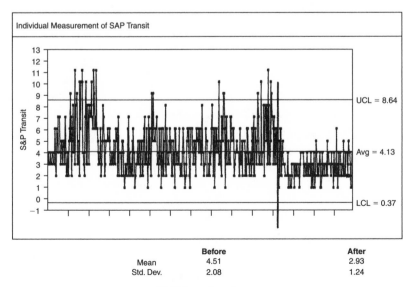

FIGURE 4-1 Lean Lanes

The transportation lane depicted in Figure 4-1 represents the lane from Columbus, Ohio, to Atlanta, Georgia. This firm reduced total cycle time from 4.51 days to 2.93 days, a reduction of 35 percent. In addition, it reduced the variation in that time as measured by the standard deviation by more than 40 percent. The company achieved this improvement by first developing a large visual map of a transportation lane. It called the large visual map a "value stream map," using the standard terminology employed by Lean experts. The highly detailed map included not only the transit time, but also the loading and unloading time on each end. After creating a value stream map for this transportation lane, the improvement team looked for opportunities to reduce both cycle time and variation and found them, creating the large reduction in both cycle time and variation shown in Figure 4-1. This company discovered that reducing both cycle time and variation caused a corresponding improvement in inventory *and* fill rates.

# TREND 3: AGGRESSIVE MANAGEMENT OF COMPLEXITY

At the University of Tennessee Global Supply Chain Institute, we find that companies that have a documented, active process for managing SKU complexity at either the beginning or the end of life had higher profit margins than their competitors. Those companies managed inventory levels more effectively, had better fill rates, and had a lower cost structure.

Complexity in the supply chain can take the form of product complexity or process complexity. Some amount of complexity is unavoidable. For instance, customers routinely drive complexity by demanding more choice in products and services. However, based on working with hundreds of companies, much of the complexity in supply chains is unnecessary. *Unnecessary* complexity is one of the greatest and most intractable impediments to supply chain performance.

## Product Complexity—Forces Driving the Change

Gone are the days when consumer choice was limited by the geographic proximity of a supplier and shelf space at the store. Today, consumers wield far more power than ever before. The complexity of modern supply chains stands as a testament to the shift of power from the company to the consumer. Consumers expect value, features, and further innovation at an unprecedented rate. Take, for example, Coca-Cola. Walking down the aisle of your favorite retailer, you'll find 16 different types of Coke in the United States alone. The Coca-Cola Company has more than 450 brands in over 200 countries worldwide.[5] This expansion of products to fill market niches has caused an exponential increase in supply chain complexity.

Companies today act quickly to provide the variety demanded by their customers, forced by their competitors, or driven by aggressive internal marketing organizations. New innovation, environmental trends, vendor demands, and global forces can also force manufacturers to develop new products and retailers to carry them. The problem is that many of the new product lines that companies create can require a separate supply chain, with more SKUs, more inventory, and even more employees. This can spiral out of control as inventories continue to increase and move forward in the supply chain, and complexity increases with the necessity to store more product variety at more accessible locations.

## A Foundation for Managing Product Complexity

Product life-cycle management is essential to managing product complexity. Product life-cycle management means managing complexity both at the *beginning* and at the *end* of a product's life. The focus of management should be to simplify product lines as much as possible. This includes minimizing finished product SKUs, as well as minimizing unique components. Most firms have a lot of work to do in this area in that they fail to manage product complexity aggressively in the new product introduction process, and further lack any process to manage that complexity as products reach the end of their life. The supply chain strategy especially needs to include an end-of-life process so that products can be retired as new products are brought on line. Otherwise, the number of SKUs continues to grow, along with cost and inventory, with older SKUs contributing very little to overall profitability. Companies should have a process to continuously rationalize their SKUs, not only to keep their product lines fresh and competitive, but also to streamline their supply chains.

In our supply chain assessments, we heard in one company: "We are great at creating new products, but have no clue about how to kill them off." Unfortunately, the problem in that company involved more than end of life. The product complexity problem was born in its new product introduction process. It, like most firms, never asked the one simple question in its new model introduction stage gate process: "How many SKUs can we justify for this new product?" Why companies fail to go through a rigorous justification of SKUs when products are born continues to be a mystery, especially in light of the devastating impact that unnecessary complexity has on supply chain performance.

Complexity can slow a company down in nearly every functional area. An increasing rate of product proliferation has a negative impact on inventory management, product availability, product development, IT systems, and logistics operations. Virtually every executive we talk with recognizes this situation. As the forces that drive complexity continue to grow, supply chain managers must establish a disciplined process to manage supply chain complexity as part of their strategic planning process.

## TREND 4: NETWORK OPTIMIZATION

Supply chain professionals have been working to optimize their physical distribution networks for decades. They have struggled with identifying the best locations for their warehouses, and with the quandary of which customers should be served from which warehouses. So, why is network optimization still a game changer today? A large part of the answer is linked to the huge swings in fuel prices since 2006, and in particular the surge in fuel prices in 2008. This extreme volatility brought network optimization front and center.

One executive told us that his CEO stared at him in a staff meeting and said, "Your transportation costs are growing faster than any other item on the income statement, and that includes healthcare!" That stark warning indicated that the executive not only needed to cut costs in the short term, but also needed a plan to make sure that transportation costs never ended up on top of the CEO's agenda again. He and his team had to rethink their distribution network and reconsider how many warehouses they had, where those warehouses were located, and which customers should be served from which warehouses. They also had virtually ignored the network issue for their emerging dot-com business, as well as the growing reverse logistics (or returns) portion of their business.

This scenario plays out differently in company after company, with the same basic theme. Supply chain professionals across the breadth of industry tell us that to control transportation costs in the long term, they will have to optimize the flow of product in their distribution networks. They have to consider the details of how they will operate if diesel fuel consistently costs $5 per gallon, $10 per gallon, or more. In such an environment, supply chain executives will face many options. For example, should they create create more warehouse locations to reduce the average distance to customers and make it possible to deliver full loads to points closer to the customer? Should they move their existing warehouse locations? Should they rethink which customers should be served from each warehouse?

Fortunately, the tools for optimizing the distribution network are improving rapidly. These new tools help deal with amazingly complex flows in supply chain networks, often representing millions of possible combinations.

## Network Optimization: Strategic Questions

All firms that move product among physical locations must deal with a number of major issues, such as how many warehouses they should have; where those warehouses should be located; what size they should be; and which customers' retail stores should be served from each warehouse. Answering such questions is a major undertaking for a company of any significant size. Firms tells us that they can spend three to four months of intense effort simply gathering and cleansing the data required to complete a network optimization study. On the positive side, they tell us that the effort yields huge savings when it is finally complete, totaling between 5 and 15 percent of their total logistics costs, at a minimum.

In summary, companies need a strategic network optimization capability in order to address questions such as:

- How many warehouses do we need?
- Which customers should be served from which warehouses?
- When we add a new customer (or store), how should we physically serve that customer?

- How can we best handle returns?
- How should we serve the dot-com business?
- Should we be shipping directly from vendor to customer (or store), bypassing our distribution centers (DCs)?
- How can we best handle the import flow?
- Where should we build a new warehouse or a new factory, or, for retailers, where should we locate a new store?

## Global Issues in Network Optimization

The trend toward outsourcing manufacturing to low-cost countries, as well as the need to sell product in those countries, has changed the focus of many firms from domestic-oriented networks to global and import-oriented networks, requiring companies to reanalyze international distribution routes. As major global trends swing back and forth, firms need a way to quickly evaluate the cost impact of moving production and distribution to different global locations. Network optimization takes on a different level of urgency for global supply chains, which are addressed in Trend 5: the global supply chain.

## The Technical Challenge of Network Optimization

As software and hardware capabilities continue to advance, optimization technology (finding the best answer while accommodating realistic constraints) advances with them. Today, companies achieve great benefits by using software with optimization capabilities. By modeling and optimizing their current operations, companies can identify opportunities to achieve breakthrough savings in cost and working capital. Network optimization can also be a critical input for decisions on modes of transport, routes, and carrier selection. However, completing a network optimization project can be a formidable challenge, and supply chain professionals should avoid underestimating the challenge of doing a network optimization. The task requires a vast quantity of data, which, in most firms, also requires a much longer than expected process of getting cleansed data into the right format.

A network optimization study can also be outsourced to a third-party company consultant. Whether the software comes from in-house, a consultant, a third-party logistics provider, or a university, assembling the huge amount of accurate data required for the study always represents the greatest challenge. Despite the initial pain of doing network optimization, a firm that successfully builds and maintains an optimization model can look forward to consistent returns (that is, cost savings in the millions).

We recommend that a full network optimization study follow the completion of the supply chain strategy. The need for the study is very likely to be confirmed by the strategy, with a network study becoming one of the major projects spawned by the supply chain strategy. A different distribution network may be the only way you can satisfy your customers' needs while still meeting cost and inventory targets. Your strategy work is likely to identify this gap, and call for a network optimization analysis.

# TREND 5: THE GLOBAL SUPPLY CHAIN

A supply chain strategy clearly must accommodate the global environment. Events such as the invention of the lightbulb, the printing press, the internal combustion engine, and the Internet were all points of discontinuity that changed the world of business forever, just as globalization has changed and will continue to change the way business is done, and in particular how supply chains operate. Never has the world operated as a single market as much as it does today. As developing countries and emerging markets grow dramatically in power in a world that is increasingly without economic boundaries, the idea of a truly global supply chain has become a reality. Today ideas, capital, and material flow freely across many borders.

However, some caution is in order. It seems as if one natural disaster after another has had devastating impacts on globally interdependent supply chains. Examples include the unpredictable earthquake, tsunami, and nuclear disaster in Japan; major floods around the globe; and the uprisings in the Middle East. Intel warned in the fourth quarter of 2011 that its revenue would be down about $1 billion because of flooding in Thailand.[6] The product availability problems caused by long global supply lines can cause a serious loss of sales and market share. In a Nestlé study presented at our Supply Chain Forum, customers shopping in retail stores have only a 4 percent chance of getting everything on a 40-item list. The study further revealed that when a customer is faced with a stock-out for a CPG item, it results in a lost sale 40 percent of the time; when a shopper experiences an empty shelf three times in a row, he or she normally leaves forever.

As companies create a larger global footprint, they need to deal with more suppliers and more customers from more locations at a rapidly increasing pace, further multiplying the risks to their supply chain. Global forces place tremendous strain on the capabilities and requirements of the supply chain. As the supply chain globalizes, lead times expand, logistics cost and inventory investment grow, information flow becomes more complex and error-prone, and the amount of required working capital increases, all adding exponentially to the challenge of managing the supply chain.

## Globalization Implications: Port Issues

Port congestion abated temporarily with the Great Recession economic slowdown and with a slowing in global outsourcing, but all the experts agree that there will be major infrastructure challenges in the future. It is essential that the contemplated improvements to deal with port congestion continue to move forward.

The Panama Canal is a testament to the congestion that transportation lanes across the world are facing. Originally built in the early 1900s, the 48-mile canal handles more than 14,000 ships per year at a maximum capacity of about 5,000 TEUs (one TEU is the size of a container measuring 20 × 8 × 8.5 feet) per ship. The largest container ships built today carry more than 10,000 TEUs worth of cargo and are "panamax" ships, meaning that they are unable to traverse the canal. To allow for more shipments through the Gulf and East Coasts of the Americas, the Panamanian voters approved a $5 billion expansion plan that will roughly double the canal's capacity when it is completed in 2014. The ports along the Gulf and East Coasts are preparing for the increase in traffic from the Panama Canal, but the expansion may not be enough to handle all the cargo ships of the future.

## Insourcing Will Become a Trend

When many companies went offshore, it often involved a myopic pursuit of cheap labor. Some countertrends are now forcing supply chain managers to reevaluate that decision. These include transportation cost increases, supply chain complexity, visibility issues, long lead times, higher inventory requirements, larger carbon footprints, quality, and labor and economic issues in host countries. Some companies have found it beneficial to move manufacturing operations to the market where the goods will be sold because of the combination of lower cost and more control over operations. Time to market matters, as supply chains switch from pushing products to customers to delivering the product with demand-driven models. Bringing manufacturing closer to home allows supply chains to quickly react to changes and nimbly deliver product as required by the customer.

Higher fuel costs especially dilute the cost advantage of outsourcing to the cheapest production location. The growth of the lanes between the United States and China has slowed partly because of the rising costs of transporting goods; inexpensive products are particularly affected, since there is less opportunity to pass increased costs on to the customer. In 2008, the cost of shipping a container from Shanghai to Los Angeles surged 150 percent and stood at $5,500 before settling back down with the global recession. If oil hits $200 per barrel or higher in the next decade, the cost to ship a container from Asia to the United States could approach or exceed $10,000.[7]

Currency issues also loom in the background, and labor costs in China are increasing quickly, causing manufacturers of some types of products to relocate to other areas of Asia, such as Vietnam, where labor rates are lower. This trend could play a part in the potential migration of jobs and production back to North America, where markets are closer and there is a higher level of control with less risk. Yet, as one supply chain executive told us, "We would love to move our production back to the United States. Unfortunately, the vendors of our raw materials have now shifted to Asia!" The major beneficiary of this surge in the cost of outsourcing to Asia may be Mexico, which can provide lower-cost labor and proximity to the United States.

Many firms now tell us that they are evaluating whether to shift from suppliers in Asia to ones in the Western Hemisphere, particularly the United States and Mexico. The economics definitely now tilt in that direction. As this new "near-shoring" trend plays out, companies will have to reevaluate their global supply chain operations.

# TREND 6: THE SUSTAINABLE SUPPLY CHAIN _____

Considering green sustainability in a supply chain strategy was once optional; those days are past. Today's supply chains must be designed to be cost-effective in delivering customer value, maintain appropriate on-shelf availability with minimum inventory, and do it all with the least possible impact on the environment. The issues of traffic congestion, growing fuel consumption, $CO_2$ emissions, and permanent increases in transportation costs increase the need for green or sustainability programs. Supply chain professionals need to continue to cut costs while they rethink old ideas about the environment.

Many companies take sustainability initiatives very seriously. Small steps in warehousing operations include converting to energy-efficient fixtures, using LED lighting, installing motion-activated lighting, adding skylights, insulating walls and roofs, installing rooftop wind power units, painting roofs with energy-efficient colors or planting vegetation on roofs to provide climate control, solar power, and using geothermal heat pumps for cooling and heating. However, the green initiatives with the most impact involve increasing the efficiency of the transportation fleet so that it not only is fuel-efficient, but also drives fewer miles. These extremely powerful supply chain sustainability initiatives pay back quickly in bottom-line cost reduction.

Companies must cut costs, especially when government regulations force sustainability upon them. One typical example was the EPA mandate of new stormwater regulations that came without corresponding federal funds to pay for them. Warehouses in affected cities needed to pay to meet those stricter regulations themselves. In Minneapolis, every square foot of warehouse space includes a cost of 12 cents per year in stormwater fees. This means that a 550,000-square-foot warehouse pays close to $65,000 per year in such fees alone. Warehouse managers have found that stormwater management is one key to operational success, deploying creative ideas such as permeable pavements, using green roofs to act as retention basins, or using native plants to reduce heat and stormwater.[8]

## The Supply Chain Is at the Tip of the Spear

Most companies see environmentalism as a necessary effort in marketing to an increasingly environmentally conscious consumer population. They view such efforts as essential to both their reputation and their competitive advantage. After all, the supply chain organization often produces the lion's share of the greenhouse gases generated by a firm. Therefore, supply chain leaders find themselves at the tip of the spear in leading the company's strategy to reduce the carbon footprint.

Some recent supply chain research that we conducted asked companies whether they were considering a greater emphasis on environmental and sustainability initiatives. A few answered that they "couldn't afford it now, and their customers didn't care." But most companies (just over 80 percent) answered a resounding yes, confirming that environmental considerations are a major and very new trend that supply chain professionals have to face. Few companies will tolerate a significant increase in cost to pursue envionmentalism. On the other hand, a number of companies cited reasons such as the "moral imperative" as a motivation for moving forward in this area. Some noted that their customers demanded that they meet certain environmental standards, even though it might lead to cost increases. However, most firms see sustainability and cost reduction as consistent concepts, while some simply repackage their normal cost reduction initiatives and call them sustainability efforts. When a firm finds a way to reduce the number of miles driven by its fleet of trucks and calls that an environmental initiative, it's as much a matter of public relations as it is of sustainability.

Unfortunately, this additional environmental responsibility comes in addition to the other massive challenges that companies face. The pressures to cut costs do not abate in the slighest. Yet some firms pursue environmental supply chain initiatives in spite of a very low return on investment and a very long payback period. One retailer, for example, replaced oversized diesel delivery trucks with lighter cargo vans that have twice the fuel efficiency. It offsets some of this incremental cost by increasing the number of packages on a delivery truck from 130 to 190 through optimizing the delivery routes of these vans in urban areas.

Suppliers don't always make it easy for their supply chain partners to achieve their environmental goals. However, megacompanies can demand and get compliance. One Walmart supplier told us that he was summoned to Bentonville for a supplier meeting. The Walmart executive in charge of environmental efforts spoke to the group. At the beginning of the talk, he passed out his business card. It was only one inch wide by one and a half inches long!

He said that the group immediately got the message. But not every retailer has the luxury of demanding and getting what it wants. Some suppliers are larger and more powerful than the customers they supply, and can resist environmental efforts that they view as an unnecessary cost increase.

## How One Retailer Saves Money with its Environmental Efforts

In spite of the barriers, some firms are making tremendous progress. A good example is a midsized retailer with about $8 billion in sales. In this company, the supply chain group leads the way in implementing sustainability efforts. The company has reduced the number of miles driven by 22 percent through an intense focus on increasing trailer cube utilization and optimizing the routes from the DCs to the stores.

The retailer worked aggressively with its contract carrier to fill empty backhaul miles. It launched a reverse logistics effort to use the trucks, which deliver from the DCs to the stores, to haul slow-moving merchandise back to the DCs. This effort yielded an additional fringe benefit of helping the company avoid severe price markdowns in the stores. Instead, merchandise that moves slowly in one location, but at a faster clip in another, flows to the store that needs it. In that same returning truck, the company hauls back all of the cardboard and reusable totes, again for free, and does the same thing for other shipping supplies, such as air pillows. The firm bundles and sells all of the used cardboard for a very nice return. It reuses delivery totes. These actions reduce its carbon footprint and also result in very substantial savings for the firm. This comprehensive program avoids having each of the nearly 1,000 stores handle slow-moving inventory and delivery detritus in a haphazard manner.

In addition, this company implemented a reverse logistics process to recycle its customers' outdated computers and printers. It further implemented a process to consolidate vendor returns so that such products could be shipped in full loads rather than having the supplier make individual pickups. Finally, it worked with its paper supplier and a number of universities on a project to recycle paper. The used paper is picked up when deliveries are made to the university, and, in a closed loop, it is transported back to the paper supplier to be recycled in its paper mills.

## The Untapped Gold Mine of Returns

As part of their "green" supply chain strategy work, firms should seriously consider returned merchandise. In studies at our Global Supply Chain Institute, we find that most firms do not have a disciplined process for managing returned merchandise. Also, most firms have a shockingly low understanding of the total cost generated by returns. We have almost never seen a comprehensive cost analysis of returns that includes such cost of returns factors as:

- Space cost and constraints
- Labor to receive and process the return
- Inventory holding cost
- Transportation to receive returns and then eventually ship them out
- Scrap and liquidation cost
- Warranty and/or repair costs
- The cost impact on the other normal warehouse operations
- The bottom-line impact on the firm if returns are not handled efficiently
- How much of value is salvaged
- Brand equity

We recommend that any project to optimize returns management follow the development of a supply chain strategy. If such a project emerges from the strategy process, we recommend a seven-step process to guide that project:

1. Identify the root causes of returns.
2. Measure the full cost of returns, which most companies grossly underestimate.
3. Review product design, packaging, and consumer instructions.
4. Manage better customer education and expectations on the front end of the purchase.
5. Segment returns with a different approach for each category.
6. Develop an operations plan to minimize the processing cost.
7. Put in place a liquidation plan to maximize asset recovery—a decision tree framework.

### Sustainable Packaging

Many companies find that packaging is another huge untapped opportunity. Walmart, for instance, plans to reduce vendor packaging content by 5 percent by 2013. This effort will result in a decrease of about 700,000 metric tons of carbon emissions, saving the company roughly $3.4 billion over a five-year period. To help achieve its goal, Walmart has introduced a "Packaging Scorecard"[9] that tracks a supplier's "greenness" against that of other suppliers. It bases the scorecard on metrics that include greenhouse gases per ton, material value, product/package ratio, cube utilization, transporation, recycled content, recovery value, renewable energy, and innovation.

By reducing packaging for just 277 SKUs, Walmart was able to use 727 fewer shipping containers, saving $3.5 million on transportation costs. In addition, by using less packaging, the supply chain was able to use 5,100 fewer trees and prevent 1,300 barrels of oil from being used for package creation.[10]

# TREND 7: THE FOCUS ON COST AND WORKING CAPITAL

The culmination of a supply chain strategy hopefully results in major reductions in cost and working capital, while *at the same time* continuing to improve product availability and service to customers. The Nineteenth Annual *State of Logistics Report* published by CSCMP (the Council of Supply Chain Management Professionals) reveals that companies in the United States spend $1.4 trillion on logistics. This is equivalent to 10.1 percent of U.S GDP (gross domestic product).[11] These costs directly affect the bottom line. Fuel costs have more than tripled in the past decade, even though the Great Recession temporarily slowed the rapid increase. The outlook for the future is not any brighter, considering the threats of a return of higher fuel costs, stricter government regulations, capacity constraints, infrastructure issues, the emergence of China, and a fragile U.S economy. To combat these forces, companies must somehow manage costs more efficiently at the same time that they also optimize working capital and improve service to their customers.

## Managing Working Capital

While minimizing cost has always been important, it cannot be the only goal. Cost should be managed in tandem with working capital. Working capital, or current assets minus current liabilities, basically consists of inventory plus accounts receivables minus accounts payable, and it has a direct impact on a company's cash flow. By managing costs and working capital together, companies strive to increase the economic value added (EVA) of operations, directly benefiting shareholders. EVA is a metric that measures a company's overall financial performance, and it is of great importance to investors because it is a true measure of their return on investment. A very simplified version of how to calculate EVA is shown in Figure 4-2.

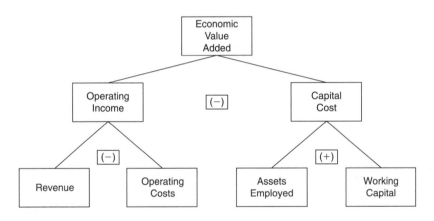

FIGURE 4-2 Economic Value Added

## Strategies to Improve Working Capital

More firms are now using their supply chains as the prime lever to reduce working capital, improve cash flow, and increase EVA. Supply chain organizations always find themselves at the forefront of managing the inventory component of working capital. However, they also have an opportunity to use their supply chains to improve the accounts receivable and accounts payable components of working capital.

For example, supply chain cycle times can be a major determining factor in setting payment terms for both payables and receivables. If replenishment cycle times to the customer decline, the customer should be able to turn its inventory faster and get payment from its customers more quickly, with less need to finance inventory with payment terms. Therefore, as cycle times to customers decrease, so logically should payment terms, which would decrease accounts receivable, decrease working capital, and increase cash flow. Regarding payables, the supply chain should manage the total strategy with the firm's vendors. There should be collaboration opportunities to make the right trade-off between vendor payment terms and vendor collaboration benefits. This should create an opportunity to increase payment terms to the vendor, increasing accounts payable, which in turn reduces working capital and increases cash flow.

## Managing Working Capital with Your Supply Chain

As indicated, more firms are now attacking working capital with their supply chain partners. An office supplies retailer recently announced plans to pull more than a billion dollars out of its inventory by moving inventory back up the chain into an RDC (regional distribution center) network.

We recently assessed a midsized retailer that cut its inventories by nearly $500 million, almost a 50 percent reduction, while still greatly improving fill rates in its stores. We were impressed with its approach. Following the development of a supply chain strategy, the company launched a targeted effort to reduce inventory and increase fill rates, an effort that was identified in the strategy as a priority. The 11-step approach that the company developed is a good checklist for anyone that is striving to simultaneously reduce inventory and increase fill rates. Those 11 steps consisted of:

1. Aligning the company's replenishment plans with actual sales by enhancing the S&OP process.
2. Improving forecast accuracy, especially at the store level.
3. Improving forecasting for promotions by creating a promotions database.
4. Reducing availability targets on very slow-moving SKU-store combinations
5. Optimizing delivery frequency to stores by varying the number of deliveries per week depending on the store.

6. Setting safety stock inventory properly to avoid unnecessary overstocking.
7. Kitting at import origin (such as China) to eliminate case-pack inventory drivers.
8. Reducing lead time.
9. Reducing case count to better align delivery quantities with demand.
10. Managing SKUs and clustering of SKU assortments by store.
11. Increasing collaboration with suppliers.

## TRANSFORM YOUR GAME OR IT'S GAME OVER

These seven supply chain game changers are having and will continue to have a huge impact on any supply chain strategy and, in general, on your company's ability to compete. Any firm that is developing a supply chain strategy should ask: "Does my company have a supply chain strategy that addresses the major supply chain game-changing trends that will affect it in the future?"

## THE SEVEN MEGATRENDS

Trend 1: Collaboration
Trend 2: Lean and Six Sigma Applied to the Supply Chain
Trend 3: Aggressive Management of Complexity
Trend 4: Network Optimization
Trend 5: The Global Supply Chain
Trend 6: The Sustainable Supply Chain
Trend 7: The Focus on Cost and Working Capital

## THE NEXT STEPS IN STRATEGY DEVELOPMENT: ANALYZE YOUR COMPETITORS AND THE TECHNOLOGY

The trends discussed in this chapter move the strategy effort from an internal to more of an external focus. Two additional external issues will affect your strategy in a major way. Those two forces, the changing face of your *competitors* and newly emerging supply chain *technologies,* are the subjects of the next two chapters.

## CHAPTER 4 ACTION STEPS

1. Discuss with your strategy team how you will address each of the seven game-changing trends in your supply chain strategy.
2. For each key trend, assign someone to research it, and define how it applies in your particular industry.
3. Review with your team whether there are any other trends that are unique to your business that should be addressed in your strategy.

# CHAPTER 5

# Analyze Your Competition's Supply Chain

In the last chapter, you made the transition from the internal to the external environment in your strategy process by considering seven supply chain game changers. The next step in this process is to continue this outward focus by considering your competition and technology trends. This chapter will address how to evaluate your competitors from a supply chain perspective; the next chapter will tackle technology.

The essence of strategy sometimes lies in choosing what *not* to do. Every company must place its bets carefully. Some companies operate on the razor's edge of survival and cannot afford to make mistakes. For example, one well-known retailer holds a number three position in sales in its segment. When the Great Recession of 2008–2010 hit, the company found itself in an especially vulnerable position. It survived only because of excellent supply chain management, which freed up hundreds of millions of dollars of working capital, reduced costs by tens of millions, and improved fill rates in stores. The company had developed much of its supply chain management capability, with the resulting benefits, before the recession hit, so it had the cushion it needed to weather the storm. The supply chain team accomplished this feat by making the right strategic choices. Not all of the bets that the team placed paid off, but most of them did. The supply chain leaders had to decide what supply chain capabilities would allow the company to compete, survive, and thrive. They were able to make good strategic choices only because they had good insight into what the competition was doing.

Failure to understand your competitors amounts to letting your competitors manage your profits for you! Yet some firms unknowingly allow their competitors to manage their profits by always being a step or two behind. They may even go through the motions of gathering competitive data, but they stop short of really analyzing those data. The real art of competitive analysis is reading between the lines and anticipating the implications of certain competitive actions. But before the analysis is done, a more basic question concerns the not-so-trivial issue of who really are your competitors.

## WHO ARE YOUR COMPETITORS?

The answer to who your competitors are may not be so simple. For example, the office supplies company Staples competes with its two direct retail competitors, Office Depot and OfficeMax. But the competitive landscape for Staples is far more complex. For example, in the annual report of Form 10-K report (an annual report required by the U.S. Securities and Exchange Commission [SEC] that includes a comprehensive summary of a public company's performance) that Staples submits each year, the company lists its competitors as:

- Online retailers like Amazon on a range of products
- Best Buy in the electronics space
- Mass merchants like Walmart and Target
- A myriad of retailers in the office furniture arena
- In the business-to-business (B2B) space, a broad assortment of firms that sell to office supply retailers
- And finally, Office Depot and OfficeMax

In an incredibly complex competitive environment like this, Staples must choose carefully whom it will try to outpace. It clearly cannot meet Amazon or Walmart head on. Success requires competing effectively in the right niches and targeting the growth markets of the future.

Staples must determine where it stands relative to its competition over the full range of supply chain capabilities. Furthermore, as Staples determines the *new* supply chain capabilities it will need in the future, it must close the loop and evaluate how it will compare to its competition. Just as a quarterback throwing a football must lead his receiver, Staples must make sure that five years from now, it is not striking a target that is well behind the industry's best. Hitting such a moving target in the dynamic, fast-moving world of business is as challenging to do as it is exhilarating to accomplish. The challenge is great because it goes beyond benchmarking a firm's direct competition and extends to being best in class for industry in general.

How much do supply chain executives understand their competition? In our discussions with supply chain managers, we find that they often consider gathering competitive intelligence somewhat of a mystery; certainly there is broad concern that collecting intelligence may be at the far edge of legality, or at least of ethics. These concerns are usually unfounded. In reality, there is an enormous amount of public information that can be used to develop competitive intelligence, and gathering it is neither illegal nor unethical, nor is it all that difficult. Using the simple processes described in this chapter, I offer ways in which you can determine the makeup of the competitive landscape. But first you will need to decide what you really need to know.

## WHAT DO YOU NEED TO KNOW?

To develop your supply chain strategy, what do you need to know about your competition? Most companies would say that it would be nice to compare basic performance data, such as cost, inventory, and customer availability. But, an "apples-to-apples" comparison of such information does not always give you the insight you need; in the worst case, it might even be harmful.

It is far more useful to understand the process, technology, and network capabilities of your competitors so that you are in a better position to interpret data like inventory turns or cost as a percent of sales. Also, seeing the signals for future process changes can give a firm an invaluable advantage. As Wayne Gretsky said, "I skate to where the puck is going to be."

For example, a grocery retailer that is strong in the southeastern United States told us that it was getting 12 inventory turns (that is, annual sales divided by average inventory levels) in its distribution centers (DCs) and 3 turns in its stores, for an average of 6.0 turns for all inventory for the company. The annual report of its major regional competitor claimed that the company achieved 5.5 inventory turns overall, with roughly the same prices and gross margins. As a result, the grocer felt comfortable that it was in a strong competitive position in this area of working capital management. But then the grocer hired someone from that same competitor. The new hire said that the competitor had recently acquired a midsized company that had very poor inventory management practices; the combined data for the acquirer and the acquired had depressed the competitor's inventory turnover number, but the competitor was now addressing that issue aggressively. The new hire told his employer that without the acquisition, turnover in the competing company ran closer to 8 turns. He further said that the competitors' stores had much more advanced replenishment processes, and that it actually turned its *store* inventory at more than 5 turns compared with 3 turns for this company. In short, the competition could support the same level of sales with 40 percent less inventory! He further revealed that the competitor's process allowed it to hold more inventory at the DC level, respond quickly to store demand, and avoid stocking items that weren't selling. Instead of having an advantage in inventory and working capital management, the grocery retailer was suffering from a severe disadvantage.

The numerical inventory turnover comparisons in this example were less useful than information on the processes and technologies that the competitor employed, because the processes and technologies explained why the differences existed. That is an important lesson for companies conducting competitive analysis: always look for the process information. For example, has your competitor implemented Lean and/or Six Sigma techniques in a mature way? Has it broken the code on cross-docking? Understanding process advantages and disadvantages offers much more insight into a competitor's capability.

In the example just given, the grocery chain acquired this process information through a lucky accident, but you don't need to recruit from the competition in order to gain competitive intelligence. You can still gather process and technology information using the techniques described later in this chapter. (See the section "How to Conduct a Competitive Study.") Before I get there, however, let's consider some basic supply chain process issues that you will probably want to explore as they relate to the competition.

## Warehousing Operations Versus the Competition

What processes and technologies does your competitor use in its warehousing operations? Many large and seemingly sophisticated firms do not use even the most basic technology. One $50 billion retailer told us that it does not use ASNs (automatic shipment notices). ASNs have been standard practice for more than 20 years, and they can greatly reduce the amount of labor needed to receive product in DCs. Another multibillion-dollar company admitted that its WMS (warehouse management system) had only basic receiving and put-away functions. It did not manage workflow or interweave tasks to optimize labor performance and cycle times in the warehouse. If companies like these learn that their direct competitors are using much more advanced technology, they can rightly surmise that they may be at a competitive disadvantage, assuming that the technology was properly implemented.

If your competitor uses Lean and Six Sigma techniques extensively in its warehouse operations and you don't, you may face a competitive disadvantage. However, without more knowledge, even this can be misleading. The competitor's implementation may be deficient. Not everyone truly understands and lives the philosophy of continuous improvement, waste elimination, cycle-time compression, problem solving, and respect for people. Some just do a Lean improvement project when a crisis breaks out. In the Lean journey, companies frequently have to make two or three attempts before the culture takes hold, if it does so at all.

Is your competitor about to revamp its distribution network? Is it about to rationalize or expand the number of DCs that it employs? Will it start shipping direct from factory to customer, bypassing the DCs? These changes can have enormous implications for your competitor's cost structure. Finding the answers to these questions is tricky, but not impossible, as described later in the chapter.

## Cross-Docking Versus the Competition

Cross-docking can bring a major competitive breakthrough. If you don't have the extra step of putting product away, only to then pick it later, with all of the associated systems and people required for those activities, you save a lot of money in the logistics operations. But if cross-docking were easy, the advantage would not be as great, because everyone would be doing it. As one executive told us, "Despite all of the talk regarding cross-docking, there is often very little done because of the enormous challenge of it."

In fact, we believe that successful cross-docking requires expertise in six areas:

1. *Supplier support.* Suppliers must provide excellent availability, which requires a stable order pattern. Also, cross-docking requires reliable service providers: logistics service providers must provide fast, reliable, consistent service.
2. *Process improvement capability.* The firm needs to have a strong focus on continuous improvement, aided by the use of Lean and/or Six Sigma techniques.
3. *Committed organization.* Documented, standardized methods and great training must support good people.
4. *Computerized systems.* Integrated systems for order management, ASNs, yard management, cross-docking management systems, and track and trace capability must exist.
5. *Facility design and layout.* Inbound and outbound doors at the facility should be designed to maximize efficiency. Also, work must be balanced throughout the day, as must dock door utilization.
6. *Right products.* The most appropriate products for cross-docking should have relatively consistent, high-volume sales and a single method of handling.

One company we know of learned from comments in an annual report that its major competitor emphasized cross-docking. The executive we spoke to said, "I figured talk is cheap, and I'd believe it when I saw it." But a year later, that same executive read an independent study of cross-docking practices in industry and found his competitor listed among the companies heralded for their best practices. That report noted that only a small percentage of volume is cross-docked in industry today. But, the study did highlight the competitor as using an advanced and effective cross-docking process. With this information, the executive feared that his company was at a significant competitive disadvantage.

## Transportation and Supply Management Versus the Competition

To understand your competitor's supply chain, you must understand how it manages transportation, both inbound to its facilities and outbound to its customers. How does your competitor handle transportation in general? Does it have a private fleet? If so, how well is the fleet managed? Does your competitor manage inbound freight (freight collect), or does it allow suppliers to manage their inbound deliveries (freight prepaid)? Firms that control and manage inbound transportation often achieve great cost savings. One small grocery company told us that it saved more than $10 million by managing the transportation flows from its suppliers. If your competitor manages inbound flows and you simply leave this to your suppliers, you are undoubtedly at a cost disadvantage.

How does your competitor work with its suppliers? Does it pursue win/win collaborative relationships, or does it employ a tough guy, confrontational tone? If the latter, it may be possible to exploit that style by working collaboratively with the same suppliers.

## SHOULD YOU HIRE A CONSULTANT TO GATHER COMPETITIVE INFORMATION?

One approach to acquiring all of this competitive knowledge is to hire a consultant. An array of firms specialize in competitive analysis and competitive intelligence. How do the competitive intelligence firms gather such information? One supply chain executive told us that he hired a firm that claimed to gather both "primary source" intelligence and "secondary source" intelligence. The executive asked for definitions. Secondary source information consisted of:

- Anything published or on the Internet
- Anything in the major business databases of journals and periodicals, such as Business Source Premier
- Any information from people who might have worked for the competitor in the past, including, of course, those who are currently working for your firm

"OK," the supply chain executive said. "But I thought that was about all you could get. What is this primary source intelligence?" The consultant told him that primary source information came from people who were currently employed by the competitor. "Is that legal?" asked the supply chain executive. The intelligence expert responded that it was legal as long as the people from her firm didn't misrepresent themselves in gathering the information. The supply chain executive asked, "How exactly do you do this?"

The consultant explained that her firm hires graduate students to contact middle managers in the competitor's firm. The students tell the managers, "I am a graduate student conducting a research study, and I heard that you are a major expert in the field. Could you answer a few questions for me?"

"It's amazing," said the consultant, "how many people respond to that line without asking the obvious question: who is funding the study? If they ask that, we would of course tell them the truth, which would no doubt end the call. But we find that few companies warn their employees about this approach."

The supply chain executive started to feel a little queasy. "I don't know about legality here, but at the least it sounds a little unethical to me." "It may be uncomfortable to you," said the consultant, "but your competitors might do this *to* you at some point!" The supply chain executive ultimately agreed to move forward, and the consultant obtained a significant amount of information for him. Every firm must gauge its appetite for such tactics. But whether a firm uses such tactics or not, it must assume that its competitors may do so. Needless to say, all employees need to be extremely cautious in responding to any survey over the phone or on the Internet! You may be responding to a survey from your competitor.

One area where the supply chain executive drew the line involved a practice known as "dumpster diving." This involves obtaining internal company documents without using outright theft. The supply chain executive said, "I don't want you to use any documents that were meant for internal distribution within the competitor's operation, including anything tossed in the trash." Luckily, supply chain executives don't always have to resort to such tactics. A huge amount of competitive information can be gleaned from secondary sources as described here.

## HOW TO CONDUCT A COMPETITIVE STUDY

A consultant is not always necessary. A surprising amount of competitive information can be obtained via Internet and database searches. For example, a midsized retailer decided to see what it could discover about its major competitors in this manner. It found that 10-K submissions for public companies contain a wealth of information. The annual 10-K report required by the SEC provides a comprehensive overview of a company's business and financial condition, and it must be filed within 90 days after the end of the fiscal year. The 10-K includes audited financial statements; it also must include a description of the company's priorities for the future. Since these descriptions influence investors and Wall Street analysts and, by law, must address anything that will have a material impact on the company's results, they can be quite detailed and specific. Often a close reading of a 10-K reveals a great deal of supply chain information, and even strategy. And looking at 10-Ks over time often yields great insight into strategic trends. For companies that are privately owned, owned by a private equity firm, foreign owned competitors, or firms having divisions embedded in a large parent company, all of this becomes more difficult, but not impossible.

## Example Using Publicly Available Information

We worked with a company (RetailCo) that did an excellent competitive evaluation, and we believe that this company's analysis is a good model for you to follow in doing your competitive analysis. RetailCo started its analysis by accessing its competitors' 10-Ks and supplemented that with searches of the Internet and periodical databases. It found a wealth of information. Some examples are listed here to give you a detailed feel for the type of information and insights you can obtain:

- RetailCo found an interview given by its main competitor's EVP of supply chain that revealed a plan to add a new position in each of the company's retail stores. The new position would focus exclusively on maintaining accurate inventory records (this amounted to more than 1,000 new positions over the retailer's network—clearly a huge commitment). RetailCo feared that this would significantly raise availability and lower inventory in the competitor's stores; otherwise the 1,000 people could never be justified. This move by the competition motivated a study within RetailCo to determine the cost-benefit of doing the same thing. RetailCo conducted the study in five pilot stores, and found that the accurate inventory records resulting from this move did in fact lead to very significant improvements in both fill rates and inventory levels. RetailCo was now convinced that it would be at a major disadvantage if it did not match the competitor's action.

- RetailCo found that its competitor revised its availability metrics so that they reflected the customer's perspective more accurately. The competitor also admitted that the 98 percent availability level that it had previously announced was really only 94 percent, implying a major new focus on fill rates. In another story found through an Internet search, RetailCo discovered a quote from its competitor acknowledging that the company had a widely divergent range of stocking practices at individual stores, which it was addressing. (To RetailCo's chagrin, it had the same problem.)

- RetailCo discovered a surprising amount of information about the systems that its competitor used. It found that some of its customers (common customers for its competitor also) actually used the competitor's system to manage in-house inventory. This clearly gave the competitor a huge competitive advantage, because it could favor its own products when recommending inventory changes. The only course of action RetailCo could take was to understand the logic behind its competitor's inventory management program, which it did by asking one of its customers that was using the system. Knowing the logic embedded in the system, it could position its offering to best take advantage of the ordering logic.

- RetailCo found that that its competitor claimed that it had reduced its Asia supply chain lead time from 120 days to 55 days, with a plan to get to 45 days for private-label products made mainly in South China. RetailCo's lead times were still in the 120-day range, which translated into more inventory and lower product availability for the growing private-label segment.

RetailCo obtained this information and much more about its main competitor using only publicly available information that was fairly easy to access. Yet this information transformed RetailCo's supply chain priorities. Unfortunately, it had to play "catch-up" because of its prior lack of knowledge of its competitor's supply chain improvements. How did RetailCo get so out of touch with competitive activity? Surprisingly, we find that even major corporations have little factual information about their competitors, especially in the supply chain area. Supply chain professionals are often out of their comfort zone here, and anecdotes and rumors carry far too much weight. Some supply chain professionals we talk with are so focused on achieving their incredibly demanding internal goals that they have little time to think much about their competition. In this example, though RetailCo fell behind, it employed an excellent approach to catch up and gather competitive intelligence.

## Don't Overlook Your Own Employees

Next, RetailCo identified all current employees who had previously worked for its competitors. It found 12 such people and asked them if they felt comfortable being interviewed about their old company; 11 of the 12 gladly and even enthusiastically agreed to the interviews. RetailCo asked us to interview them. In most cases, the information we obtained was dated and probably no longer relevant. But we did find the following:

- We were impressed by the extent to which the competitor had implemented Lean in the supply chain.
- We heard about an S&OP (sales and operations planning) process in the competitor that dominated the management process, unlike the lip service paid to S&OP at RetailCo. In fact, we discovered that the competitor's CEO actually said that the S&OP meetings were the most important meetings in the entire company! RetailCo's CEO didn't know how to spell S&OP.

Each of these findings pushed RetailCo to reevaluate and ultimately strengthen its internal approaches to Lean, S&OP, and cross-functional accountability.

## Don't Forget Your Suppliers and Customers

A final phase of the competitive analysis involved polling key suppliers and customers who also interfaced with RetailCo's competitors. Of course, a supplier or a customer cannot divulge much information without making all parties extremely uncomfortable. As one supply chain professional said, "If they talk about them, they will talk about us." Asking for specific information on any individual competitor was a nonstarter. However, RetailCo struck gold when it asked its suppliers one key question, which proved to be extremely enlightening: "Based on what you see in the industry in general, what can we do better?" Its suppliers basically confirmed what RetailCo had discovered from publicly available information. Very little was new, but it was good to get independent confirmation.

RetailCo found that accessing publicly available information and talking with employees, suppliers, and customers yielded a fairly detailed and rich description of the competition, with no need for consultants.

## SUPPLY CHAIN COMPETITIVE EVALUATION: CASE STUDY

A consumer packaged goods (CPG) firm, CPG, Inc., approached the competitive assessment using an intriguing process to rank its capabilities relative to those of its competitors. We highly recommend the approach it used to get to the next level of sophistication in its competitive analysis, building on the excellent process that RetailCo used.

CPG, Inc., found that only five significant competitors remained after nearly 50 years of intense competition. Its process for competitive analysis involved first determining the qualities that were most important to retail customers. It started exactly where it should: with the needs of its customers. It identified capabilities that were important to its customers by actually traveling and talking to many of its retail partners. Those customers emphasized 10 supply chain capabilities, in order of priority:

1. "Shorten your replenishment lead time. It needs to be 48 hours at the most."
2. "You need better order integrity. When you give us a delivery date, hit the date!"
3. "Please be able to hit tight delivery windows of plus or minus two hours at our DCs."
4. "We want all products we order to be delivered in a single shipment."
5. "Please correct the periodic errors in your invoicing."

6. "We want real-time order tracking and inquiry."
7. "We need enhanced reverse logistics capability. In other words, the process of returning product to you needs to be more flexible and efficient."
8. "You need to provide the right level of manpower to collaborate effectively on joint improvement projects. We want to collaborate, but there's no one to work with."
9. "Please develop more advanced e-business capabilities, such as electronic data interchange (EDI), ASN capability, online proof of delivery (POD), paperless transactions, electronic funds transfer (EFT), and radio-frequency identification (RFID) capability."
10. "For some of our products, we want you to manage the inventory levels to our specifications. In other words, you need to be good at vendor-managed inventory (VMI)."

CPG, Inc.'s, second step involved a process much like that described for RetailCo, including searching all publicly available information and interviewing suppliers and employees. Building on that foundation, it took an impressive next step.

## Aligning Customers' Needs with Competitors' Capabilities

Next CPG, Inc., ranked its five competitors according to their capability in each of the areas that were important to customers. When the team finished ranking each of the five competitors on each of the ten qualities just listed, it discovered that it matched or exceeded four of the five competitors on all dimensions. But one competitor stood out, equaling or exceeding CPG, Inc., on eight of the ten characteristics, as shown in Table 5-1.

One item especially worried CPG, Inc. Customers identified the fourth item in the list of priorities (all items ordered delivered in a single shipment) as critically important. CPG, Inc., discovered that its major competitor achieved single shipments more than 85 percent of the time. CPG, Inc., almost never delivered an order in a single shipment; in fact, it could take up to four shipments to deliver the complete order. This clearly multiplied cost for the company and its customers. Addressing order completeness became a high priority.

When CPG, Inc., completed its supply chain strategy, it resolved to have a plan in place to equal or exceed its dominant competitor's

TABLE 5-1 Competitor Comparison

Current State 2010

1 = Poor, 10 = Estimate of World Class

▓▓▓ = Worse than Competition, ▒▒▒ = Parity, ▓▓▓ = Exceeds Competition

| Capability Valued by Customer in Priority Order | CPG, Inc. | Dominant Competitor |
|---|---|---|
| 1. Replenishment lead time | 5 | 5 |
| 2. Give a date; hit the date | 7 | 8 |
| 3. Tight delivery windows | 5 | 5 |
| 4. Complete order delivery | 2 | 8 |
| 5. Accurate invoices | 9 | 9 |
| 6. Real-time order visibility | 3 | 5 |
| 7. Reverse logistics | 6 | 3 |
| 8. E-business capabilities | 8 | 4 |
| 9. Collaboration capability | 4 | 7 |
| 10. Vendor-managed inventory | 3 | 8 |

TABLE 5-2 Future Competitive Position

Expectation at End of Planning Horizon 2014

▒▒▒ = Parity, ▓▓▓ = Exceeds Competition

| Capability Valued by Customer in Priority Order | CPG, Inc. | Dominant Competitor |
|---|---|---|
| 1. Replenishment lead time | 7 | 7 |
| 2. Give a date; hit the date | 9 | 9 |
| 3. Tight delivery windows | 7 | 7 |
| 4. Complete order delivery | 10 | 9 |
| 5. Accurate invoices | 9 | 9 |
| 6. Real-time order visibility | 8 | 6 |
| 7. Reverse logistics | 7 | 5 |
| 8. E-business capabilities | 9 | 8 |
| 9. Collaboration capability | 8 | 8 |
| 10. Vendor-managed inventory | 9 | 9 |

capability in *each* of the ten categories. It faced a moving target, and it would have to determine where it expected things to be at the end of the five-year planning horizon. Looking ahead, CPG, Inc., set goals for performance that would equal or exceed its competitor's on every dimension, as shown in Table 5-2.

CPG, Inc., lacked the resources to be green (that is, to exceed the competition) everywhere. Instead, it picked the areas where exceeding the competition's capabilities both was feasible and would have a high impact, and aimed for parity on all other factors. The VP of supply chain couldn't resist saying with a smile, "It's not easy being green."

## Scenario Planning

Once CPG, Inc., had assessed its current and expected future position against its dominant competitor, it worked through several scenarios that could affect its strategy in a major way. Again, we recommend that you take this next step in your competitive assessment. For one scenario, CPG, Inc., posed the question: what if a major competitor sold its consumer durables business to a Chinese company that was at that time seeking to gain a strong foothold in the market? The team felt that it needed to answer some key questions regarding the potential introduction of a major Chinese competitor into the mix:

1. What specific threats to our supply chain strategy emerge?
2. What opportunities exist?
3. Is our strategy still valid if this sale takes place?

A high-level summary of the team's findings is shown in Table 5-3.

TABLE 5-3  Foreign Competition High-Level SWOT Analysis

Scenario: Major Competitor Sells Its Consumer Durables Business to Major Chinese Firm

| | |
|---|---|
| Threats | The Chinese firm is extremely capable and exerts extreme cost pressure, resulting in market share loss. |
| Opportunities | The new Chinese competitor has less supply chain expertise, allowing us to gain advantage and market share. |
| Strategic impact | Our supply chain can truly be a differentiator if we execute the strategy properly. Furthermore, it is even more important that we keep moving forward aggressively. |

The insight provided by this exercise did two things:

1. It provided an even stronger motivation to complete the strategy and execute it flawlessly.
2. It motivated a study to find out much more detailed information about the Chinese competitor. The findings of that analysis indicated that the Chinese competitor would be likely to stumble in the U.S. market initially, given its total lack of experience. But this firm also had a history of extremely short learning curves. It could be expected to close the gap quickly, maybe even within a couple of years. This implied a short window of opportunity. A plan needed to be in place to attack the temporary weakness were this scenario to play out.

Did CPG, Inc., make a mistake by focusing so much of its attention on its dominant competitor? Perhaps. What happens if some firm like Apple emerges from nowhere to change the business model? It's interesting to reflect on how Apple, a company in a completely different business, was able to shift revenues in the music business away from the labels and analog retailers and toward hardware and digital retail (iTunes). No one saw that coming. The labels underestimated the demand for singles and negotiated such low rates for singles sales that Apple was able to charge $0.99 for a song. As with the Staples example, competitive intelligence may need to extend to nontraditional competition.

## COMPETITIVE ANALYSIS SUMMARY

You should use a process similar to RetailCo's in your initial competitive evaluation. Then you should follow the CPG, Inc., process to go deeper in evaluating your competitors relative to your own capabilities, as well as play out some likely competitive scenarios. It may be helpful to use some outside assistance, but you can learn a great deal by utilizing publicly available information. Once you complete an analysis like this, you can stay current and keep it all in proper perspective by continuing to benchmark best practices, as described in the next section.

# GET OUT THERE AND BENCHMARK

Great golfers play the course, not the other players. That may be true on any given day, but make no mistake: great golfers are constantly assessing their competition and using that to motivate improvements in their own game. In the business world, executives can actually become so concerned about confidentiality that they avoid going to industry forums and seminars where competitors may be present. That kind of isolation is a big mistake. Arrogance can also be a major barrier to improvement. One executive actually told us that he hated to speak at conferences because it was all "give." He learned nothing, and he felt that everyone else benefited from his leading-edge presentations. In effect, he decided to play his home golf course. Yet we strongly believe that a firm can remain competitive only by constantly focusing outward on the best in class.

In working with companies, we unfortunately often hear some version of the comment: "We're different, so that doesn't apply to us." We encounter this disease all too often. It induces complacency and is quite simply a huge impediment to progress. One staff analyst in a major multibillion-dollar company confirmed that his company suffered from the "we're different syndrome." He told us that in many cases, an industry best practice would be stonewalled with this killing attitude. The GM-Toyota joint venture NUMMI is a classic example. When Toyota took over the failed Fremont, California, GM facility in 1984 in a joint venture with GM, it gave GM an astonishing early opportunity to understand the power of Lean on U.S. soil. But GM executives brushed it off, and instead launched a tremendously expensive automation strategy that ultimately failed.

One progressive executive from a company whose supply chain was rated in the top 5 by Gartner told us that he often agreed to benchmarking requests from companies that had clearly inferior supply chains. He said that he always benefited from these encounters, and they helped him further tighten the logic for the approaches he employed. He said, "When you have to explain what you are doing to an outsider, you find that there are many gaps in your thinking and logic. The mere act of verbalizing your strategy to an outsider always results in a more robust internal strategy." For example, in one benchmarking meeting, he explained a new inventory management process that would further improve the already excellent fill rates that the company provided. But then his guest asked, "How will you measure the improvement your customer sees and be certain that your internal measures aren't misleading you?" This led to a rethinking of the fill rate metrics. In our view, benchmarking exchanges almost never fail to benefit both parties.

## GLOBAL CONSIDERATIONS

Complexity expands exponentially in the global environment, and most firms today operate in a global arena. As in a military campaign, it is important to engage your competitors on all fronts. If you don't, your firm might cede a profit sanctuary that your competitor could use to its advantage. The competitor will use the profits from its uncontested sanctuary to overcome competitors in other regions. The global environment demands that we fight the competitive battle on all sides, in all regions of the world. Each region in a global company must conduct the same kind of analysis we have just described. Clearly this can be daunting, especially if the results are different in each region. It is necessary all the same.

To complete a competitive analysis in other regions of the world, you should rely on your counterparts in those regions, assuming that you have such counterparts, and train them to follow the processes described in this chapter. It will be your challenge to bring all of this together into one comprehensive competitive analysis, and that analysis will be essential to building your global supply chain strategy.

## CONCLUSION

A good supply chain strategy cannot be completed without knowledge of the competition. By employing a disciplined approach, you can gather the intelligence you need. The basics are quite simple:

- Review all publicly available information, using the Internet and electronic databases. For public companies, the 10-K report is also quite valuable.
- Interview all employees who have worked for a competitor in the past.
- Engage suppliers and customers.

Consultants can provide valuable additional insights using a variety of methods. With their experience and resources, they can take competitive analysis to a depth that would require far more resources and time if it were done internally. If you do decide to use a consultant, checking references is crucial. Supply chain analysis demands highly specific knowledge. There is no guarantee that even the largest consulting firms have the requisite knowledge and experience to perform an insightful competitive analysis in such a specialized area.

Once competitive data are gathered, they need to be put in a disciplined framework such as that described in the case study and shown in Tables 5-1 and 5-2. It is especially important to anticipate trends. Nothing in this world is static, least of all your competitors. The real art lies in anticipating the possible scenarios that may emerge three, five, or even ten years hence, a problem that is further exacerbated by the global environment.

Given the challenge of doing competitive analysis, many firms skip this step in their strategy development efforts. These firms merely develop a static strategy using poorly informed assumptions concerning the competitive status quo. If you make this mistake, you'll find one day that you are at the mercy of competitors who have assessed the competitive landscape and are attacking your weaknesses, weaknesses that you may not even know you have.

## CHAPTER 5 ACTION STEPS

1. Choose the key strategic competitors you need to follow.
2. Decide what you really need to know, focusing specifically on your competitors' processes.
3. Use publicly available sources and assess your key competitors.
4. Survey your suppliers and employees who have worked elsewhere.
5. Brainstorm strategic scenarios for competitive actions—threats, opportunities, and strategic impact—and develop a plan to counter various threats.
6. Compare your capabilities with your competitors' and set improvement goals.

# CHAPTER 6

# Survey Supply Chain Technology

We considered seven game-changing supply chain trends in Chapter 4 and showed how to analyze your competition from a supply chain perspective in Chapter 5. That brings us to the final step in evaluating the external environment: the assessment of supply chain technology. Technology should be viewed as an enabler of the new processes that your strategy will require. You need to understand the state of supply chain technology in order to use that technology appropriately in the implementation of your supply chain strategy.

## THE ROLE OF TECHNOLOGY

Technology plays a vital role in helping you enable and sustain the new processes and capabilities that you create as you execute the strategy. It could be argued that technology should be considered *after* the new supply chain capabilities have been identified, not before. The reason I put the technology review at this stage of strategy development is because new and emerging technologies could point to new supply chain capabilities. This is in fact a bit of a chicken-egg question, and an example may help.

A manager from a manufacturing company in our Supply Chain Forum told me that her company had discovered recently that new software was available that could prioritize orders and inventory in unique ways to serve a segmented customer base. That functionality appealed to this company because it had recently completed a customer survey and had found widely varying needs for supply and service. Initially the company had had no idea how to address these needs and had frankly tabled the whole issue for another day. But now, seeing that new technology that could help the company address those customer needs was available gave the manager confidence that the company could implement this new capability for its customers, and it launched an initiative to do exactly that.

Reviewing technology at this stage of the strategy development process may cause your strategy team to connect new technical capabilities with the customer requests you heard in Step 1 and visualize a new supply chain process that can address customer needs directly. The important thing to keep in mind is that the customer request, not the technology, must drive the new capability.

A proper technology assessment begins with a comparison of your current technology capabilities with the best in class in each of the areas in Table 6-1. The purpose of this is simply to establish a baseline foundation for your strategy team. Determining the gap between your current technical competence and best in class will be invaluable input when you identify new strategic supply chain capabilities.

Most supply chain strategies will have to be supported with new tools. These tools serve as essential components of the plan to move to new processes and sustain them. Choosing and implementing new technologies present a range of challenges, but technology selection and implementation are far less difficult than defining new processes and integrating those processes into the firm. In fact, technology implementation becomes much easier and more purposeful when firms have first taken the time to identify, develop, get support for, and even implement the processes and capabilities they need. Once those processes are in place, the proper technology can enable their smooth execution.

We believe that Honeywell, an incredibly diverse firm with many different business lines, has an outstanding way of balancing the different considerations that are at play when implementing a new supply chain initiative or strategy. Honeywell's view is represented in the Table 6-2.

This assignment of 10 percent to technology is not intended to say that tools and technology aren't critical to business. Technology is often the cornerstone of a supply chain strategy initiative— without it, the whole effort would collapse. Technology compares equally in *importance* to the other factors. But the technology element of any effort represents only 10 percent of the total implementation *challenge*. Anyone who has gone through a difficult SAP

TABLE 6-1 Sample List of Supply Chain Technologies

| Supply Chain Technology Category | Examples |
|---|---|
| Software | Forecasting systems |
| | Transportation management systems (TMS) |
| | Warehouse management systems (WMS) |
| | Distribution requirements planning (DRP) |
| | Inventory optimization software (multiechelon inventory optimization) |
| | Network optimization and simulation software |
| | Production optimization software |
| | Collaboration software |
| | Enterprise resource planning (ERP) systems |
| | Customer relationship management (CRM) systems |
| E-business technologies | Automatic shipment notices (ASNs) |
| | Electronic data interchange (EDI) |
| | Web-based data interchange and communication |
| | Electronic invoicing and payment, linked to shipments and receipts |
| | Exchanges and auctions |
| | Early warning and visibility systems |
| | Collaboration software |
| Visibility and productivity | Bar codes (UCC 128, stacked bar codes, QR codes, and so on) |
| | Radio-frequency data transmission |
| | Radio-frequency identification (RFID) |
| | Pick to light |
| | Voice picking |
| | Automated picking |
| | Cellular/satellite tracking |
| | Carousel and conveyor systems |
| | Automated storage and retrieval systems (ASRS) |
| | Event management: visibility with real-time alerts |
| Process advances | Lean |
| (Note: Though these are not technology per se, we recommend assessing the firm's sophistication on these and other leading supply chain processes along with the pure technology assessment.) | Six Sigma |
| | Vendor-managed replenishment (VMR) |
| | Collaborative planning forecasting and replenishment (CPFR), and sales and operations planning (S&OP) |
| | Activity-based and total landed costing |
| | Carbon footprint management |

TABLE 6-2  Tools, Processes, and Culture: The Challenge

| Area of Challenge | Challenge in the Implementation |
|---|---|
| *Tools:* implementing the tools and technology to support the new strategy | 10% |
| *Processes:* defining and implementing the new processes required for the strategy | 30% |
| *Culture:* changing the culture of the organization so that the new processes will be successful in both the short run and, more important, the long run | 60% |

implementation might shudder at that statement. Yet most will also recognize that the steps required to choose and implement a new technology tool are straightforward compared to the cultural challenge of getting people excited about and supportive of change. In fact, the difficulty found in most major technology projects is not a challenge with the technology per se but a challenge with the processes codified into it and the people who have to use it.

## IMPLEMENTING NEW SUPPLY CHAIN TECHNOLOGY _____

Choosing the right technology to support your supply chain strategy should not be taken for granted. Because of the extreme cross-functional and cross-company nature of supply chains, technology implementations can be especially challenging. A primer for implementing new technology can be found in *The New Supply Chain Agenda.*[1] In that book, we proposed three caveats in implementing new supply chain technology:

1. Make sure you use leading-edge (beta) technology carefully and appropriately.
2. Realize that people issues are tougher than technical issues.
3. Make sure your supply chain technology project has a business case showing a strong return on investment.

In addition, we posed seven questions that you should ask in advance of any supply chain technology implementation; these are shown in Table 6-3.

TABLE 6-3 Questions Supply Chain Leaders and Senior Executives Need to Ask Before Acquiring or Implementing Supply Chain Technology

| Question | Action |
|---|---|
| 1. Can we eliminate the need for the technology by eliminating non-value-added supply chain operations? | Eliminate before you automate. |
| 2. Who else has implemented this supply chain technology, and have you spoken with them? | If this has not been done, stop the project until it is. |
| 3. Are you implementing a cross-functional change management communication plan, and is it tailored to the individuals and functions that are critical to this effort? | This has to be done. Ask to see the written plan with dates, assigned responsibilities, and a timeline. |
| 4. Will this make line jobs in the supply chain easier or more complex? | If it will make them easier, great. But more likely the answer is "more complex." If it is, make sure that there is a clear training program and that the people doing the work understand and support what the expected return on the investment will be. |
| 5. Do you have a plan for sustaining the cross-functional change once it is made? | If not, write up such a plan, make assignments, and hold people accountable for date-driven tasks. |
| 6. What is the complete business case to generate economic profit for this project? | Make sure the benefit is quantified and clearly communicated. |
| 7. What is the business case vs. the next best option for generating generate economic profit? | This is a tough but necessary question. If the answer shows that your ROI disappears, you have a problem. Stop the project and evaluate it further. |

# THE NEXT BIG THING IN SUPPLY CHAIN TECHNOLOGY ⸺

Times of dramatic change offer incredible opportunities, yet even the most visionary people struggle to recognize the true nature of these opportunities. The emergence of the automobile, electronic communication, the integrated circuit, and the Internet represent clear departures from the past. When such technologies emerge, some companies are able to capitalize on them, while others struggle—and even fail—to adjust. Fortunes are made and lost very quickly at such discontinuities.

The place of technology in your supply chain strategy can be put in proper perspective only by following the process outlined so far in this book. Decisions about technology make sense only after you have determined the needs of your customers, analyzed your internal capabilities relative to the best in class, determined the implication of the game-changing supply chain trends, and discerned the current and future capabilities of your competition. At that point, it is appropriate for supply chain executives to ask, "Do we need to anticipate the next big thing?" Do we need to try to get out in front of the next big technology trend in order to avoid being left behind? Supply chain professionals often ask this question as they survey the landscape of supply chain technology. So what is the "next big technology thing in supply chain"? The following four topics are possible candidates that, whether they reach "next big thing" status or not, represent areas of technology that you should consider in your supply chain strategy.

## Is RFID the Next Big Thing?

The Beer Game[2] and other classroom simulations have a common theme, namely, that cross-enterprise data transparency and visibility are paramount for breakthrough supply chain performance. For example, if Emerson, a supplier of washing machine motors for Maytag, could see the demand for Maytag washers at retail, it would be in a much better position to anticipate disruptive spikes in demand caused by the classic supply chain "bullwhip." (The bullwhip refers to the fact that modest changes at the retail level grow in size for firms positioned further back along the supply chain; thus, Emerson experiences larger swings in inventory and greater supply chain shocks as a result of smaller retail-level adjustments.) The promise of data visibility in the supply chain is one of several major benefits promised by radio-frequency identification (RFID). Embedding RFID chips into products allows them to be accurately identified at various phases in the supply chain.

The RFID tag provides much more information than can be held in a bar code. The RFID industry is expected to grow at about a 20 percent clip for the next several years. One day in the not too distant future, ubiquitous RFID tags will enhance the visibility of data throughout the supply chain and provide many other advantages, such as:

- The ability to hold vastly more information than advanced bar codes—30 times more with even inexpensive chips—and the capability to contact a web identifier, which can hold an unlimited amount of information
- The advantage of not requiring a line of sight to be read
- The ability to work in tough environmental (factory floor or warehouse) conditions
- The ability to embed the chip in the product or packaging
- The time savings of not requiring scanning
- The capability to read thousands of tags per second

Unfortunately, RFID was prematurely imposed on many companies by the exuberance of Walmart. In June of 2004, Walmart announced that it would require its top 100 suppliers to put RFID tags on shipping crates and pallets by January 1, 2005, and later announced that it would expand its RFID efforts to its next 200 largest suppliers by January 1, 2006. Even when the cost structure, accuracy, and reliability of RFID chips fell far short of acceptable levels, Walmart soldiered on. Yet the initial energy created around Walmart's mandate spurred an enormous amount of innovation in the RFID industry, and new investments in reader technology, chip technology, and software arguably accelerated RFID progress. The Department of Defense also pushed RFID and the innovation surrounding it.

At present, the future of RFID is bright. The cost of RFID chips continues to fall, and great advances in reliability and data accuracy are occurring steadily. Uses in retailing and manufacturing are increasing all the time. In retailing, for example, the idea is to use RFID technology to improve the accuracy of store-level inventory records. Many retailers are now placing an RFID read point where goods leave the stockroom and go to the retail floor, in order to update inventory records automatically. This helps avoid the chronic and common problem that the system shows that the product is available, but it is actually out of stock for the shopper on the retail floor.

## Are Computing Power and Internet Speed the Next Big Thing?

Some people argue that the combination of Moore's law (computer power doubles every 18 months with no increase in cost) and rapidly expanding network capacity and bandwidth has been and will continue to be the next big thing. This may seem an odd choice for the "next big thing," given that Moore's law has been around since the 1960s. However, the speed and power with which information is available nearly instantly on the Internet continue to provide astounding possibilities. The computing power and network capacity and speed added by the digitization of content are leading to disruptive change. Google is not only a company name, but also a cultural verb. Software as a service accessible through the Internet is an expanding way to delivery application functionality. Moore's law and the increasing availability of broadband are dragging us all along an accelerating pathway leading to who knows where, but leading us there quickly.

## Is Optimization the Next Big Thing?

One intriguing possibility for supply chain professionals that is further enabled by the continued growth in computing power is the promise of optimization. Optimization is the ability to minimize cost or maximize profit, subject to existing constraints such as the structure of the current warehouse network or the capacity of transportation resources. We believe that in the future, the ability to use optimization tools will make the difference between average and outstanding performance. Moore's law, along with better model design and more accurate detailed data, will provide ever-greater access to the true power of optimization in the future.

Optimization models based on linear programming and its cousins have been used for many decades (since the 1940s). However, computing power limited their application. For most of optimization's history in industry, optimization analysts have had to dumb down their models to get them to run.

One team in a multibillion-dollar manufacturing company told us of designing an optimization model in 2002 that encompassed the firm's 17-warehouse network. The team wanted to find the network configuration that minimized total logistics costs. Team members suspected that they had added too much detail to the model, but they didn't want to simplify it too early because they wanted to get the most accurate results possible. So they loaded all the data into the model on a Friday and set the model to optimize, expecting that it would compute an answer over the weekend. When the project team members arrived early on Monday morning, however, they found the model still churning, with no realistic hope of completion. The only way to get an answer was to simplify the model significantly and hope to get directionally correct results.

A great deal has changed since 2002, as Moore's law continues its inexorable advance. Today, very realistic models can be designed, optimized, and run in narrow time frames. We are entering an era of supply chain systems capability that represents a real discontinuity with our past of relatively *kaizen*-like continuous improvement. Optimization tools will allow us to reach a supply chain capability that represents an entirely different level of performance.

## Are Advanced Planning and Scheduling Systems the Next Big Thing?

Operations planning technology for the supply chain is growing increasingly more powerful over time, as advances have augmented the functionality available in the previous generation of tools. It all began with the tremendously successful emergence of materials requirements planning (MRP) more than 40 years ago. Today, the new planning engines can routinely consider questions such as:

1. What is the optimal warehouse and transportation network to minimize logistics costs while still achieving better service for customers?
2. How do we schedule production to provide the minimum disruption to the factory and distribution network?
3. What is the true trade-off between inventory and capacity?
4. How can we schedule production to optimize the number of shipments directly off the assembly lines?
5. How can we handle the flow of orders through the supply chain to provide an accurate available-to-promise (ATP) capability to ensure reliable customer delivery dates?
6. How should we prioritize customers in shortage situations?
7. How do we simulate our supply chain to deliver a capable-to-promise (CTP) functionality to ensure that capacity exists to meet customer requirements?
8. Is it possible to integrate manufacturing planning, distribution planning, and transportation planning when demand is volatile and essentially unpredictable?

Supply chain professionals could not answer questions like these satisfactorily in the past. Today, we are at the frontier of new decision support capability, and we see more and more companies addressing these issues today.

## WILL HUMAN RESOURCES LIMIT THE POTENTIAL OF THIS NEW TECHNOLOGY? _____

The universe of supply chain technology, of course, extends far beyond the examples just addressed. The scope is broad, including warehouse productivity tools such as conveyor and picking systems, transportation innovations to improve driving efficiency, and a multitude of web-based applications.

How effectively these new technologies improve or transform the supply chain depends greatly on how successful a company is at hiring and keeping people who can use them. Human resource limitations are not a trivial issue. Optimization models, for example, are often based on linear programming applications that few supply chain professionals understand. The supply chain profession, to be blunt, needs more technically qualified people.

How qualified do they have to be? The optimization and forecasting tools used today are complicated. That will hopefully improve over time, as vendors try to enhance their sales opportunities by investing in greater user simplicity. Having said that, the skill sets of the supply chain professional need to expand at the same time that the technology tools evolve.

Take forecasting systems as an example. Sophisticated forecasting models need to be used by people who, while not highly trained statisticians, have the skills and know-how to ask the right questions and can understand when there is a problem with the answer. When the output doesn't make sense, forecasters need to be able to identify a false result and have sufficient knowledge to fix the problem. More people who have the sophisticated technical skills normally found in the engineering sciences are needed in the supply chain field.

Not only are such people scarce, but many companies fail to recognize the need for them. In one large firm ($17 billion in sales), the forecasting area consisted of 20 people who handled various product lines of the company. Not one of them had any educational background in statistics! The leader of the group had a background in

sales and felt that the key to forecasting involved developing relationships with customers and the sales organization. Though cross-sector
collaboration is an important skill, it would have been helpful to
have had at least one member of the group who had been schooled
in the nuances of the statistical forecasting model that the team used.
Without that knowledge, the forecasters had no idea how to adjust
the model when it produced clearly incorrect numbers. When errors
occurred, most of the forecasters bypassed the multimillion-dollar
forecasting package with an Excel workaround. Although the group's
leader often boasted about the system's statistical forecasting capability, few of his people actually used it, and none of them used it to its
maximum capability. Training and talent planning need to be part of
any technology strategy.

## THE POLITICS OF SUPPLY CHAIN TECHNOLOGY

Your supply chain strategy will probably require you to implement
new technologies to support the processes that are essential to your
strategy. A good change management plan, discussed in depth in
Chapter 10, will be key to a successful implementation. Other stakeholders have a vested interest in the technology component of your
strategy. The information technology (IT) department in particular
will play an important role. IT naturally pushes for tools that are built
on platforms that it supports and that it can integrate and maintain
conveniently. Given that IT will be responsible for maintenance and
troubleshooting of the tools, the department should be involved early
in the strategy development process, and even represented on the
core strategy team. However, IT should not dominate the discussion
of the technical functionality needed by the supply chain professionals running the business. IT has a right and a duty to communicate
the cost and integration implications of these decisions, but in the
end, the business should make the final decision.

Failure to include IT's input and weigh it appropriately can create a situation like the one described to me by one supply chain
executive. He told me that his IT department insisted that all supply chain decision support software be sourced from the company's
enterprise resource planning (ERP) supplier, given the huge investment that the firm had made in the transactional software. However,
the supply chain group felt that the business functionality offered by

this vendor was inferior. For example, the warehouse management system module had no capability to pick multiple orders simultaneously (task interleaving), and it did not have the yard management capability to manage the massive trailer yards outside the warehouse. Unfortunately, the supply chain department lost this battle. The CIO prevailed, with the supply chain VP saying, "This was just a hill I don't want to risk dying on." Sadly, his logic was that if problems with the implementation occurred, he didn't want to be criticized. What could the supply chain VP have done differently? In retrospect, he should have involved the IT department at the very beginning of the strategy development process so that the IT liaison was part of the strategic decision-making process and understood the capabilities that the business needed.

Once it is complete, the supply chain strategy is very likely to require major IT resources to implement and maintain a range of new systems. IT needs to support the strategy and do its part to ensure its success. The intensity of IT resources required and the important and ongoing role that IT plays cause many companies to put IT exclusively in charge of supply chain technology implementation projects. And yet, at the end of the day, the responsibility for delivering critical results for the company in the form of cost and inventory reductions and customer service improvements lies with the supply chain team. In my view, the supply chain organization that uses the application should at least co-lead the technology implementation project. Unfortunately, we often see supply chain managers abdicate their role to IT. As one CIO said, "I would love it if the supply chain group would take the lead. Unfortunately, they look to us traditionally to accept that role. I suppose I need to push back harder than I have in the past."

The IT organization often fills a project management leadership vacuum in companies. Complex systems projects are always difficult and often exceed their expected budgets and timelines. These project failures have forced IT organizations to develop disciplined project management skills. The IT group, more than any other, seems to understand that managing projects requires more than being organized and keeping good to-do lists. IT professionals often lead the way in becoming certified project managers, such as getting the Project Management Institute's PMP (Project Management Professional) certification. Sometimes they have to face the wrath and frustration of business departments that want projects to move faster.

However, IT has learned the hard way that cutting corners, especially in the early phases of needs assessments and process documentation, leads to disappointing results. Because many IT organizations have dedicated themselves to project management excellence, IT often finds itself by default in the role of managing systems implementations that ought to be managed by the business function that will own the new tool once it is implemented.

Ironically, when we ask IT managers if they would like supply chain managers to step up and lead project implementations, they invariably say yes! But in the absence of business leaders that are willing to engage with technology-related projects, IT must step into the void. IT does its best, but in case after case, we hear of a supply chain business area that expected IT to deliver a certain function in a user-friendly application, only to find that the functionality either doesn't get delivered or is packaged in such as way that it is virtually unusable by the people who are doing the work.

Supply chain functions routinely deal with the implementation of complex new systems that result from their strategy work. They must not abdicate their responsibility to lead these initiatives. They must involve the IT organization in the strategic planning process from the beginning, and step out and truly lead systems initiatives to a successful conclusion.

## DOES NEW TECHNOLOGY MAKE OUR JOBS HARDER OR EASIER?

New supply chain strategies often require sophisticated technology. However, many supply chain professionals feel that new technology makes management processes more complex. On the one hand, this is simply progress, as our thinking and sophistication become ever more intricate to deal with a business environment that is expanding in complexity. However, additional complexity should pass a rigorous screen to assess the real cost benefit, with a goal of making the system as simple as possible.

Most companies identify a few subject-matter experts whom they rely on to use the new technology systems, and without whom, companies believe, the systems would fail. Common phrases we hear are, "If Joe is ever run over by a Mack truck, we're all sunk," or, "If Joe ever wins the lottery, you can kiss your bonus goodbye." Of course,

Joe does invariably leave, and the company magically finds a way to carry on without him. Perhaps the bigger problem is that Joe constrains creativity because all new ideas relating to a certain system must flow through him. This common situation of relying on one technology-savvy user is one key downside of increasing complexity in tools and systems, making it essential that management require clear documentation and cross-training.

## CASE STUDY: IMPLEMENTING AN ORDER ALLOCATION CAPABILITY AT A LARGE MANUFACTURING COMPANY____

We audited a $6 billion manufacturing company as it worked on the technology stage of its supply chain strategy. At that juncture, the company realized that it did not have the tools it needed in place, especially those for managing customer orders. The company's systems could not set and protect customer priorities, for instance—the current system treated all orders the same: first come, first served. Even worse, order-processing agents would react to irate calls from retailers and override the system in random and unpredictable ways. The promise dates that the system generated were a bad joke. The large megadealers threatened to move their business elsewhere.

The supply chain strategy team formed an improvement team to address the problem. The improvement team worked in parallel with the strategy team for 60 days and developed a solution to the problem. The team members identified a process and software that they called allocated available to promise (AATP). This new system and process would allow priorities to be set and followed. For example, in a shortage situation, where not all orders could be filled on time, the system would allocate the available inventory to customers based on a set of preassigned priorities. The decision rule might be to allocate 50 percent of the inventory to the top two retail dealers, 20 percent to the next tier, and finally spread the remainder proportionately among the remaining retail customers. In some cases, some customers would simply not be served, and would be told to either substitute a different product or re-place the order later.

Once the strategy work ended, the team launched the AATP project and discovered, to its dismay, that the implementation would be hugely difficult, largely because the software was a beta version that had not been implemented anywhere else. The new system also created a layer of complexity in the fulfillment system that no one fully understood. These technical issues seemed daunting, but they were actually relatively minor compared to the larger challenge of getting the sales organization to agree on the priorities and discuss them with the company's customers. If the team had involved the sales organization early in the strategy work, this problem could have been avoided.

By the time all of these implementation challenges had been identified, enough time had passed that the improvement team had no choice but to narrow the scope of the project and focus on what it could accomplish by the project deadline. The team basically punted and altered the logic within the company's existing application to make the promise dates to customers slightly more accurate. The improvement also included some obvious, noncontroversial priorities, such as the priority to satisfy back orders for the largest customer before releasing inventory for other orders. The project was renamed "Phase 1" to signify that the prioritization issue would hopefully be revisited over time.

To avoid problems like this, supply chain strategy teams need to deeply involve key stakeholders in the strategy development process. Cultural issues always trump technology challenges.

## CHAPTER 6 ACTION STEPS

1. Assess where you stand on the dimensions of supply chain technology (see Table 6-1).
2. Determine what technology can do to facilitate your supply chain strategy.
3. Strive to hire people with more advanced technical skill sets.
4. Make sure that technology enables but doesn't dominate or lead the supply chain strategy.
5. Plan to step up and take leadership of any new supply chain technology project.
6. Involve all key stakeholders at the beginning of the strategy development process.

## CHAPTER 7

# Manage Risk in the Global Supply Chain

At this point, you have considered your customers' needs and analyzed the internal and external environment, including competition and technology. Now is the time in your strategy development journey to consider the risks your supply chain will face and how to deal with them. The lack of a robust process for identifying, prioritizing, managing, and mitigating risks is a clear threat to your supply chain and its strategy. Among the hundreds of companies in our database, we rarely find a formal risk management process in place. Frankly, most firms ignore risks, sometimes with dire consequences.

The supply chain arguably faces more risk than other areas of the company because of its global nature and its systemic impact on the firm's financial performance. The scope and reach of the supply chain argue for a formal, documented process for managing risk. Without a crisis to motivate action, however, risk planning often falls to the bottom of the priority list. Supply chain executives too often find themselves at the center of the daily storm, striving to balance very demanding operational objectives while satisfying customers, cutting costs, and helping to grow revenue. They must deliver results today, while working on capabilities that will make their companies competitive in the future. They operate in the same maelstrom of competing priorities and limited time as their executive peers—but their scope of activities is broader, while at the same time they have less direct control over all the moving parts. In this environment, risk management doesn't receive the priority it should.

But there's a silver lining. Developing a supply chain strategy presents an invaluable opportunity to address risk within a strategic framework. Risk cannot be eradicated, but it can be planned for.

Having a risk management plan can even be used as a competitive advantage, since so few firms have one. Preventing disruptions down the supply chain can have a dramatic impact on a firm's competitiveness in general.

## RISKS ARE A FACT OF LIFE

Risks are a fact of life for the supply chain professional; in fact, there is a long list of forces that drive supply chain risk. These include quality and safety issues; shortages of supplies, especially critical commodities; legal, security, regulatory, and environmental compliance; weather and natural disasters; and terrorism. Companies with diverse and global supply chains face an addition potential for risk, including, but not limited to, the longer lead times needed in the global environment; supply disruptions caused by global customs, foreign regulations, and port congestion; political and/or economic instability in a source country; changes in economic factors such as exchange rates; and so on.

Supply chain risk management is a critical requirement, largely because failure to manage risk can be so devastating to the bottom line. Professor Vinod Singhal of Georgia Tech analyzed 800 supply chain disruptions that took place between 1989 and 2000.[1] Firms that experienced supply chain disruptions saw the following consequences:

- Shareholder returns were 33 to 40 percent lower over a three-year period.
- Share price volatility was 13.5 percent higher.
- Operating income declined by 107 percent.
- ROA declined by 114 percent.
- Sales declined by 93 percent.

The repercussions of supply chain disruptions are far-reaching and devastating to the financial health of the firm. Risk in the supply chain can cause companies to suffer missed customer commitments, stock-outs, reduced earnings, higher inventory levels, increased time-to-market cycles, reductions in product quality, and negative impacts on brand perception.

# GLOBAL SUPPLY CHAIN RISK CAN MANIFEST IN DEVASTATING WAYS _____

Global supply chains are a source of competitive advantage. They provide access to cheap labor and raw materials, new financing opportunities, and larger product markets. Unfortunately, those benefits, which entice firms to establish global supply chains, come with uncertainties and risks that many global supply chain managers fail to consider sufficiently.

Once a firm is committed to the decision to outsource globally, some risks are easier to avoid than others. For instance, many years ago, Whirlpool decided to outsource the production of dishwasher water seals to a Chinese supplier for a net savings of $0.75 per unit, or a total of $2 million in annual savings. But soon after the arrangement was made, the Chinese supplier changed to a different rubber supplier. The seals made from this new rubber leaked in dry climates, causing nearly a 10 percent failure rate. By the time Whirlpool discovered the problem, more than two million dishwashers with the defective seal had been produced. This cost the company millions of dollars and destroyed all savings for more than three years. Whirlpool could have avoided this problem by doing some basic planning and putting robust quality controls in place. Those controls now exist at Whirlpool and are excellent for the company as a whole, but it took a crisis to motivate action.

Not all risks can be fully mitigated in a cost-effective way. Natural disasters like the 2011 earthquakes in Japan or the floods in Thailand are predictable in the sense that Japan is a volcanic region and Thailand is prone to flooding, but the scale of the 2011 events proved more extreme than most risk managers had taken into account. The Honda factory in central Thailand was under 15 feet of water at the high point of the flooding. This incident was minor compared to the March 11 earthquake, tsunami, and subsequent nuclear crisis that engulfed Japan. Toyota suspended production of the Prius in Japan after this event, losing 140,000 badly needed vehicles.

Hundreds of other companies faced major disruptions to their supply chains from this disaster, some of them lasting through the end of the year. For instance, Boeing experienced major delays as a result of the tsunami, because the Japanese suppliers that were affected produce 35 percent of the Boeing 787 components and 20 percent of the Boeing 777 components. General Motors had to halt production at several plants because of shortages from Japanese suppliers. Honda faced severe problems because 113 of its suppliers were located in the affected region of Japan. These twin disasters in Asia in 2011 produced an estimated $240 billion in losses.[2]

In another global example originating in the United States, the supply chains of Nokia and Ericsson were disrupted when a brief fire broke out in a Phillips plant in Albuquerque, New Mexico, in March 2000. The fire crippled the plant's production of chips that were used by Nokia and Ericsson. Both firms were told that it would be one week before operations would be up and running again. Nokia acted swiftly, sourcing from other locations and collaborating with Phillips to use capacity at other plants temporarily. Ericsson, on the other hand, did not react quickly, and by the time the company responded, it was already too late. Nokia had captured the excess capacity, and Ericsson had no choice but to manage as best it could. Nokia survived relatively unscathed, while Ericsson reported losses of $340 million that quarter. At the end of the year the company's mobile phone division announced a loss of $1.68 billion.[3]

Sourcing offshore clearly carries a wide range of risks, as is evident in the examples just given. Long supply chains offer more opportunities for disruption by unforeseen events. Because of the impact on the corporation, global supply chain strategies especially must include a thorough risk analysis.

## ONLY 10 PERCENT OF FIRMS CONSIDER RISK WHEN OUTSOURCING GLOBALLY

Despite the importance of identifying and mitigating risk as part of the supply chain strategy, we rarely find robust risk practices among the firms that pursue a global outsourcing strategy. For example, when companies analyze global outsourcing decisions, we find that they fall into three categories:

- Category 1 (35 percent) considers unit cost plus transportation only.
- Category 2 (55 percent) also includes inventory as part of the assessment.
- Category 3 (10 percent) adds a risk assessment.

In other words, 90 percent of the firms *do not* formally consider risk when outsourcing production.

As part of a strategic planning process, firms should invest time in considering disaster scenarios like those described here. Although it is impossible to know when such events are going to occur, it is not impossible to develop some possible scenarios based on the location, geography, climate, and political environment of the places where you outsource, and to engage in disaster contingency planning mock exercises to prepare the company better to react to supply chain disasters. As an outcome of these exercises, firms can develop a risk management process that employees can follow in the event of a crisis. An important part of this process is always a clear plan for communicating quickly with all stakeholders.

In summary, your supply chain strategy must identify possible global supply chain risks and develop probability and impact assessments and risk mitigation plans. Executing this process at the strategy phase, before you begin to implement the supply chain projects that come out of your strategy, can help you avoid much pain later. Examples showing how to do that are included later in the chapter. However, before going there, it would be helpful for you to have a deeper perspective on supply chain risk, especially with respect to global outsourcing, which represents perhaps the greatest risk to your supply chain.

## GLOBAL OUTSOURCING TRENDS

As you develop your supply chain strategy, your strategy team will have to decide how much risk to take on globally. As part of that process, it is helpful to understand the current global outsourcing trends in industry. *World Trade* magazine and the University of Tennessee recently conducted the first of what will be an annual survey of global supply chain trends across industries. More than 240 business executives from a broad array of firms participated in the study. As the increased risk of outsourcing becomes more apparent to today's companies, the survey asked whether firms were reducing their reliance on global outsourcing and planning to do more insourcing or near-shoring in the future.[4]

Results from this inaugural survey proved both interesting and surprising. They showed that 72 percent of companies consider financial factors such as unit cost, freight, and/or inventory when evaluating an outsourcing decision. Shockingly, the remaining 28 percent use *only* nonfinancial factors in evaluating their outsourcing decision. Surprisingly, only 48 percent of companies consider the cost of inventory in their outsourcing decisions, which compares to 55 percent found in the University of Tennessee survey described above. Inventory almost always increases significantly when production is outsourced. For most firms, inventory represents a major cash flow challenge as well as a major holding cost expense. The fact that only around half of the respondents consider inventory in their outsourcing analysis definitely sets off alarms and calls for further study. Consistent with the results from our database, only 11 percent of respondents formally quantify risk in their outsourcing decision.

Despite the increasing buzz in the supply chain community about global risk, only 12 percent of respondents thought that outsourcing would *decrease for their company* in the next two years. In what might seem a contradictory finding, 52 percent expected near-shoring back to the United States to *increase for industry in general* in the next two years. This dichotomy no doubt reflects the confusion, debate, and concern that are going on in firms regarding the future of outsourcing.

In spite of these concerns about risk, the low cost of labor remains an overwhelming motivation for global outsourcing, with 57 percent of the respondents pointing to the low cost of labor as the greatest inducement. In addition, when companies need to increase production capacity, a significant percentage, 33 percent, look offshore. India and China still remain the top two countries for outsourcing, followed by rapidly growing Vietnam. Regardless of the recent negative publicity, Mexico is holding its own as an outsourcing destination: 43 percent expect outsourcing to Mexico to increase in the next two years.

Juxtaposed against these cost advantages, the concerns about risk in global outsourcing are increasing. In fact, 52 percent of the respondents indicated that they were very or extremely concerned about the quality of outsourced products. When selecting an outsourcing partner, respondents said that they consider commitment to quality as the most important factor, with 86 percent listing it at the top of their concerns. After quality, respondents were most concerned about the changeable economics of the outsourcing decision (43 percent).

The threat to intellectual property came next on the list of concerns, with 38 percent of the companies being very or extremely concerned about this issue. In spite of all of the recent publicity, piracy ranked last on the list of outsourcing concerns. Surprisingly, the survey said that having a good cultural match was the next to last factor in importance in selecting an outsourcing partner.

Regardless of the concern about the risks inherent in global outsourcing, most of the respondents do not formally analyze and quantify risk in making their outsourcing decisions. On the other hand, companies do take ad hoc measures to reduce risk. The number one way (75 percent) is simply to do business with an established and trusted supplier. Of the respondents, 45 percent employ technology to track shipments, and 38 percent participate in government programs such as C-TPAT (Customs-Trade Partnership Against Terrorism). Also, 35 percent manage risk by adding inventory to the supply chain, 33 percent employ Lean principles to reduce the long and risky lead times in global outsourcing, and 30 percent plan to rely on airfreight when necessary.

Most executives we talk to feel that a major factor in mitigating risk in the global environment is having people with the right talent in the right positions. The majority of respondents to this survey (59 percent) said that they use domestic talent in the home country to supervise their global relationships. To manage the global supply chain at the corporate level, firms rely most (49 percent) on hiring people with expertise in global supply chain management. The least common way of developing global talent (26 percent) is through expat assignments; the extremely high cost of that approach probably makes it less attractive.

In summary, this study confirms that the global nature of outsourcing, and its associated risks, will be with us for the foreseeable future. Supply chain professionals are becoming more concerned about the risks they face in a global environment, but few of them have a process for formally including risk in a supply chain strategy. The growing anxieties about global outsourcing motivate a wide range of ad hoc actions to reduce risk, but these actions normally fall outside any strategic framework. Therefore, companies that include a formal risk assessment in their global supply chain strategy have a significant advantage in avoiding or mitigating those risks that affect all global supply chains.

## SUPPLY CHAIN RISK IS ALSO A LOCAL PHENOMENON

Before moving on to ways in which companies can deal with risk, I want to dispel any impression that readers may have that supply chain risk is an exclusively global phenomenon. The global nature of the modern supply chain increases the possibilities of risks developing from end to end, but supply chain risk is not unique to the global context. A *Supply Chain Digest* article in 2006 detailed the "eleven greatest supply chain disasters of all time." All of these events took place within the borders of the United States.[5] For example, Robert Smith, GM's CEO in the 1980s, invested billions in robot technology during his tenure. The company deployed 14,000 sophisticated robots, yet GM plants continued to have more employees per plant than the competition (1,500 more than a Mazda plant producing the same volume). Toyota employed the Lean philosophy, and the rest is history. The cost of the GM robot investment exceeded the market capitalizations of Toyota and Nissan combined at the time.

In 1996, Adidas tried to implement a warehouse management system in a U.S. warehouse; the attempt failed, and was followed by another failed attempt. The new technology was too complex and untested, and it resulted in the company's filling only 20 percent of the orders for one 30-day period.

Countless other examples of local supply chain disasters and their devastating impact on the firm's performance exist. These range from natural disasters to software failures. Whether local or global, supply chain risk must be identified, prioritized, and mitigated.

## IDENTIFYING AND PRIORITIZING RISK

Your supply chain strategy team should set aside time to evaluate the risks facing your supply chain. You should be in a good position to do that, assuming that you have established a good foundation that allows you to place those risks in perspective. Risks come into focus once you have determined your customers' needs, completed an internal best practices evaluation, considered supply chain megatrends, and evaluated your competition and technology. In doing this risk evaluation, your strategy team will need to identify the risks, then prioritize them, and finally determine ways to mitigate them. This section includes examples of several approaches your team could use in completing its risk analysis.

The examples rely on a version of a process that engineers developed long ago to identify and prioritize risks: the failure mode and effects analysis (FMEA) approach. The military first used the FMEA approach as far back as the 1940s. It prioritizes risks based on three factors:

1. Seriousness of consequences
2. Likelihood of the problem ever occurring, or frequency of occurrence
3. Likelihood of early detection of the problem

Several firms in our database have successfully applied this approach as a way of identifying the high-priority risks to the supply chain. The goal is to determine which risks require a mitigation plan and which are too low-impact or unlikely to warrant the effort. We believe that the real power of this approach lies in its use as a framework for discussing and debating risks with your supply chain strategy team. Given that risk analysis has a large subjective component, reaching group consensus is critical. Two examples of this approach are included here.

## Addressing Supply Chain Risk at a Food Manufacturer Using FMEA

As part of its supply chain strategy, a food products manufacturer was considering outsourcing its warehouse operations to a third party. To assess the risks associated with this move, the manufacturer used a table much like the one in Table 7-1 to guide the risk discussion. The supply chain group identified 13 risks and, using the approach outlined, prioritized these risks. Eventually, the group decided to launch mitigation projects for the top five prioritized risks. Table 7-1 demonstrates an example using just *two* of the risks that were identified.

After using the FMEA process to prioritize the various risks, the company established a risk mitigation plan, called "recommended action" in Table 7-1. Once the supply chain group completed and

TABLE 7-1 Food Manufacturer Risk Analysis

|  | Risk 1: Safety of Food Product | Risk 2: Freshness of Product |
| --- | --- | --- |
| Severity (1–10) | 9 | 6 |
| Probability of Occurrence (1–10)<br><br>High probability = 10<br><br>Low probability = 1 | 2 | 4 |
| Probability of Early Detection (1–10)<br><br>High probability = 1<br><br>Low probability = 10 | 6 | 2 |
| Probability Index (Multiply Three Previous Items) | $9 \times 2 \times 6 = 108$ | $6 \times 4 \times 2 = 48$ |
| Recommended Action | Enhance testing process | Audit inventory and ensure stock rotation |
| Responsibility | Safety engineering | Third party with company oversight |

gained approval for the supply chain strategy, it assigned responsibility for each of the five high-priority risk management projects and made those projects a standard part of the weekly strategy implementation meeting.

## Addressing Supply Chain Risk at a Durable Goods Manufacturer

In another example, a durable goods manufacturing company felt that its supply chain strategy should include some important outsourcing decisions, and it decided to test that assumption by evaluating the risk associated with outsourcing a key manufacturing component to a Vietnamese manufacturer. The manufacturer used a modified version of the previous approach, but this firm focused on two factors. First, the group estimated, through consensus, the *probability* of occurrence of each risk, and then it multiplied that by the *estimated cost* of the occurrence. Although the data are heavily disguised, the analysis, done in a group setting, looked very much like that shown in Table 7-2.

TABLE 7-2  Outsourcing Risk Analysis

| Risk | Estimated Potential Loss, Stated as Cost in $ per Unit | Subjective Probability of Occurrence | Net Loss per Unit (Multiply the Prior Two Columns Together) |
|---|---|---|---|
| Quality failure | 25.00 | 0.10 | $2.50 |
| Safety failure | 100.00 | 0.01 | $1.00 |
| Unexpected demand spike | 30.00 | 0.25 | $7.50 |
| Currency change | 20.00 | 0.25 | $5.00 |
| Intellectual property problem | 10.00 | 0.25 | $2.50 |
| Source disruption | 30.00 | 0.10 | $3.00 |
| Force majeure | | | |
| Port problem | 25.00 | 0.025 | $0.62 |
| | | Total | $22.12 |

The firm used this analysis in two ways:

1. The supply chain team made sure that the ROI on the outsourcing project included the "cost of risk," which in this case was $22.12 per unit. The outsourcing savings without risk stood at a net $55.00 per unit, which safely exceeded the risk estimate. The group fully recognized the subjective nature of this analysis, yet the act of discussing the potential sources of disruption and estimating their costs gave the group some assurance that the project would still be viable, even if it encountered one or more of the potential risks.
2. Once the supply chain team had completed the supply chain strategy, it launched several projects designed to reduce the probability that any of these risks would occur. These mitigation actions decreased the estimated cost of risk from $22.12 to $12.74, which included the cost of the mitigation activity, giving them further assurance of the project's feasibility.

Your strategy team should use a process like those described here to identify and prioritize supply chain risks. This process will provide a framework for engaging in a group discussion to reach consensus on the subjective issues associated with risk evaluation. Then your team is in a good position to brainstorm ways to mitigate the highest-priority risks facing your supply chain.

# THE MANAGEMENT OF RISK IN INDUSTRY TODAY

Your strategy team can also benefit from a deeper understanding of the management of risk in industry today. This section presents recent research that uncovered six categories of risk management activity that companies employ to manage the three primary types of supply chain risk they face. You should use these categories as checklists when identifying the risks you face and deciding how to manage them.

In 2008, Dr. Ila Manuj and Dr. Tom Mentzer at the University of Tennessee conducted fourteen in-depth qualitative interviews with senior supply chain executives across eight companies, and used that information to create a risk management framework.[6] In addition, they also conducted a focus group meeting involving seven senior executives of global manufacturing firms. Five of these seven executives were later interviewed separately for this study and became part of the fourteen in-depth interviews. In total, the study had sixteen unique participants. In the interviews, Manuj and Mentzer spoke specifically with managers involved in making and executing global supply chain decisions from a variety of manufacturing companies, including home appliances, electronic component suppliers, pharmaceuticals and over-the-counter products, office products, heavy equipment, and consumer goods. In addition, they supplemented these observations with general comparisons from our database at the University of Tennessee, amassed over several years.

## Three Types of Risks in Global Supply Chains

The supply chain is subject to numerous types of risks, but based on the interviews, it seems that the vast majority of risks can placed into three categories:

1. *Supply and demand:* risks that deal with inbound and outbound flows
2. *Operations:* risks that deal with the possibility that an internal issue will affect the company's ability to produce

3. *Security:* risks that have recently played a more important role because of globalization and the ever-increasing requirements for inventory minimization, precision, and availability

This risk categorization model is depicted in Figure 7-1.

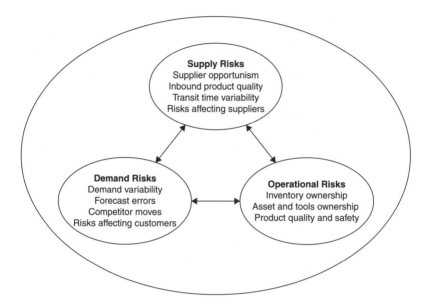

FIGURE 7-1 Risks in Global Supply Chains

### Supply Risks

Supply risks refer to the possibility of a failure of inbound supply that renders a provider unable to meet customer demand within anticipated costs, within a stated time frame, or in a way that does not cause threats to customer safety. Supply risks can occur at any point along the chain, from the movement of materials from a supplier's suppliers all the way to and through the firm and movement to its customers.

### Demand Risks

Demand risks arise from the movement of goods from the firm all the way to the final customer. Demand risks can result from such events as delayed or inappropriate new product introductions (leading the firm to either miss market opportunities or have inventory write-offs or stock-outs as a result of inaccurate forecasting), variations in demand (caused by fads, seasonality, and new product introductions by competitors), and chaos in the system (caused by overreactions, unnecessary interventions, and distorted information from the downstream supply chain members). Demand risks vary with the nature of the product, with functional products being less at risk than innovative products.

### Operational Risks

Operational risks affect the firm's internal ability to produce goods and services, the quality and timeliness of production, and/or the profitability of the company. Sources of operational risk may include a breakdown in core operations; inadequate manufacturing or processing capability; high levels of process variation; changes in technology, which may render the current facilities obsolete; and/or changes in operating exposure. Exchange rates are an example of a change in operating exposure that often affects the operating profits of companies that have no foreign operations or exports, but that face important foreign competition in the domestic market.

## Ways Companies Manage Risk

The interviews confirmed that companies deal with risk management in many ways, including:

- Adding inventory (for outsourcing, they typically add 30 days in transit, 30 days safety stock, additional cycle stock, and so on).
- Planning for a realistic percentage of the shipments to be sent by airfreight when emergency shortages occur.
- Developing excellent import processes and optimizing INCO terms (international commerce terms, which assign responsibility for a shipment at each stage of the process).
- Developing a second domestic source that can be quickly used.
- Dealing only with competent, world-class suppliers. (It can take two years to develop and certify an excellent source in some global regions.)
- Designing for globalization, including parts standardization and postponement.
- Implementing event management technology to provide real-time alerts when shipments are delayed.
- Applying Lean and/or Six Sigma principles to compress cycle time and reduce variation in the new longer supply lines.

The study grouped the wide range of risk management strategies into six categories based on the interviews with global supply chain managers: postponement, speculation, hedging, control/share/transfer, security, and avoidance (see Figure 7-2).

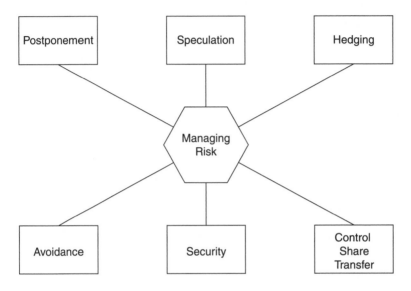

FIGURE 7-2  Risk Management Strategies

### Postponement

Postponement maintains the company's flexibility and reduces cost by delaying the actual commitment of resources to build or move product in the supply chain. *Form* postponement involves labeling, packaging, assembly, and manufacturing. *Time* postponement involves moving goods from manufacturing plants only after customer orders are received. The following quote from one of the interviews conducted by Mentzer and Manuj illustrates the usefulness of postponement strategy:

> Let's just say you architect your product into modules, and then you separate the module production from the assembly of the product. Right now, in our operation, subassembly production and building the final product all happen at the same time. If you separate those, you have tremendous flexibility. You can then do assembly of your product close to where you need it, at your distribution center, and then distribute it into the marketplace when needed.

### Speculation

Speculation (also called selective risk taking) is a management strategy that is the *opposite* of postponement. It includes such actions as forward placement of inventory in country markets, forward buying of finished goods or raw material inventory, and early commitment to the form of a product, all in anticipation of future demand. In spite of the cost impact, speculation emerged in the interviews as the most commonly used strategy to address uncertainty in the business environment. However, deciding when and where to speculate becomes a complex issue.

### Hedging

In a global supply chain context, firms hedge their exposure by having a globally dispersed portfolio of suppliers and facilities, so that a single event (like currency fluctuations or a natural disaster) will not affect all the entities at the same time and/or with the same degree of magnitude. Managers in the study mentioned having "qualified backup" suppliers in the United States because their supply chains are not in a position to accommodate even short-term disruptions. An example quote illustrates the impact of the absence of a hedging strategy:

> We got burned a number of times in the past with currency fluctuations due to outsourced product. In 2008, the Euro had been strengthening, and had a dramatic impact on our profitability. The import of that European product was very profitable previously, but a lot of profitability got wiped out due to the currency issues. I think there's a huge risk we face right now as we outsource more and more stuff to China, that the Yuan or the RMB is going to strengthen. And that could wipe out a good chunk of the savings.

### Avoidance

Firms use an avoidance strategy when they determine that the risks associated with a given product, a particular geographic market, given suppliers, or even certain customers are unacceptably high. Avoidance takes the form of exiting through divestment of specialized assets, delay of entry into a market or market segment, or participating only in low-uncertainty markets. The following quote illustrates:

If it was all easy, then there's not much reward in assuming the risk. It is a risk/benefit trade-off. We get benefit from moving to China through lower cost, and we can quantify how much we think we can save by moving product to China. But if that probability of risk times impact is greater than the benefit, then you make a conscious decision that that's probably not a good idea.

Many attractive markets have hugely problematic corruption and crime metrics that make this avoidance strategy an issue of employee safety as much as of profit. For example, crime ranks among the most urgent concerns facing Mexico, as Mexican drug trafficking rings play a major role in the flow of cocaine, heroin, and marijuana between Latin America and the United States. Drug trafficking leads to corruption, which has had a deleterious effect on Mexico's federal representative republic. Drug trafficking and organized crime have also been a major source of violent crime in Mexico.

### Security

Global supply chain security encompasses information systems security, freight breaches, terrorism, vandalism, crime, and sabotage. Firms that use a security strategy focus on increasing a supply chain's ability to sort out unusual or suspicious elements as their goods are moving. A security strategy also encompasses working closely with government and port officials to proactively comply with regulations and avoid unnecessary delays at border-crossing points. Several government efforts such as the Container Security Initiative, the Customs-Trade Partnership Against Terrorism (C-TPAT), and the overarching Operation Safe Commerce initiative provide directions to gradually enhance the security of global commerce.

Many companies go beyond the statutory regulations to secure their supply chains. Almost all managers in the study reported concern over supply chain security and indicated that they are taking proactive actions to secure their supply chains. Private initiatives mentioned by the study participants included tracking and monitoring the integrity of cargo containers with GPS, use of tamper-proof seals, and working with port officials to understand and implement C-TPAT guidelines. Managers facing all varieties of supply and demand risks reported having more security checks in place because of increasingly stringent global regulations.

Supply chain managers need to include the costs of implementing security strategies with all other risk management strategies. Some strategies, such as vertical integration and avoidance, may reduce security strategy costs, while others, such as transferring risks, may increase the cost of implementing security strategies.

### Control/Share/Transfer

Control, share, or transfer of risk takes the form of vertical integration, contracts, and agreements. Vertical integration increases the ability of a member of a supply chain to control processes, systems, methods, and decisions. It may take the form of forward (downstream) or backward (upstream) integration, and is therefore both a supply-side and a demand-side risk management strategy. Integration may also be used to create entry or mobility barriers. Desirability of control, and hence the level of integration, also depends on the commitment of the focal firm to the target market. Vertical integration may increase control and reduce risks in a supply chain, but it changes variable costs into fixed costs.

## CONCLUSION

Any risk to a firm's supply chain puts the entire financial health of the firm in jeopardy.

In the global supply chain environment, risks should be evaluated intently. By addressing risk, companies have a much greater chance to preempt devastating disruptions in the supply chain and insulate themselves from the ensuing negative effects. Since the supply chain determines the overall financial health of the firm, any risk is magnified in importance. *It is essential that firms have a disciplined process in place to identify, prioritize, and manage the risks that can affect their supply chain.*

At this stage of the strategy process, you and your team have identified, prioritized, and defined ways of mitigating the risks your supply chain faces. This, along with the prior five strategy steps, is definitely a lot of work and a great accomplishment. So, congratulations are in order! You have done the difficult preliminary work, and you are now ready to move on to the exciting part of strategy development, namely identifying the specific new supply chain capabilities that you will need to implement. That is the subject of the next chapter.

## CHAPTER 7 ACTION STEPS _____

1. Brainstorm with your supply chain strategy team the risks that your supply chain faces.
2. Prioritize these risks, using the techniques described in this chapter.
3. Develop a risk mitigation plan for each of the high-priority risks.
4. Make sure you include a formal risk evaluation as part of any global outsourcing plan.

CHAPTER 8

# Determine the New Supply Chain Capabilities and Develop a Project Plan

You have analyzed the needs of your customers and completed an honest internal assessment. You have completed an analysis of your competitors, and you have reviewed the landscape of supply chain technology. And finally, you have realistically looked at the risks facing your supply chain. Congratulations! You have built the necessary foundation for developing an outstanding supply chain strategy. Now comes the exciting part, when you bring all of this together. Now is the time to identify the new supply chain capabilities that your firm needs, prioritize them, and decide what to do and how to get the right things done first.

## A SUPPLY CHAIN STRATEGY SHOULD SPAN AT LEAST THREE YEARS

Identifying the new supply chain capabilities your firm will need is certainly exciting, but it is also highly complex when it is executed over a multiyear planning horizon. In a survey of 40 firms, we asked participants how many years a supply chain strategy should cover. The responses varied widely, but centered around three years:

- One year: 15 percent
- Two years: 12 percent

- Three years: 43 percent
- Four years: 3 percent
- Five years: 18 percent
- Beyond five years: 9 percent

A supply chain strategy must look at least three years into the future. Shorter time frames, which 27 percent of the respondents favored, tend to focus more on the tactical problems of the day rather than on a pathway to move the firm to true competitive advantage. Developing an effective supply chain strategy means laying out a project road map three years or more into the future that delivers your company's goals for product availability, cost reduction, working capital improvement, economic profit, and ultimately shareholder value.

One supply chain executive told us that he hesitated to formalize a three- to five-year plan because it might make the firm less flexible and less responsive to the highly changeable business environment. This concern is based on a misunderstanding. Crafting a three-year strategy does not mean that the business then follows that strategy for three years with no change or variation. The global business environment is far too dynamic to *not* make midcourse corrections. If the competitive landscape changes in a major and dramatic manner, if customers change their demands or their structure, if a new technology suddenly becomes available, or if a new major risk to your supply chain emerges, it is time to modify the strategy. But these corrections must be integrated with the multiyear road map to ensure that the firm does not "tilt at windmills," chasing the idea du jour without regard for its fit with the overarching strategy and goals.

## IT'S FINALLY TIME TO DEVELOP THE STRATEGY

It's finally time to develop the supply chain strategy, using all of the information you've assembled thus far. I recommend that your team meet off-site, away from its normal workplace. The members of the cross-functional strategy team should check their iPhones, laptops, iPads, and BlackBerries at the door and devote their entire attention to the task at hand. This work will guide the firm for years and will be the road map that will lead it to success. It deserves the full attention of everyone involved.

Prior to assembling the group, the leader should assign various team members a lead role in accumulating all the inputs developed so far.

There should be a team member assigned to assemble and review with the team the following information:

- Customer requirements
- Internal supply chain assessment
- External megatrend analysis
- Competitive valuation
- Technology appraisal
- Risk assessment

In the strategy session, a facilitator should keep a running list of the potential supply chain capabilities that could be developed or enhanced. That list will start with the capabilities needed to satisfy the customer requirements and build from there. There is no need to debate the priorities at this stage. That will come later. Table 8-1 gives an example of how this process will unfold:

TABLE 8-1 New Supply Chain Capability Determination

| Strategy Foundation Element | Example of Finding | Example of Supply Chain Capability Needed |
|---|---|---|
| Customer requirements | Customers want their order shipped in one complete shipment and delivered at one time. | The capability to consolidate orders from more than one location into a single shipment |
| Internal assessment | A clear weakness is that we have no ability to consolidate orders. | The capability to consolidate orders from more than one location into a single shipment |
| External megatrend analysis | Collaboration with our customers is critical. In meetings, they keep asking us to consolidate orders. | The capability to consolidate orders from more than one location into a single shipment |
| Competitive evaluation | Our major competitor can consolidate orders from more than one location in to a single shipment. | The capability to consolidate orders from more than one location into a single shipment |
| Technology appraisal | We don't have the information system and visibility to consolidate orders. | The information system to consolidate orders |
| Risk assessment | If we don't develop the capability to consolidate orders, we will lose market share. | The capability to consolidate orders from more than one location into a single shipment |

The list of supply chain capabilities needed is likely to be very long at this stage. I have seen lists that exceeded 100 items in length at this early stage; that kind of volume can be quite daunting for the team. Still, the leader should encourage the team to capture everything at this point. The list does not represent what the company *will* do, just everything it *could* do. Again, prioritization will come later. Once this process is complete, your team will have a list of the new supply chain capabilities needed. (As another aid in this process, the addendum to this chapter gives a checklist of supply chain capabilities that other companies have identified, which your strategy team could review after first identifying the supply chain capabilities you need.)

## SETTING PRIORITIES

It's now time for the strategy team to work on what is perhaps the most challenging yet rewarding part of the strategy process: setting priorities. This is the culmination of the entire process, where your team identifies the real work that will result from the strategy. The overarching goals for the supply chain are likely to call for over-aggressive multiyear targets for cost reduction, inventory reduction, and product availability improvement. The task at hand is to prioritize the new supply chain capabilities into a multiyear road map that delivers those critical goals.

The team will be faced with a bit of a dilemma at this point. Priorities can be set only by quantifying the costs and benefits of implementing *each* capability and comparing that to the goals. This tedious and time-consuming work may be overwhelming, assuming that the list of capabilities is a long one.

You should pare down the list of supply chain capabilities to a manageable size by subjectively estimating the costs and difficulty of implementation of each potential initiative relative to the benefits. At this stage, the strategy team can subjectively rank costs and benefits on a scale of 1 to 10. Those rankings can be used to reduce the list to a reasonable number of potential initiatives. (In my experience, a "reasonable" number falls in the range of 10 to 25 initiatives, but of course this depends on the judgment call by the team.)

Once that is done, the leader should assign to the team members the challenging task of working with finance to quantify the costs and benefits of the initiatives that make the cut. After completing that work, the team should reassemble, review the results, and use them to lay out the multiyear road map that will achieve the corporate goals. This process is much easier to visualize with some actual examples of how other companies have made this journey.

## HOW ONE RETAILER IDENTIFIED THE NEW SUPPLY CHAIN CAPABILITIES AND PRIORITIZED THEM

A medium-sized retailer with $10 billion in sales used a process much like the one described in this book to determine the new supply chain capabilities it would need in the future. The company reviewed everything it knew about its customers, as well as the company's internal strengths and weaknesses, competition, technology, and social and demographic trends. The supply chain team also brainstormed the possible risks it faced in the future and the corporate goals that the supply chain organization had to deliver, such as cost, inventory, and product availability. All of that became grist for the mill as the supply chain team debated what new supply chain capabilities it would need in the future. It portrayed this process as shown in Figure 8-1.

The next step for this retailer involved an interesting process of categorizing these new supply chain capabilities into three buckets:

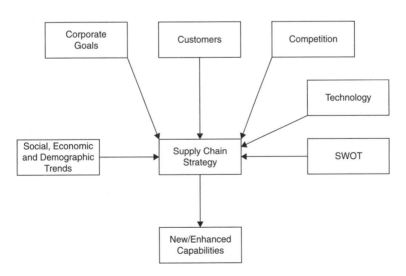

FIGURE 8-1 Determining New Supply Chain Capabilities

adaptive, innovative, and radical initiatives. Continuous improvement initiatives were identified as *adaptive*. A major step improvement in supply chain capability fell into the *innovative* category, and the company decided to categorize truly transforming initiatives as *radical* initiatives. It did this to satisfy a request from the CEO that the final supply chain strategy include initiatives that would not only achieve the company's goals, but also be innovative and transforming. The final list of initiatives is given here; it may serve as another checklist for your team, but only *after* you have completed *your* process of identifying initiatives.

### Adaptive Initiatives

1. Revamp supply chain metrics to focus on the consumer.
2. Develop a logistics process to serve geographic areas that are not being served now.
3. Address supplier on-time delivery.
4. Focus on supplier collaboration and supplier lead-time reduction.
5. Move to more inbound freight controlled by the firm.
6. Better utilize labor in the network.
7. Implement better supply chain decision support capability.
8. Evaluate the right mix of private fleet and common carrier.
9. Develop a culture of benchmarking and join industry forums that promote that culture.
10. Embrace sustainability as a cost reduction strategy.

### Innovative Initiatives

1. Implement a sales and operations planning process.
2. Apply Lean and Six Sigma tools to the logistics operations.
3. Expand the cross-docking operations from 30 percent to 50 percent of goods moved.
4. Implement a stock-keeping unit (SKU) management process.
5. Optimize product design for low logistics transportation and storage costs.
6. Implement a world-class inventory management process, along with modern decision support tools.
7. Commit to the dot-com business and develop a logistics strategy to serve it.

### Radical Transforming Initiatives

1. Create a true supply chain organization, combining logistics operations with inventory management and procurement.
2. Totally reengineer the store backrooms, and use them in the future for dot-com order picks.
3. Establish a logistics subsidiary to use excess logistics assets to carry freight for other companies.
4. Optimize the network. Execute a complete, all-encompassing network optimization and deal with issues like:
   a. Dot-com business.
   b. Serving the urban markets.
   c. Product/inventory placement: the right products (inventory) in the right places.
   d. Returns.

The combined lists had a total of 21 separate initiatives. The supply chain strategy team next formed a subteam to quantify the costs and benefits of each initiative. With this information, the team could create a three-year plan that would deliver on the supply chain goals set by the corporation and accommodate the constraints on the capital and expense available for the implementation. The plan also needed to satisfy the CEO's directive to include innovative and transforming initiatives, in addition to adaptive initiatives, in each year of the project plan.

The process this retailer followed had some unique elements in it, but it basically consisted of the same steps I recommend that you follow in your strategy process:

1. Identify all the new supply chain capabilities that need to be developed based on an analysis of customers, internal SWOT, megatrends, competition, and technology.
2. Quantify the costs and benefits of each initiative, and use that to prioritize the initiatives.
3. Develop a three-year project plan that delivers results related to the company's goals for cost and working capital reduction and customer service improvement.
4. Iterate and revise until the plan fits within the negotiated constraints on expense and capital requirements.

## HOW A CPG COMPANY IDENTIFIED THE NEW SUPPLY CHAIN CAPABILITIES AND PRIORITIZED THEM_____

The consumer packaged goods (CPG) firm described in Chapter 2 also followed the four-step approach described here. However, it added a few excellent enhancements that you might consider as you develop your process for identifying and prioritizing the new supply chain capabilities for your strategy.

To identify new supply chain capabilities, this company started, as it should, with the needs of its customers. But the strategy team enhanced the quality and relevance of its customer information by also considering the future supply chain operating models it felt it would have to support. The strategy team identified four future supply chain models:

- The base model that it currently used to serve customers, but with enhanced service and efficiency
- The shared supply chain approach, which pooled distribution assets with its retail customers
- The home delivery model in which the retailer takes the order
- The home delivery model with no retailer involvement

CPG Co. needed new supply chain capabilities in order to operate successfully in each of these future customer environments. The supply chain team next considered all known information on competition, technology, and internal strengths and weaknesses. Unfortunately, this company did not complete a megatrends analysis, and thus risked missing some key capabilities it might otherwise have identified.

Next, CPG Co. held a two-day planning session, evaluated all of the inputs, and identified 57 new supply chain capabilities. This number far exceeded what the business could reasonably tackle, so the supply chain strategy team formed a subteam to cull this list down to a more manageable number based on high-level estimates of how each capability would benefit the business and how difficult each would be to implement. One week later, the entire group reassembled, and the subteam proposed 18 new supply chain capabilities that should be prioritized over the next three years. After a full day of discussion in which the team refined the work of the subteam, the group settled on the following list of 20 capabilities, detailed here as another checklist for you to consider after you finish identifying your new supply chain capabilities:

1. Ship each purchase order complete.
2. Reduce replenishment lead time.
3. Ensure date integrity and available-to-promise (ATP) capability—that is, when you give a date, hit the date.
4. Meet tight delivery windows at the retailer's distribution centers (DCs).
5. Provide expedited deliveries when needed.
6. Provide a reverse logistics service to pick up returns.
7. Provide real-time order tracking.
8. Provide customized packaging and labeling when needed (delayed differentiation).
9. Provide a home delivery service for certain dot-com product areas.
10. Offer direct-to-store deliveries (DSD) for high-volume stores.
11. Put in place a single point of contact for all availability and delivery issues.
12. Provide proofs of deliveries (PODs) online.
13. Deliver damage free.
14. Provide collaborative planning, forecasting, and replenishment (CPFR) capability.
15. Have a mature sales and operations planning (S&OP) process.
16. Provide a sophisticated cost to serve capability.
17. Develop a disciplined process for managing SKUs at the beginning and end of life.
18. Provide a world-class e-business business-to-business (B2B) capability.
19. Introduce allocated available-to-promise (AATP) capability to enforce priorities among customers during product shortages.
20. Have the ability to optimize production schedules based on constraints.

The team next determined which of these 20 new supply chain capabilities were required to support each of the four customer operating models. Table 8-2 shows 5 of the 20 capabilities.

TABLE 8-2  Supply Chain Capabilities by Operating Model

| Supply Chain Capabilities | Four Possible Customer Operating Models | | | |
| --- | --- | --- | --- | --- |
| | Base | Shared Supply Chain | Consumer Direct Through Retailer | Consumer Direct |
| 1. Ship each purchase order complete | | | | |
| 2. Reduce replenishment lead time | | | | |
| 3. Date integrity and ATP capability—when you give a date, hit that date | | | | |
| 4. Meet tight delivery windows at the retailer's DCs | | | | |
| 5. Provide expedited deliveries when needed | | | | |

TABLE 8-3  Prioritized Selling Model by Operating Model

| | Base Model | Shared Supply Chain | Consumer Direct Through Retailer | Consumer Direct |
| --- | --- | --- | --- | --- |
| Retailer with distribution assets | 4 | 1 | 2 | NA |
| Retailer with no distribution assets | NA | NA | 5 | NA |
| Consumer direct | NA | NA | NA | 3 |

Some of these new supply chain capabilities would be required for all four future customer models, such as number 3, date integrity. Others would be needed to support only two of the operating models. Given that variability, the team needed to first prioritize the future supply chain operating models, since that prioritization would drive the prioritization of the *individual* initiatives. The priorities set by team consensus are shown in Table 8-3.

Once all of this was done, the supply chain team was able to take the next step in prioritizing the 20 individual supply chain capabilities. For, example, since "shared supply chain" ranked number one as a customer model, the corresponding supply chain capabilities to support it would have a higher rank.

Next, the team needed to estimate the cost, benefit, and ROI of each initiative as further input into how each initiative should be prioritized. This company clearly endured an extremely complex prioritization process, but in the end, its supply chain strategy and the corresponding prioritization of capabilities were firmly grounded in the future needs of its customers and how those needs would be served.

## HOW AN AUTOMOTIVE SUPPLIER IDENTIFIED THE NEW SUPPLY CHAIN CAPABILITIES AND PRIORITIZED THEM____

In the previous examples, the two firms had somewhat different methods for prioritizing new supply chain capabilities. Regardless of the process, the final priorities must fit within corporate constraints on personnel, capital, and expense. This third example is a good description of how to deal with the added issue of limited resources. Resources are almost always limited, regardless of the ROI. A strategy team should not shy away from requesting more resources if it needs them, but in the end, there will be a limit—often a much narrower limit than you want—beyond which the team cannot go. Therefore, the process must be iterative. Prioritization should allow the company to lay out a strategic project plan that delivers the goals, then revise that group of projects until it falls within the constraints for capital and expense.

I worked with an automotive supplier whose supply chain team used an excellent process to fit the project plan into the constraints on capital and expense imposed by the corporation. The strategy work generated 27 possible initiatives. The strategy team next tackled the challenge of prioritizing these initiatives and laying out a three-year road map that both delivered the goals and accommodated the corporate constraints on capital and expense. This team faced extremely demanding three-year goals given to it by the senior executive committee:

1. Customer service improvement: 93.5 percent to 97.5 percent
2. Working capital reduction: down $450 million, or 40 percent
3. Cost reduction: down $38 million.

This supply chain executive told me that if he were in a position to take on one goal at a time, he would want customer service to lead the way. But he knew all too well that his management expected him to deliver all three simultaneously. Working with his team, he first detailed by year the team's annual targets toward achieving the end three-year goals (see Table 8-4).

TABLE 8-4  Supply Chain Objectives

| Project Benefits | 2012 | 2013 | 2014 | Total |
|---|---|---|---|---|
| Customer service fill rate | 95% from 93.5% | 96% | 97.5% | 97.5% |
| Working capital | $75 million reduction | Additional $150 million | Additional $225 million | $450 million |
| Logistics cost reduction: transportation, warehousing, and administrative cost | 4% $15 million reduction, ignoring inflation effects | Additional 3% $10 million | Additional 3.7% $13 million | $38 million |

His team initially felt that these goals were impossible, but supply chain professionals face daunting challenges like this routinely. Aggressive senior executives regularly ask them to do the impossible, and they often enable that behavior by actually achieving the impossible!

Once the supply chain executive had laid out the annual breakdown of targets, he and his team needed to identify the year-to-year list of initiatives that would allow the company to achieve its goals. The team did not have carte blanche to pursue its goals. It was constrained by the people resources and the availability of capital. The team had 27 project possibilities that needed to be prioritized based on how they, individually and collectively, would deliver on the availability, cost, and inventory goals, while staying within the budget for expense and capital resources. This is where the "rubber meets the road" in strategy work. It is a very complex and challenging undertaking.

The team rightly decided that it needed more information before deciding which projects to pursue. It didn't want to sink into analysis paralysis, but without some basic data, it was reduced to guesswork.

The team faced the major task of defining each project in terms of what it was expected to accomplish and its probability of success.

The team decided to take each of the 27 initiatives and complete Table 8-5. This required some significant analysis as well as some good basic management judgment. The team split the initiatives among the team members and asked each to develop a set of estimates for the capital and expense required for each project (that is, columns D and E in Table 8-5). For each project, the team members carefully documented the assumptions they used in calculating these estimates.

Then the entire project team assembled for a three-day off-site planning meeting. The purpose of that meeting was to complete the rest of the table, that is, the benefits expected from each initiative, the ROI, and an estimate of the probability of delivering each initiative on time. The team first estimated the improvement that each project would deliver in terms of availability, cost, and inventory reduction (columns A, B, and C). A member of the corporate finance department attended the meeting to work with the supply chain team in turning its improvement information into an ROI calculation. This work led to the values in column F.

Once the supply chain team had taken these steps, it had only one final column left to fill in: column G, the estimated probability that the project would deliver its expected results. Some projects involve more variability and risk than others. The group finally reached consensus on each subjective probability.

Note that the total benefits exceed those required over the next three years, but as it turned out, so did the resources required.

The next step was to construct a three-year project plan for each of the three corporate goals. The projects were to deliver the annual results and come as close as possible to the constraints of expense and capital budget. For example, for the inventory goal, the supply chain team designed a plan that involved implementing 10 projects over three years, as shown in Table 8-6.

This approach was impressive in its detail and discipline, and I would recommend it as a good approach to use. Just be sure to maintain some flexibility. If a project runs into trouble and stalls out, there needs to be a process to reset priorities quickly. If the environment or needs of the business change, priorities may need to be adjusted. Overreaction to change can be just as devastating to a strategy as underreaction. That's why this team resolved to meet on a quarterly basis to reassess the strategy and project priorities. It wanted to change

TABLE 8-5 Project Data Needed for Prioritization

| Project | A Improvement expected in availability because of this project | B Annual logistics cost reduction | C Inventory reduction and payables reduction: working capital | D Expense resources required and people required to complete the project | E Capital resources required | F ROI | G Subjective probability of delivering results on time |
|---|---|---|---|---|---|---|---|
| Project 1 | 0.2% | $25,000 | None | $45,000 One-half person-year | $55,000 for software | 33% | 90% |
| Project 2 | None | None | $250 million | $90,000 One person-year | None | 49% | 80% |
| Project 3 | 0.1% | $10 million | None | $65,000 | $1.2 million in the warehousing operation | 15% | 75% |
| Project 4 | None | $12 million | 137 million | Negligible | None | 55% | 65% |
| Remaining Projects | 7% i.e., 7 percentage points | $23 million | $200 million | $8.5 million | $13 million | | |

TABLE 8-6  Benefits and Resources Required by Year for the Inventory Reduction Goal

| Projects to Implement a New Supply Chain Capability | 2012 Goal: $100 million | 2013 Goal: $200 million | 2014 Goal: $150 million | Total Working Capital: $450 million |
|---|---|---|---|---|
| Project 1 | $25 million | $35 million | | |
| Project 2 | $75 million | $5 million | $5 million | |
| Project 3 | $15 million | $2 million | | |
| Project 4 | $36 million | | | |
| Project 5 | | $11 million | $5 million | |
| Project 6 | | $47 million | $5 million | |
| Project 7 | | | $85 million | |
| Project 8 | | | $89 million | |
| Project 9 | | | $55 million | |
| Project 10 | | | $2 million | |
| Estimate of inventory that will be reduced | $151 million | $100 million | $246 million | $497 million |
| Total expense required | 12 people $1.7 million | 13 people $2.1 million | 11 people $1.4 million | Total: $5.2 million |
| Total capital required | $17 million | $2.4 million | $5.3 million | Total: $24.7 million |

when it absolutely had to, but to hold firm otherwise. This prioritization process also allowed the team to fit the project load into the capital and expense limitations imposed by the corporation.

## RECOMMENDED APPROACH TO SELECTING AND PRIORITIZING THE NEW SUPPLY CAPABILITIES

Based on the three examples described in this chapter, the following are the steps you should take to select and prioritize your new supply chain capabilities. This is the culmination of all of the prior work, and it will determine what you are actually going to do as a result of all of the strategy work, and when you will do it. The steps are:

1. Identify all of the new supply chain capabilities that need to be developed, based on an analysis of customers, internal SWOT, megatrends, competition, and technology.
2. Reduce the number of initiatives to a manageable number, using estimates of benefits and difficulty of implementation.
3. Lay your goals (for example, for cost, inventory, and product availability) over the multiyear planning horizon, as in Table 8-4.
4. For each supply chain initiative, quantify, as in Table 8-5, the following items:
   a. The benefits each initiative will yield (for example, how much it will cut cost, reduce inventory, and/or improve availability).
   b. The expense and capital required to implement each initiative.
   c. The ROI of each initiative.
   d. The subjective probability of success for each initiative.
5. Use this information to iteratively develop a multiyear road map that achieves each goal and stays within the capital and expense constraints, as in Table 8-6.

## DEALING WITH CAPITAL AND EXPENSE CONSTRAINTS

When you follow the process described here, you are very likely to encounter capital and expense constraints far sooner than you would like. Capital and expense resources required almost always exceed those available. For example, at the automotive supplier discussed in the previous example, the supply chain team had an expense budget of $9.5 million for all projects. This budget was dominated by additional IT resources and people resources, along with the associated costs required to do the project. The cost of additional people involved salary, benefits, travel, and so on. The supply chain project plan ultimately required 85 additional people: 53 IT professionals and 32 professionals in various business functions.

In most companies, adding head count is traumatic. Even when you expect a very high return on investment from the initiatives with which those professionals will be involved, most firms cringe at adding "heads." One executive I worked with recently promised his boss that he would generate more than $1 million in savings if he had just one more person. His request for head count was still denied. I believe that head-count requests are rejected even when there is a strong case for them because executives do not really believe that adding a new employee will generate the promised savings. A return on investment is just talk until it is actually achieved, and experience has taught good business executives that a return on investment estimate is usually optimistic despite the best efforts of team members to be "conservative." Also, there's the innate belief among many senior executives that more people beget more people, and that's how costs get out of control. Therefore, actually getting the 85 people that this supply chain project plan required would be highly problematic.

The $13 million in necessary capital was no less of a challenge. This budget would be spent largely on computer software, which the supply chain team expected to purchase and capitalize. However, this company faced capital constraints everywhere, and the CFO and the CEO felt that everyone would have to do some belt tightening. In the firm's overall capital budget, the supply chain organization, independent of its strategy work, had already asked for $22 million to upgrade its stable of 13 DCs. The team offered to delay receiving half of its core budget in order to get the capital it needed to buy the software to support the new supply chain strategy. That request was approved. Trade-offs such as this occur constantly in well-run companies, and are essential to properly manage the company's resources. Strategy teams should consider trade-offs between existing and ongoing initiatives as they deal with capital constraints.

As could be predicted, the senior executive committee denied the request for 85 additional people. Instead, it asked that the supply chain team deliver results with only 50 new people. The project team responded by showing how not receiving the full head count requested would reduce the ROI. A compromise of 65 additional people was reached, along with a challenge from the CEO to not let the ROI suffer.

## After the Cuts, Then What?

In this case study, the supply chain organization found a way to get the capital it needed, but it got only 65 of the 85 additional people required. Nonetheless, the supply chain team was still expected to achieve the targeted ROI, despite having fewer resources. Fortunately, all of the projects taken together yielded *higher* estimated benefits in terms of availability, cost reduction, and inventory reduction than were *required* by the strategic goals, but the proper pathway was not clear. Therefore, the team decided to break each project into a high, medium, and low scenario related to both the level of capability it delivered and the number of people it would require. For each project, the supply chain team prepared a table like the one shown in Table 8-7. The people resources required were tied directly to the level of capability that would be produced. Invariably, a higher level of capability required more personnel. The team defined the high-investment scenario as world-class capability, medium investment was related to an above-average capability, and low investment produced an average capability level.

With analysis like this for each supply chain project considered, the team could see where the best return occurred. In fact, it wished it had taken this approach in the first place. With this information,

TABLE 8-7  High, Medium, and Low Investment Scenarios for Supply Chain Capability A

| People Requirements | Fill Rate Benefit | Cost Reduction | Inventory Reduction |
|---|---|---|---|
| Low: average capability | 0.2% | $12.5 million | $16 million |
| Medium: better-than-average capability | 0.3% | $17 million | $30 million |
| High: world-class capability | 0.5% | $22 million | $40 million |

the supply chain team found a project and investment pathway that operated within the head-count constraint and delivered the corporate goals.

## How to Avoid Cherry Picking

When a CEO or a CFO sees the final project plan, with all of the detail on costs and benefits, it's like putting raw meat in front of a hungry lion. He or she feels an unavoidable urge to "cherry-pick." He or she is likely to immediately say something like, "I see we achieve 90 percent of the benefit if we spend only 70 percent of the resources. Isn't that good enough? Can't we stop there and avoid spending the remaining 30 percent?"

There are two possible strategies for dealing with this situation.

1. Don't show the senior executive data like these! (But that's dangerous on a number of levels.)
2. Prepare for the inevitable questions.

In the case of the automotive supplier, the supply chain teams anticipated what the business executives would ask, and prepared answers that cleverly showed how all the projects were interconnected—and were critical to meet the competition. Even though a project looked like it might yield only a small benefit on paper, the supply chain team demonstrated how it was integral to the success of the other projects, critical to satisfying customers, and essential for competing given the capacity of the competition.

For example, one new capability involved "shipping each order in one complete shipment"; this required a new systems capability, but the sales organization believed that it would generate enough additional market share to yield a huge ROI. Another project involved a web-based system to suggest a substitution for products that were not available. This project had a significant cost with very a modest benefit tied to it, yielding a low ROI. The strategy team felt that this substitution tool was a critical enabler for the "ship PO complete" capability, and it needed a way to tie the two projects together so that the low-ROI project wouldn't be eliminated. In this case, the team hit upon on a very simple solution to avoid the cherry-picking problem. It simply combined both projects into one large project and let the ROI of the combination carry the day.

# HOW WILL THE PLAN STACK UP
# AGAINST COMPETITION?

One final refinement to consider involves comparing your final plan against the competition. Each new project identified by the strategy team should establish a new supply chain capability or greatly enhance an existing one. These new capabilities should achieve a major step forward in serving customers, and also yield significant reductions in cost and working capital. Each new capability should also meet competitive threats. The strategy team for the automotive supplier decided to compare the new capabilities the company would develop with those of the firm's toughest competitor. The team benchmarked the competition using the tools described in Chapter 5 and found the situation shown in Table 8-8.

This comparison required a lot of analysis and some guesswork, especially since the company was facing a moving target—the competition was also working every day to get better, establish demanding goals, and aim to achieve outstanding results. On the other hand, the automotive supplier had uncovered no evidence that its main competition was working on a true supply chain strategy and would devote the same level of resources. Therefore, the strategy team felt confident that the company would close the gap and move ahead in many areas.

TABLE 8-8  Plan Versus Competitor Capability

| Supply Chain Capability (e.g., Supply Chain Project) | Year 0 Capability Compared to the Competition | Year 3 Capability Compared to the Competition After the New Initiatives Are Implemented |
|---|---|---|
|  | Equal | Superior |
| B | Equal | Equal |
| C | Inferior | Equal |
| D | Superior | Superior |
| E | Inferior | Equal |
| F | Inferior | Inferior |
| G | Equal | Superior |

The team had the time and resources to complete a study like this for only a few competitors, and therefore limited its analysis to those competitors that it deemed most important. There could be a small competitor that may someday come out of nowhere. However, given the high capital barriers to entry in the automotive industry, the company was not likely to be surprised. The supply chain team did spend part of a day in one of its planning sessions discussing the competitors who were not threats today, but might be in the future. After this discussion, the team resolved to monitor one particular small competitor that seemed to be doing innovative work in the marketplace.

## DEVELOPING THE PROJECT PLAN

Once the strategy team has prepared the multiyear road map of initiatives for its new supply chain capabilities, it is time for basic project management. Project management is covered more thoroughly in other books, but some advice is included here because it is so critical to a successful strategy outcome. Projects must be monitored on a weekly basis. This is not optional if a major strategy initiative is to stay on track. It is a good idea to appoint a Project Management Professional to man a PMO (Project Management Office). The PMO should track and monitor the projects, conduct weekly meetings, and ask each project leader to answer three questions:

1. What did you accomplish last week?
2. What will you do this week?
3. What barriers are you facing that you need help with?

Two of the firms I have worked with had an excellent approach. The project management director obtained a commitment from the VP of supply chain that either he or a member of his staff would always be present during weekly reviews to give those meetings the weight they needed. The project management meetings were conducted with great discipline. Project leaders could be in and out in 15 minutes. If issues arose that needed extensive discussion, they were tabled and scheduled for discussion the next day. In both of the companies, the project director published a report each week that offered a short synopsis of each project and also produced a stoplight chart that quickly showed whether or not an initiative was on track with a red, yellow, or green indicator.

If one of the projects ran into trouble and became "red," the root cause of the schedule delay almost inevitably arose from cross-functional issues. In several cases, the VP of supply chain needed to step in and help resolve issues that impeded the supply chain initiatives. It is important not to "punish" the red project leaders. Senior executives need to stay in a "support and help" mode.

## CHANGES IN THE PROJECT PLAN

As discussed at the beginning of the chapter, a strategy needs to be stable, and priorities cannot blow with the wind. Yet a change in the business environment could make a change essential. For example, each of the two major home improvement retailers, Home Depot and Lowe's, must always be cognizant of the other's strategy. Recently Home Depot undertook a major change in its distribution strategy to move closer to the Lowe's model. The new Home Depot distribution network involved moving to a regional distribution center (RDC) network and pulling inventory back from the stores. This approach was expected to save a billion dollars in inventory. Lowe's had a superior supply chain, but Home Depot closed the gap rapidly. Fortunately Lowe's had independently anticipated the need to make a major advance in its supply chain years earlier and was already well on the way to implementing a new strategy to reestablish its superiority in the supply chain space.

It is important to decide which environmental changes justify a change in the strategy. The strategy needs to change as often as absolutely necessary, but no more. One company I worked with set up a "priority council" consisting of senior executives from all functions. Every six months, the executive priority council convened to discuss the changing environment and whether it warranted a revisiting of the strategy. The team considered changing the strategy only if the members of this council *unanimously* agreed that external changes warranted such a change in the supply chain strategy. This process prevented excessive changes because of the six-month schedule of the meetings and the fact that the process required unanimous agreement.

In one instance, the VP of sales learned that his company's major competitor was about to build a DC in St. Louis in an attempt to penetrate that market. He requested that the PMO leader call an emergency executive priority council meeting to discuss whether this justified a change in the supply chain strategy. In this case, the group met and decided that significant change was not necessary. The current strategic plan met that threat effectively.

## CONCLUSION

Choosing the critical new supply chain capabilities and prioritizing them into a project plan that delivers the company's goals and falls within resource constraints is the final result of all the intense work that goes into strategy development. As described in the examples in this chapter, this step requires a great deal of highly complex analysis. However, the strategy team has the right foundation on which to build this analysis if it has been diligent in carrying out all of the prior steps. The strategy process is now close to being finished, but not quite. Once the projects are identified, it is time to consider the organization, people, and metrics required to make sure everything gets done. That is the subject of the next chapter.

## CHAPTER 8 ACTION STEPS

1. Identify all of the new supply chain capabilities that need to be developed, based on the analysis of customers, internal SWOT, megatrends, competition, and technology.
2. Quantify the cost and benefit of each initiative, and use that to prioritize the initiatives.
3. Develop a three-year project plan that delivers the company's goals for cost and working capital reduction and customer service improvement.
4. Iterate until the plan fits within the negotiated constraints for expense and capital.
5. Prepare arguments to avoid the cherry-picking problem described in the chapter.
6. Evaluate how the list of strategic projects, when complete, will stack up against the competition.

# ADDENDUM: SUPPLY CHAIN CAPABILITIES CHECKLIST ___

The following is a list of detailed questions that could point to the need for new supply chain capabilities.

### Transportation

1. Do you manage inbound transportation flows from your vendors, or do you abdicate that and let the vendors deliver and charge as they wish?
2. Do you have a world-class transportation management system (TMS) that dynamically optimizes routes and helps select carriers?
3. Are transportation flows completely visible across the supply chain?
4. Have backhauls been optimized?
5. Do you have a clear policy for intra-DC transfers and how to minimize them?
6. Do you track cube utilization or load factors and have a plan to continuously improve the fullness of your loads?
7. Do you have a disciplined process for selecting transportation providers and 3PLs (third party logistics operators)?
8. If you have a private fleet, do you routinely compare the real cost and quality inside with that which could be obtained outside?
9. Do you have a process to track transportation flows and an event management process that enables you to see any problems quickly?
10. Do you have a world-class process for managing global movements, including optimizing INCO terms, freight classification, customs clearances, and security?

### Warehousing

1. Do you use automatic shipment notices (ASNs)?
2. Have you maximized the cross-docking potential?
3. Do you fully employ slotting and profiling by locating SKUs optimally in your warehouse according to volume or other criteria?
4. Do you have a world-class yard management capability?
5. Do you employ Lean and Six Sigma extensively in your warehouse operations?

6. Do you manage the returns and reclaim area for minimum cost and maximum customer service?
7. Do you use world-class picking techniques as appropriate for your operation, such as voice picking, pick to light, put to light, A frame, smart conveyors, and so on?
8. Do you use radio-frequency identification (RFID) or enhanced bar codes?

### Network Optimization

1. Based on the location of your suppliers and customers, have you done a complete network optimization in the past three years in order to determine:
   a. How many warehouses you should have?
   b. Where they should be located?
   c. What size they should be?
   d. Which customers or, in the case of retailers, retail stores each should serve?
2. Do you have an in-house network optimization capability so that at least once a year you can:
   a. Reassess transportation flows to make sure that the right suppliers are serving the right warehouses, and the right warehouses are serving the right customers?
   b. Answer a myriad of ad hoc network questions that come up routinely, such as:
      • When we add a new customer (or store), how should we best serve that customer?
      • How can we best handle returns?
      • How should we serve the dot-com business?
      • Should we do more shipping direct from vendor to customer (or store)?
      • How can we best handle the import flow?
   c. Address where to build a new warehouse or where to locate a new store?

### Inventory Management

1. Do you have a distribution requirements planning (DRP) system and process to calculate the correct and even optimum inventory level needed to:
   a. Meet a preestablished service level?
   b. Place inventory in the correct network location?

    c. Decide how much should be ordered from the supply
       source (factories or vendors)?
2. Are all functions in the company that affect inventory levels
   held accountable for them (sales, marketing, planning, manufacturing, procurement)?
3. Have you analyzed the correct strategic place in the extended
   supply chain network to carry inventory and in what form
   to carry it: at the vendor, factory warehouse, RDC, store, or
   customer (that is, do you have a multiechelon inventory optimization capability)?
4. Has inventory management been centralized in order to manage DC levels (and store levels for retailers)?
5. Do you have a strategy to reduce system inventory while still
   improving customer service by employing such tools as:
    a. SKU management?
    b. Lead-time reduction and intense focus on each step from
       vendor to customer?
    c. Forecasting improvement?
    d. Segmenting SKUs into, say, an ABC classification and
       applying different inventory policies for each class?
    e. An aggressive plan to track, monitor, and dispose of
       excess and obsolete inventory?
    f. A world-class S&OP process?

### SKU Management

1. Do you know the operating cost and inventory implications
   of carrying an SKU in the supply chain?
2. Have you segmented SKUs, and do you have a different
   management process for each class (that is, do you have a different customer lead time or availability targeted depending
   on the SKU classification)?
3. Do you have a disciplined process at the beginning of life
   to determine how much variety is appropriate for a new
   product?
4. Do you have a disciplined end-of-life process to phase out
   SKUs that are no longer performing?
5. Have you considered whether a postponement strategy is
   appropriate?

### Order Management

1. Is order management fully integrated with the supply chain process?
2. Are you easy to do business with, and can you accept orders from your customers any way they wish to submit them?
3. Do you have an ATP capability based on supply capability?
4. Do you have an AATP capability to make sure orders get filled according to preestablished customer priorities?
5. Is order management integrated with a customer relationship management (CRM) process?

### New Product Introduction

1. Do you have a stage gate process to guide the introduction of new products?
2. Is the supply chain function integrated into the stage gate process, and do the following questions get asked:
   a. How can you design the product to reduce warehousing and transportation costs?
   b. Have you done everything you can to reduce component and finished product complexity?
   c. Can you design for postponement (that is, delaying the commitment to a specific SKU until as late as possible in the supply chain)?
   d. Do you have a plan to phase out old product and phase in the new in order to maintain excellent customer service and minimize obsolete inventory?
3. Do you have a disciplined phase-in/phase-out process to guide the introduction of a new product and its inventory into the distribution system?

### Forecasting

1. Do you use a modern statistical forecasting package with all of the latest features?
2. Are users fully trained in the use of the statistical forecasting system?
3. Do you have statistical expertise in the forecasting group?

4. Is forecasting accuracy measured on a mean absolute percent error (MAPE) basis and on a bias basis?
5. Is the responsibility for forecast accuracy assigned to all areas that affect it, especially sales?
6. Is there a good process for obtaining and using input from sales on a routine basis?
7. Do you have a collaborative forecasting process with your major customers?
8. Are financial and sales goals kept separate from demand forecasts?
9. Is forecasting fully integrated with inventory management and the S&OP process?

### Procurement and Vendor Management

1. Is vendor-managed inventory (VMI) supported appropriately?
2. Are vendor lead times tracked and aggressively reduced?
3. Does vendor on-time delivery performance get tracked, and are vendors held accountable for delivering on time? (Early is not on time.)
4. Have vendors been quality-certified so that inspection is not necessary?
5. Are vendors required to use ASNs and bar codes (or RFID labels) that integrate with the DC receiving systems?
6. Have collaborative relationships been established with the core vendors, and are there projects underway to improve the supply chain on a win/win basis?

### Organization Design and Metrics

1. Do you have a complete supply chain organization that includes both logistics operations and inventory management? Do you follow the best practice of grouping *demand creation* activities in one area of the company and *demand fulfillment* (logistics and inventory management) activities in another because:
   a. These two major activities require totally different skill sets?
   b. Such a separation allows competing trade-offs to be balanced most effectively?

    c. The separation better facilitates the rapid implementation of improvement projects?

    d. When logistics and inventory management are separate, this creates a problem with balancing service with cost and inventory, and aligning metrics? Therefore, separating them is a barrier to improvement initiatives that need to sweep across the supply chain.

2. Have metrics been designed to put the right cross-functional accountability in the right place? (The accountability for inventory, forecast accuracy, and availability should be shared between the supply and demand sides of the organization.)

3. Are metrics linked to the overarching goals of the company in a logical framework?

4. Do metrics meet these best-in-class criteria?

    a. Robust

    b. Stable

    c. Understandable

    d. Accurate

    e. Cannot be manipulated

    f. Must have "intelligence"

    g. Drill-down capability

    h. Know cause and effect (drivers)

    i. Must be accessible

    j. Metric guru not necessary to obtain information

    k. Reports developed and published with pertinent information

    l. Frequency of reporting must be balanced with effort

    m. Single point of responsibility

    n. Don't have to chase people to get information

    o. Direct access to data and reports

### Lean/Six Sigma

1. Have Lean concepts been applied to the supply chain?

    a. Value stream mapping of material flows to eliminate waste

    b. Aggressive cycle-time reduction for the end-to-end supply chain

    c. A *kaizen* culture of continuous improvement, with heavy involvement of all personnel

2. Have Six Sigma concepts been applied to the extended supply chain?
   a. Use of the Six Sigma tool set to reduce process variation.
   b. Use of the Six Sigma tool set to reduce cost and inventory throughout the supply chain.

## CHAPTER 9

# Evaluate the Organization, People, and Metrics

You have completed all of the difficult and intense work of developing an outstanding supply chain strategy. This new strategy could very well create the need for a new supply chain organization, including additional people. Also, new metrics will undoubtedly be required. As Eli Goldratt said, "Tell me how you will measure me, and I will tell you how I will behave. If you measure me in an illogical way, don't complain about illogical behavior."[1] Successful implementation of your supply chain strategy will require that you reevaluate your organization, people, and metrics.

## THE EXPANSIVE SUPPLY CHAIN ORGANIZATION

The ever-broadening scope of supply chain sophistication has driven many firms to create larger, more expansive supply chain organizations that encompass logistics operations, customer service, and wide-ranging planning activities. That expansion can go quite far. Some supply chain organizations also include procurement and manufacturing on the supply side and order/customer management on the demand side.

We believe that it is better to group *demand creation* activities in one area of the company and *demand fulfillment* activities in another. The logic for this separation is threefold:

1. Demand creation (sales and marketing) requires a totally different skill set from demand fulfillment (operations and planning).

2. Grouping all demand fulfillment activities in one organization creates a single point of accountability and allows competing trade-offs to be balanced effectively. For instance, when the organization needs to cut cost and inventory, while at the same time improving customer service and product availability, a single demand fulfillment team will have a view into all the moving parts.
3. Organizations that group demand fulfillment functions can implement improvement projects more rapidly because the initiatives are managed by one organization and therefore face fewer functional barriers.

Based on hundreds of interviews done in many companies, we find that when organizations mix demand fulfillment activities with demand creation roles under one umbrella, they find it more difficult to balance service with cost and inventory, and to align metrics. Such combinations also slow or prevent improvement initiatives that need to sweep across the extended supply chain.

When you evaluate what will be the best supply chain organization to implement your strategy, you will have to make tough decisions regarding which functions to include in your recommendation. Two examples of how a manufacturer and a retailer approached this challenge are presented here to help guide you in that process.

## How an Automotive Manufacturer Redesigned Its Supply Chain Organization

The CEO of an automotive manufacturer had reviewed the supply chain team's proposed strategy and given it tentative approval, but before signing off, he asked the VP of supply chain to study the supply chain organization and come back with a proposal for how he would restructure it to best pursue the strategy. The good news was that the CEO *gave* the VP of supply chain a mandate to wade into the politically infested waters of organization design. The bad news was that in this organization, the VP of supply chain reported to the EVP of sales and marketing. Any recommendations that the supply chain executive made would either need to maintain the full organization territory currently held by the EVP or be absolutely, inarguably supported by clear evidence. He turned to us to provide an unbiased analysis, and also to serve as a buffer for the changes he expected to suggest.

When I talked with people in the company, I found that many of them were confused about the difference between the supply chain *functional organization* and the supply chain *process*. To create a foundation for organizational change, I felt it was important to make sure that management across the company understood that the supply chain process was an end-to-end horizontal process that extended across the company and beyond it, reaching backward to the suppliers and forward to the dealers and end consumers. In subsequent discussions, I stressed that the supply chain process should provide the best possible customer service at the lowest possible level of cost and working capital. I also pointed out that any new supply chain functional organization would be a subset of the supply chain process, given its vast expanse.

### Reporting Relationships

The next step I took with this company was to review organizational benchmarking data for other large firms. These data showed that there are three common reporting lines for supply chain functional organizations. Most functional supply chain organizations report either to operations, which is the most popular approach; to sales/marketing, as the organization in this case did; or directly to a senior executive officer, such as the COO or the CEO. According to our database at the University of Tennessee, 19 percent of supply chain organizations report to sales/marketing, 49 percent report to operations, and 21 percent report independently to the COO or CEO; the remaining 11 percent report to other functions such as finance or IT.

The different organizational approaches have some obvious consequences for how the supply chain operates and what it emphasizes. The supply chain group at the automotive firm felt, as do most supply chain professionals, that supply chain organizations that report to sales/marketing have a tendency to emphasize service over cost. Conversely, supply chain organizations that align with operations generally focus on cost and inventory more than on service. (Of course, the degree of bias is exaggerated or lessened depending on the metrics established within the firm.)

To avoid any imbalance between customer service and inventory/ working capital priorities, we feel that the supply chain organization optimally should report to a senior executive (the COO in this case, who had broad control and served as the company president). This level of leadership provides the appropriate balance among cost, working capital, and customer service. The supply chain VP and I both reached the conclusion that his organization should report in this manner. It's not surprising that we agreed on this point, since we are both supply chain people, and we both felt that the current reporting relationship impeded progress. The supply chain VP passionately believed that this was right, and he was willing to face the impending political minefield. More important, he was ready to commit to major, step improvements in cost, inventory, and even customer service, and he believed that he could deliver if such an organization change occurred.

Before moving forward with this proposal, the VP and his team debated one potential challenge to this reporting relationship: was the COO willing to get involved in supply chain issues, did he really understand the supply chain, and would he provide critical assistance with cross-functional coordination? After some consideration, the supply chain leadership team felt confident that they could count on his support.

### The Supply Chain North American Organization

Next, the team had to contend with geographic issues. Which functions and geographic entities should report to the supply chain function? There were two specific questions:

- Should operations in Mexico, Canada, and the United States be integrated?
- Should any specific supply chain activities report globally to the corporate supply chain functional organization?

When interviewed, people across the company were almost unanimous in saying that the supply chain organization should include responsibility for Canada and Mexico. Predictably, the only dissenters were the management teams in Canada and Mexico. A common comment in the interviews was: "Bringing together Canada, Mexico, and the United States is a real opportunity for us. Today we have a lot of duplication." Integrating Canada was less complex, and could be done in a short time frame. Mexico was more complicated, especially culturally, and would take longer to absorb. Other parts of the world would remain autonomous for now.

### Functional Integration

They study team next considered the possible options for how it would structure the supply chain organization from the inside. The preferred option involved grouping all demand fulfillment activities in one supply chain functional organization. As a general principle, this approach worked, but there were a lot of details to consider. To give them each their due consideration, the team listed all of the possible activities that could be included in a supply chain functional organization. It then engaged our help to conduct a benchmark of 10 supply chain organizations in somewhat similar companies to find out which activities were commonly housed within the supply chain organization. What we found is shown in Table 9-1.

### Final Organization Decisions

With all of this as input, the team decided to create a comprehensive supply chain organization that included almost all of these functions. (Credit and collection, which was a stretch to begin with, was excluded.) The team especially wrestled with the question of whether it should include the inventory management and forecasting functions. Those functions reported separately to the sales organization at that time, and the supply chain team feared that any proposal to consolidate them within the new supply chain organization would create conflict. Anticipating that it would need very clear justifications, they developed a table listing the pros and cons of including these functions (see Table 9-2).

After much debate, the team resolved that in spite of the political issues, it could answer the tough questions it would face; in the end, its proposal included a recommendation that these functions be moved to the supply chain organization.

Once all of this work and analysis was complete, the supply chain VP asked me to make the first presentation to his boss, the EVP of sales and marketing, from whom he expected a lot of opposition. He wasn't wrong. The EVP objected strongly, using, as expected, the "con" arguments in Table 9-2. The VP of supply chain knew that his boss was upset, but he and the team held firm. He felt that they had done the necessary work to justify the change, and the EVP could

TABLE 9-1 Likelihood of an Activity Being in the Supply Chain Organization

| Function | Number of Companies Including This Activity in the Supply Chain Functional Organization |
|---|---|
| Raw material ordering | 4 |
| Raw material transportation | 7 |
| Raw material warehousing | 6 |
| Raw material inventory management | 5 |
| Supply base management | 5 |
| Finished goods forecasting | 5 |
| Finished goods production ordering | 8 |
| Finished goods transportation | 10 |
| Finished goods warehousing | 10 |
| Finished goods inventory management | 9 |
| Finished goods inventory deployment/allocation | 8 |
| Finished goods network optimization | 9 |
| Finished goods customer service/availability | 9 |
| Service parts ordering/production planning | 5 |
| Service parts transportation | 6 |
| Service parts warehousing | 6 |
| Service parts inventory management | 6 |
| Service parts inventory deployment | 6 |
| Service parts network optimization | 6 |
| Service parts customer service/availability | 6 |
| Accessory ordering | 7 |
| Accessory transportation/warehousing | 7 |
| Accessory inventory management | 7 |
| Accessory customer service/availability | 7 |
| Export production scheduling | 7 |
| Export global transportation | 9 |
| Export warehousing | 9 |
| Export inventory management | 7 |
| Export inventory deployment | 7 |
| Import transportation | 9 |
| Customer order processing | 4 |
| Credit and collection | 1 |
| Supply chain strategy for the function | 9 |
| Supply chain strategy for the process | 7 |

TABLE 9-2 Pros and Cons of Including Inventory Management
and Forecasting in the Supply Chain Organization

| Arguments for Including Inventory Management and Forecasting in the Supply Chain Organization | Arguments Against Including Them That Need to Be Countered |
|---|---|
| Establishes clear responsibility and a single point of accountability to fulfill demand | Supply chain personnel will not understand customer needs and will be too focused on cost versus service |
| Allows all fulfillment functions to be efficiently integrated together and thus speeds improvement projects | It would disrupt vital lines of communication with the dealer base |
| Allows a better balance with operations constraints and service objectives | |

not prevent the report from making its way to the desks of the CEO and COO, since the executive suite had ordered it in the first place. In the final meeting with the CEO and the COO, there was a great deal of passionate debate, but in the end the CEO approved the changes, to the great relief of the VP of supply chain, who had in effect put his job on the line with this recommendation.

This organization's analysis includes some good lessons that could benefit anyone who is engaged in such an activity. Having a strong commitment to deliver major benefits in cost, inventory, and customer service definitely helped. The analysis was well grounded in benchmarking data. And it followed the best practice of separating demand fulfillment from demand creation activities.

## How a Retail Company Changed Its Supply Chain Organization

The previous example involved a manufacturing company. Retailers often have different organizational challenges because they have a different balance of functions. For example, retailers commonly have a logistics function, which includes transportation and warehousing. Then they have a separate merchandising organization, which often includes inventory management and vendor procurement. In other words, supply chain activities are sometimes separated and report to two senior executives in totally different parts of the organization. This might be perceived as a problem, but it's hard to argue with the success of, say, Walmart, which is organized this way. As the supply chain discipline matures, however, retail logistics executives increasingly feel that they are leaving money on the table because their structures do not allow the company to seize cross-functional opportunities between logistics/warehousing, inventory management, and merchandising.

For example, we recently worked with a VP of logistics who felt that performance at his company would improve significantly if an expansive supply chain organization were formed. He ticked off three critical improvement initiatives that had stalled recently because of a lack of alignment between functional silos. In his view, much of the problem lay in the fact that merchandising didn't understand the need to address key supply chain issues as part of its responsibilities. He mentioned, for example, that merchandising always failed to communicate clear information to customers about the cost of certain supply chain benefits, such as faster delivery.

The logistics VP asked us to help him make the case for creating a supply chain organization that combined the relevant functions. We provided data and benchmark examples to help. As one can imagine, a multitude of political tentacles surrounded this decision, not the least of which was turf protection on the part of the VP of merchandising.

After seeing benchmark data documenting how other retailers had improved their performance by developing an expanded supply chain organization, the logistics VP was convinced. He now believed that his organization needed a focused point of accountability that could deal with the trade-offs between cost and inventory reduction, on the one hand, and stock improvement and customer service, on the other.

He was not, however, naïve about the challenge he would face. One area that would change dramatically in a single organization was inventory management. The logistics VP felt confident of the argument he had developed to absorb inventory management for the distribution centers (DCs), but the company's 600-plus *stores* presented an entirely different challenge. Each store operated with a high degree of autonomy, since each was accountable for delivering on tough sales goals. Store managers and staff members had little expertise in inventory management, and there were more than 600 different "seat-of-the pants" processes. This was a huge opportunity to create significant improvement, but he expected that getting control over those processes would lead to a lot of organizational conflict.

After completing the full analysis, the logistics VP scheduled a meeting with the CEO to make the proposal. To his chagrin, when he arrived, the VP of merchandising was there at the CEO's invitation. The meeting ended with the CEO agreeing to "think about it." Sadly, he is apparently still thinking. In the meantime, performance improvements in cost, inventory, and customer service at the retailer stalled, and then, worse, another firm acquired the company one year later.

The logistics VP had a lot of insight into how his company could make improvements, but he might have had better results if he had searched early in the process for ways to show the merchandising VP how better alignment could improve merchandising performance. He also should have involved the CEO far earlier.

### Organization Summary

The two examples just given show that changes in the supply chain organization involve intense political issues. A good change management plan with early involvement of key stakeholders is critical. To evaluate your supply chain organization, you should follow these steps:

- Adopt the general principle that demand creation activities should be separate from demand fulfillment activities.
- List all possible functions that could be placed in a supply chain organization, and prepare to clearly communicate the advantages of including them. Anticipate and prepare to face arguments against consolidation.
- Commit the new organization to quantified improvements in cost, working capital, and customer service.
- Involve all stakeholders as early as possible.

# PEOPLE

Implementing the new supply chain capabilities identified by the strategy and managing them over time will no doubt require new skills. Some new faces will be added, and, unfortunately, some existing employees may have to be let go. You should identify the complete list of skills needed for each position and evaluate the existing people based on whether they already have these skills or are able to acquire them. New hires should be evaluated in the same manner.

Each person in your organization will need technical skills, whether in transportation, warehousing, inventory management, planning, forecasting, or some other relevant area. Beyond the technical skills, you will need people who have key management capabilities, such as the five listed in *The New Supply Chain Agenda:*[2]

- *Global orientation.* Almost all supply chain strategies have a strong global component, and almost all supply chain organizations will need people who can manage effectively in that environment.
- *Systems thinking.* Supply chain professionals must understand how the extended supply chain works, given its expansive cross-functional and cross-enterprise nature.
- *Inspiring and influential leadership.* The supply chain challenge requires leaders who can inspire and influence people throughout the organization to change.
- *Technical savvy.* Supply chain managers must know what questions to ask when they are faced with new technologies, and they must also be highly experienced in the disciplines of project management.
- *Superior business skills.* The supply chain professional must be able to speak the language of the executive suite and communicate comfortably using terms that resonate with senior executives, such as *revenue generation, cash flow,* and *shareholder value.*

Not only must the right talent be hired and retained, but it must also be developed aggressively over the course of a career. Certain skills become obsolete more quickly than equipment, so professional development plans for *each individual* must be established and carried out.

## MANDATE FOR NEW METRICS

New supply chain organizations and strategies demand a new set of metrics. It makes little sense to change the organization and the strategy and then rely on the same tired set of metrics. The right supply chain key performance indicators (KPIs) aligned with the right accountabilities help the organization deal effectively with trade-offs and proactively address the inevitable problems that engulf any firm in a competitive industry.

In a recent survey of our Supply Chain Forum members, we found that "choosing the right metrics" was rated third among 25 possible topics that supply chain professionals want to hear and learn more about. Many supply chain executives thirst for a better metrics framework. They worry that their existing KPIs prevent them from optimizing performance. They tell us that they want to:

- Learn how excellence is achieved in similar companies.
- Share knowledge about common problems within the company and with trading partners.
- See how to set appropriate performance measures and targets for improvement.
- Learn how others enable and empower employees to make change happen.
- Understand how to create a culture of continuous improvement.

In another of our surveys, 34 business executives from a broad range of companies ranked the supply chain issues in Table 9-3 on a scale of 1 to 10, with 10 being the most important and 1 the least important:

Performance measures and goal setting being number one surprised us, but it shouldn't have.

TABLE 9-3 Ranking of Supply Chain Executives' Interests

| | |
|---|---|
| Implementing the right metrics and setting the right goals | 8.15 |
| Establishing collaborative relationships with suppliers and customers | 7.91 |
| Advances in supply chain visibility | 7.80 |
| Professional development, training, and education | 6.71 |
| Helping with revenue generation | 6.62 |
| Managing the global supply chain | 6.55 |
| Using technology effectively | 5.21 |

## Make Sure the Right Cross-Functional Accountability Is Established

Measuring something accomplishes little unless the right account-ability is established. Good supply chain leaders should always ask themselves whether their metrics have been designed with the right cross-functional accountability in place. For example, the account-ability for inventory, forecast accuracy, and product availability should be shared between the supply and demand sides of the orga-nization. One executive told us that only the production planning function had the goals for inventory turnover in its personal perfor-mance plan (PPP). Yet the planning function controlled neither the input to inventory (manufacturing) nor the output (sales). In this case, planning had all of the accountability and none of the control!

Unfortunately, this situation is all too common. There are few companies in which sales shares accountability for inventory. Yet sales strategies have a tremendous influence on inventory levels. This particular issue is one of the greatest organizational accountability flaws in firms today.

## Make Sure Metrics Have a Logical Framework

Are your metrics linked to the overarching goals of the company through a logical framework, or are they simply a laundry list of items with no apparent logic? If the prime goal of the firm is to drive shareholder value, then a framework needs to be estab-lished so that the organization can clearly see how every submetric flows into shareholder value. One manufacturing firm we assessed selected "the efficient perfect order" as its ultimate goal. (The basic perfect order performance is calculated by multiplying together performance in four areas: on time, complete, damage free, and invoiced correctly.) Table 9-4 shows how 95 percent performance in each category of the perfect order leads to a dismal 81 percent perfect order result.

TABLE 9-4  The Perfect Order Metric

| On Time | × | Complete | × | Damage Free | × | Invoiced Accurately | = | Perfect Order |
|---------|---|----------|---|-------------|---|---------------------|---|---------------|
| 95% |  | 95% |  | 95% |  | 95% |  | 81% |

The "efficient" perfect order in this firm then included cost and inventory as key additional factors. With the efficient perfect order as the overarching goal, this firm built a metrics framework, illustrated in Figure 9-1, to show how all of the submetrics contributed to achieving the perfect order.

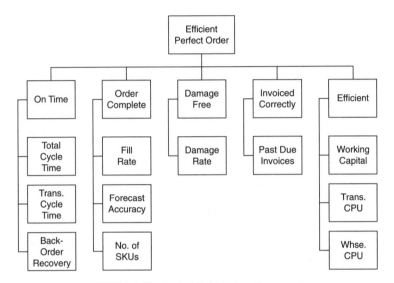

FIGURE 9-1 The Perfect Order Metrics Framework

In developing the new metrics to support your strategy, make sure you have a set of criteria in place that enables you to avoid poorly designed or seriously flawed metrics. For example, I worked with one firm that defined a set of excellent criteria to use in designing the new supply chain metrics needed to support its supply chain strategy. These characteristics became a hurdle test. Metrics had to reasonably satisfy the following criteria in order to be part of the KPI framework:

- Stable and accurate data, with few large, random, or unexplainable swings
- Understandable to everyone, along with a "line of sight" so that key personnel can see how their actions influence the metric
- Designed so that they cannot be easily manipulated or gamed
- Capable of drill-down analysis so that the root causes of changes are apparent

- Clear cause-and-effect drivers
- Easily accessible by relevant parties and available in clear reports, developed and published with clear explanations

These criteria always generated good discussion in the organization before a new metric was adopted, and resulted in a smaller number of high-impact KPIs.

## Goal Setting and the Importance of Benchmarking

It's clearly important to select the right metrics and define the associated responsibilities. Establishing *goals* is an entirely different matter. Too many companies use only internal comparisons (year-over-year performance, for instance) and feel good about achieving an internal goal. This is a very dangerous practice. For example, one consumer products manufacturer achieved a 6.7 inventory turnover level on its finished goods inventory, a 15 percent improvement over the 5.8 level in the prior year. Unfortunately, when doing a competitive assessment, the company discovered that its major competitor had achieved an 8.5 inventory turnover level. The 15 percent improvement didn't look so good in light of that statistic!

## Gaming Metrics

Many companies "game" their metrics, often by eliminating data that paint a process or function in a negative light. Doing so does the organization a great disservice because the performance level that it communicates to management is inevitably refuted by the customer. Supply chain professionals rationalize this data manipulation (for example, "It would be unfair to include that SKU in our fill rate calculation; we've had supplier problems, and we can't get enough of that product"), but in the end, it only hurts the supply chain organization because it hides real performance and creates a disconnect between the company's perception and the experience of the customer.

In a recent survey that we conducted, 81 percent of respondents believe that their company *provides* superior customer service. Yet, only 8 percent of customers say that they *receive* superior customer service. Likewise, in a recent analysis of our database, 94 percent of firms rated themselves above average in satisfying their customers.

Since it's statistically unlikely for 94 percent of companies to be above average, these respondents are either manipulating or over-estimating their capability. Overestimation is more than just naive; it actually destroys internal motivation because employees hear how well the firm is doing and feel no urgency to surpass competitors or delight customers, thereby giving its rivals an upper hand.

One supply chain vice president described the extreme pressure he faced at all levels of his organization to deliver better fill rates. He said that the sales organizations continually communicated hor-ror stories in which customers complained bitterly about not being able to get product. "The CEO called me one day and made it quite clear that fill rates had to improve. In fact, he demanded that large three- by four-foot charts be posted in prominent places around the building to show the improvement in fill rates that must come about!" He then related how, during the subsequent weeks, the com-pany struggled with manufacturing and vendor issues, which offset any internal fill rate improvements. The pressure on the supply chain organization built to an excruciating level.

Suddenly, everything changed. The metrics started to show fill rate improvements, which continued until the company's goal was achieved. The supply chain VP was amazed. He was also confused because customer complaints continued unchanged. Much later, his director of inventory management left for another company, and the replacement discovered that his predecessor had directed the inven-tory analysts to exclude certain data when they calculated fill rates.

For example, when new products entered the system, it took several months for the inventory to catch up with demand. This imbalance had a negative impact on the fill rates at this company, so the inventory analysts decided to eliminate those data from the fill rate calculation until the new product stabilized. They did not tell anyone, rationalizing that they were making the metric more accu-rate by eliminating such detail. This slippery slope became steeper and steeper, and the analysts began manipulating other "unfair situations." Eventually, the house of cards came crashing down. Several of these analysts were actually dismissed from the company, and the supply chain VP had to explain the abrupt and embarrassing fall in the fill metric once the data were corrected.

In summary, we believe that you should design a new set of supply chain metrics that support the new supply chain strategy, follow a logical framework, have clearly defined cross-functional accountability, are related to goals set with best practices bench-marking, are customer-focused and not easily gamed, and provide effective insights into how the supply chain organization is perform-ing and where improvements can be made.

## CHAPTER 9 ACTION STEPS

1. In your organization design:
   a. Adopt the general principle that demand creation activ-ities should be separated from demand fulfillment activities.
   b. List all possible functions that could be placed in a supply chain organization, and prepare to clearly communicate the advantages of including them. Anticipate and prepare to face the arguments against consolidation.
   c. Commit to quantified improvements in cost, working cap-ital, and customer service if the organization change is made.
   d. Involve all stakeholders as early as possible.
2. In assessing people:
   a. Evaluate each person relative to the new skill sets required by the supply chain strategy.
   b. Make sure leaders and potential leaders possess the five management skills described in the chapter.
   c. Ensure that each person has a tailored professional devel-opment plan.
3. In your metrics design, make sure that your metrics:
   a. Support the new supply chain strategy.
   b. Follow a logical framework.
   c. Have clearly defined cross-functional accountability.
   d. Are related to goals set with best practices benchmarking.
   e. Are customer-focused and not gamed.

## CHAPTER 10

# Develop a Business Case and Get Buy-In

People throughout your company need to support the supply chain strategy. From the senior executive level to middle management—and even to the front lines—everyone needs to understand and work toward the common goals your team has laid out and the capabilities and methods you will pursue. A firm's supply chain process is the ultimate cross-functional entity. Without explicit buy-in from the people who affect it, and are affected by it, the entire strategy creation process becomes just another example of a lot of effort delivering no results.

Buy-in is by no means a given. I've already related a number of examples of supply chain leaders who faced serious resistance to their strategy proposals. In fact, getting buy-in for supply chain projects is often quite difficult. As one executive put it, "Someone's ox is being gored with everything we try to do." But getting the company and its people to support the supply chain strategy is critical, and you are much more likely to be successful if you follow a concrete process that starts with developing a great business case. A tight business case is not a sufficient condition for buy-in, but it is absolutely a necessary one.

## DEVELOPING A BUSINESS CASE

A good business case clearly demonstrates how the personnel, expense, and capital consumed by each initiative will deliver a quantified benefit. Supply chain professionals generally place the benefits from any supply chain initiative in one or more of three categories: lower cost, lower working capital, and increased customer satisfaction. Many supply chain managers feel a great deal of trepidation about creating a business case. They worry that their business case will fail to stand up to the intense and often political scrutiny of the corporate review process. The need to make the business case credible and bulletproof haunts them. They want to be very conservative about the benefits, since they will have to deliver them. But they also want to generate the excitement that the strategy deserves.

Experienced professionals involve the finance function when crafting the business case. At this stage of the process, finance is critical in helping the supply chain strategy group develop a credible business case. In fact, I have already mentioned my belief that a finance representative should be part of the strategy team. Many executives tell us that finance can be either a valuable ally or a major barrier. If you want to have your finance department on your side, you need to have the finance professionals feel invested in the outcome—and that requires finance's involvement *from the beginning.*

Getting finance to "bless" the business case calculation is important, but it is only one step in achieving cross-functional buy-in. Approval from finance adds a level of credibility, but it cannot by itself overcome the intricacies of the corporate power game. In many supply chain initiatives, some functions gain power, and others lose it. At one retailer, for example, the strategy team came to the conclusion that the company should combine inventory management and logistics operations into a consolidated supply chain functional organization. At the time, the merchandising function owned inventory management. The strategy team developed a strong business case for this move: it showed how combining inventory management and logistics could reduce inventory by 20 percent, or $40 million, and improve customer fill rates by five percentage points, from 92 percent to 97 percent. The finance function helped develop the business case calculation and fully supported it. But despite the compelling logic and analysis, the SVP of merchandising still declared the move too risky.

The corporate political environment usually guarantees resistance like this. A business executive protects his turf the way a medieval knight defended his castle: by charging forward with lance drawn. In this case, the merchandising SVP argued that the analysis was flawed. He told the CEO that he had heard of such a change in another company, and it hadn't worked and had to be reversed. He said, "If we do this, don't blame me if sales fall." He managed to put enough doubt in the CEO's mind, even without having specific data or details, that the initiative died, and with it a major improvement in the company's performance.

In this classic situation, the business case alone failed to generate buy-in for the reorganization component of the strategy. Almost every company will have one or more influential leaders that it needs to win over to the supply chain strategy. One of the most effective ways to gain that leader's response is to involve him or her from the very beginning, and let him or her be part of the process of molding the strategy. In many cases, without that early involvement, it becomes impossible to have a conversation, especially the difficult dialogues involving organization changes. Getting a resistant leader involved in the supply chain strategy in its early stages is not without risk; you will have to craft a compelling story about how he or she will benefit both functionally and politically.

When all else fails, the CEO may be forced into the position of being the final arbiter. In many companies, this means putting the CEO in the position of deciding the outcome of a winner-take-all confrontation. This carries with it severe risks, and it is not a tactic that I recommend. A more subtle approach may be to educate the CEO and the executive team over time, with regular updates regarding the development of the strategy and the dramatic effect the supply chain has on economic profit and shareholder value. If the executive team understands the company's supply chain and its huge potential, its members may venture from their comfort zone, especially during a business crisis. (This dynamic is fully addressed in the *Harvard Business Review* article, "Are You the Weakest Link in Your Supply Chain?"[1])

## DOING THE MATH

Doing the calculations required in developing the business case need not be intimidating. Especially with finance on the team, calculations of return on investment (ROI) or economic value added (EVA) should be straightforward. But the calculations are the easy part. Estimating benefits in a credible manner is a much greater challenge. Some of the following examples illustrate this challenge.

## Calculating the Project Cost and Benefits

A supply chain executive for a components supplier told us at a recent Supply Chain Forum about a supply chain initiative at his company, the aim of which was to implement a new forecasting process with a modern, state-of-the-art forecasting package. This new technology replaced a manual Excel process that had been used in inconsistent ways by the seven people who were generating forecasts for the various products made by the firm. To calculate a forecast, each person used Excel in a manner that he or she had individually evolved. Each forecaster used totally different calculation methods, data sources, and sales inputs to generate a forecast. The only consistency was Excel. The new initiative would require all forecasters to use a modern forecasting package and a new consistent forecasting process.

The cost of implementing this new process included $2.8 million for the software, which the firm capitalized. Consultants helped implement the package and train the users at a cost of $230,000. Finally, the IT function integrated the software with other systems, charging back $380,000. In all, the project consumed $2.8 million in capital and $610,000 in expense. The project also required nearly one person-year of time (2,080 hours) from supply chain personnel, but this firm did not typically charge the cost of supply chain personnel to projects of this kind. Since no additional people were hired, the supply chain person-hours were treated as a sunk cost. (Arguably this practice underestimated the true cost, since it didn't consider the benefits of other projects that were not done.) Next, the business case team turned to estimating the project benefits.

### Estimating the Project Benefits

The next step in developing the business case involved estimating the benefits, starting first with cost and inventory reductions. The project team believed strongly that better forecasts would lead to fewer expedited emergency shipments, less emergency airfreight on inbound components, and less overtime for people in operations. In their experience and judgment, these benefits would result from reducing mean absolute percent forecast error (MAPE) at the stock-keeping unit (SKU) level. (They expected the project to reduce forecast error from 46 percent error to 32 percent.) They estimated the cost reduction benefits shown in Table 10-1.

TABLE 10-1  Cost Reduction Savings Benefit Calculation

| Cost Reduction Category | Total Amount Spent in This Area in the Prior Year | Amount Saved due to This Project | Logic |
|---|---|---|---|
| Fewer expedited shipments | $2,740,000 | 25% or $685,000 | In analyzing a sample of expedited shipments, an improvement of forecast error as planned would have .eliminated at least 25% of expedited shipments. |
| Less airfreight for inbound components | $3,240,600 | 33% or $1,069,400 | Based on an analysis of a sample of airfreight shipments, this forecast accuracy improvement would eliminate a third of the airfreight shipments. |
| Less overtime in operations | $5,782,900 | 25% or $1,445,725 | This reduction was conservatively based on the lower levels of overtime generated in the past when forecasts were more accurate. |
| **Total Savings** | | $3,200,125 | |

In addition to these cost reductions, the project team also planned to reduce inventory. Better forecasting would allow the company to carry less inventory, especially less safety stock inventory; however, the team members working on the ROI calculation had to be careful, because savings from decreased inventory could overlap with the cost reduction benefits already summarized in Table 10-1. The team members wanted to make sure they avoided double-counting benefits. After much thought and discussion, they decided to be conservative and take only half of the value of the inventory reduction benefit to avoid any controversy later. They determined the inventory benefits as shown in Table 10-2.

The project team believed that it was on solid ground with these cost and inventory reduction benefits. However, quantifying the value of an improvement in product availability was a different story.

TABLE 10-2  Inventory Reduction Savings Benefit Calculation

| Category | Total Inventory | Amount Saved due to This Project | Logic |
|---|---|---|---|
| Finished goods inventory in DCs | $425,000,600 | 5% or $21,250,000 | Slow-moving and obsolete inventory alone totaled $55 million, mostly due to poor forecasts. |
| Finished goods inventory on consignment held by customers | $35,580,000 | 2% or $711,600 | Customers would have faster sell-through with a more accurate forecast. |
| Raw material inventory and work-in-process inventory | $45,675,000 | 5% or $2,283,750 | Just-in-case safety stock inventory could be reduced if forecasts improved. |
| **Total Savings** | | $24,245,350 | |

## Estimating the Product Availability Benefits

At this stage, the team had identified enough savings in cost and inventory reduction to easily justify the project. The team members were tempted to stop and avoid the potentially controversial area of product availability benefits. However, one team member passionately felt that improved availability held the greatest benefit for the firm, and that this improvement should be acknowledged, even celebrated. The team also knew that if it failed to quantify this benefit, it would be ignored and treated as zero. Benefits that are not quantified as dollar savings are irrelevant in the eyes of senior executives; many supply chain professionals waste their time listing a number of subjective benefits without any dollar value in their business case in an attempt to lend credibility. This team had the courage to try to quantify this benefit, feeling that any number attached to it would be more accurate than "zero."

Nonetheless, the team struggled to estimate a credible product availability benefit. At the time, the availability percentage on new orders was 90.8 percent. The team expected the availability percentage to increase to at least 95 percent. In a group brainstorming session, one team member had an inspired idea: to look at cancelled orders, as these provided the only hard data related to availability that they had. The team quickly surveyed a few customers and found that 85 percent of cancelled orders occurred because of lack of product availability. Cancelled orders seemed to drop off in a linear manner as availability increased, and stopped altogether when availability exceeded 97 percent.

After much discussion and analysis, the team formulated a simple "law of lost sales." This hypothesis stated that:

$$\text{Percentage of sales lost} = 0.85 \times (97\% \text{ minus the current availability percentage})$$

Based on this "law," the team estimated that 5.3 percent of sales were lost because of a lack of available product [that is, $0.85(97\% - 90.8\%)$]. The team then asked how much of the 5.3 percent loss the company could recapture if forecast accuracy improved to the goal set by the strategy. In the end, the team decided to be extremely conservative and use only 1 percent of sales (not the full 5.3 percent). This was a big company, so modest savings nonetheless yielded a substantial benefit of $78 million. At a marginal contribution of 29 percent, the additional profit generated totaled $22.6 million.

Instead of simply saying that the new forecasting project would "improve availability," the supply chain team could now state more boldly that it would add $22.6 million to the bottom line as a result of higher customer satisfaction. However, the team did not want to go public with this analysis without the full buy-in of the sales organization, which it expected would be difficult to get. Sales goals and targets could now be pushed upward as a result of the supply chain analysis.

Before the team approached the sales vice president, one of the team members thought to seek an independent check for reasonableness. Rather than use cancelled orders as the benefit driver, the team took a macro approach. Team members first noted that the company enjoyed a 24 percent market share in a $32.5 billion industry. They found that if the firm gained only ¼ *of 1 percentage point* of market share with the fill rate increase, this would yielded another $81 million in sales and $23 million in additional margin, compared with the $22.6 million calculated previously. So, regardless of whether they assumed a 1 percent increase in sales or a ¼ of 1 percentage point increase in market share, the result was roughly the same. With such a modest and conservative benefit, it was time to go to the sales VP.

### Getting Sales to Agree

The sales VP understood the logic, but he also knew that the CEO would use the same logic to increase his sales goal. In his view, the goal he had was already a stretch, "like a hole in one on a par 5 against the wind," as he put it to the supply chain team. So the supply chain team asked him if he supported the new forecasting project, along with the goal to improve availability from below 91 percent to at least 95 percent. Of course he enthusiastically supported the project. The team then pointed out that the cost of the project, as outlined previously, made little sense if the company saw no increase in sales. After some additional discussion, the sales VP grudgingly agreed to support one-half of the proposed sales increase, or $39 million in sales and $11 million in additional margin—still a substantial benefit.

### The Bottom Line

The supply team now had a bottom line for the project, along with organizational commitment (see Table 10-3).

TABLE 10-3  Total Cost and Benefit Summary

| Cost of Project | Benefits of Project |
| --- | --- |
| $2,800,000 in capital | $24,245,350 in inventory reduction |
| $610,000 in expense | $3,200,125 in cost reduction |
| Incremental 2,080 hours of people time in supply chain | $11,000,000 in additional margin due to increased sales |

Clearly the benefits of this project dominated the cost, with an off-the-charts ROI. It was now time to manage the coming change.

## ADVICE FOR DEVELOPING A BUSINESS CASE _____

When developing the business case for your supply chain strategy, I recommend the following guidelines.

1. Involve the finance function and enlist it as an ally during the development of the strategy. Make sure that you have a finance representative on your strategy team.

2. Be conservative with benefits and liberal with project costs to make sure you will deliver on your commitment.
3. Build your credibility by estimating benefits using more than one independent method.
4. Make sure all benefits pass a reasonableness test in terms of the percentage of the total cost or inventory to be saved.
5. Make sure you quantify all benefits, even the ones that are difficult to quantify.
6. Involve sales and marketing in the strategy development from the beginning and work to get buy-in for the availability, revenue, and market share benefits expected from the supply chain strategy.

## MANAGING CHANGE: GETTING FULL ORGANIZATIONAL BUY-IN

The process of getting buy-in at all levels of the organization should begin on the first day of the strategy development. It needs to if the effort is going to be successful, since true cross-functional buy-in is rare. In our survey, companies reported the following levels of cross-functional buy-in for their supply chain strategy:

- Poor: 15.2 percent
- OK: 21.2 percent
- Average: 24.2 percent
- Good: 33.3 percent
- Excellent: 6.1 percent

Poor, OK, or average responses came from 60.6 percent of respondents, meaning that the majority of companies do not have a good level of organizational buy-in for their supply chain strategy. We have identified four key causes of resistance to the supply chain strategy, which are discussed next.

1. Political barriers
2. Impermeable functional barriers
3. A flawed communication process
4. No plan to sustain the strategy

## Got Politics?

Got politics? Who doesn't? Political issues pervade most firms. At one retailer, the supply chain executive told us that sales felt that it should own customer service, which resided in the supply chain function. In this firm, customer service personnel managed order taking and customer delivery appointments. They also resolved problems with order delays. Yet the sales EVP lived for empire building, and he argued that the customer service organization clearly was performing a sales function. The supply chain group resisted the move on the grounds that the supply chain organization was accountable for demand fulfillment, and thus needed to manage the customer service function in order to have end-to-end oversight of the fulfillment process. This controversy consumed huge amounts of time and energy that could have been better spent working together to better serve the customer. The political turmoil relegated the customer to an afterthought, and sadly the big loser in this battle. There are always politics, but sometimes things spin out of control, causing multibillion-dollar companies to behave in totally irrational and damaging ways. Many great ideas have been sacrificed on the altar of career advancement.

Sometimes executives behave in a way that actually harms the company in order to gain personal advantage, although they may sincerely believe that the company will be better off in the long run. In this case, the sales EVP felt that if the supply chain failed to deliver the needed results, he could then offer to "fix" it for the CEO. This EVP, in one particularly egregious example, actually gave a major customer an incentive to order triple the usual amount. When the order hit the system, inventory was short, causing a major availability problem and an embarrassment for the supply chain organization. This represents corporate politics at its worst, but it is far from unknown. The best way for supply chain people to respond is with excellent analysis, early involvement of key stakeholders, aggressive commitment to improvement, and dependable delivery of results.

## Impermeable Functional Barriers

A second barrier to supply chain strategy buy-in arises from the extreme breadth of the supply chain, which creates huge communication challenges when any change occurs. The supply chain is surely the most complex of all business processes, if for no other reason than its scope. Clearly the supply chain process is the ultimate horizontal cross-functional process, leading to the most fundamental of business dilemmas: "how do we manage a *process* when we are all organized *functionally?*" or "how do we operate horizontally when we reside in a vertical functional mindset?" In my experience, the best way to deal with this issue is to represent all functions on the core supply chain strategy team from the beginning of the process.

## A Flawed Communication Process

Another barrier to achieving supply chain strategy buy-in is a poor communication process. One executive from a durable goods firm described what we believe to be an outstanding process of getting buy-in for her supply chain strategy. She reported that this process worked extremely well. Her buy-in process involved three steps that are simple, obvious, and almost never done. We believe that her three-step formula is an excellent process to use in communicating the supply chain strategy.

### Step 1: Identify the Critical Few

Step 1 involved identifying the individuals in all functions who were key to the supply chain strategy implementation. She used a grid like the one shown in Table 10-4, and she placed individual names on the grid.

TABLE 10-4  Influence Grid

| | | |
|---|---|---|
| Highly influential people who oppose the initiative | Highly influential people who are taking no apparent position on the initiative | Highly influential people who are enthusiastic |
| Moderately influential people who are opposed to the initiative | Moderately influential people who are taking no apparent position on the initiative | Moderately influential people who are enthusiastic |
| People who have little influence, but oppose the initiative | People with little influence who are taking no apparent position on the initiative | People with little influence who are enthusiastic |

Her theory, which we have confirmed with every executive we interview on this subject, is that there is always a handful of key individuals who can make or break the strategy. She noted that these people do not necessarily rank the highest on the organization chart. There can be extremely influential people in the middle management ranks, experts that everyone respects. In addition, the handful of people who are critical to the strategy's acceptance may fall anywhere on a spectrum from enthusiastic supporters to overt opponents. The key is to identify them.

### Step 2: Conduct Targeted Communication Sessions

Next, she developed a targeted communication plan like the one pictured in Table 10-5, and executed it almost flawlessly. She told us that it would have been easy to skip some of these steps, especially when her team complained constantly about the time they took. But she persevered.

She found that her message needed to change depending on the audience. In the extreme stereotype, operations people love to hear about cost reduction projects, and sales managers get excited about plans to increase revenue. Although the situation is never this simplistic, the message must be tailored to the audience. She would gather suggestions for her supply chain strategy from the key stakeholders, work them into the strategy, and then meet again to show the stakeholders how their feedback was being used. This created strong cross-functional ownership, and she found it well worth the substantial time investment. She determined that the individual communication plan should have a tailored message that demonstrated the benefits to each individual—the WIFFM (what's in it for me) or, even better, the WIIFW (what's in it for we).

She managed communication sessions in a very disciplined way. She scheduled these sessions as tasks on the strategy development project plan and Gantt chart. She met with each key individual and asked for his or her thoughts. Invariably the person would suggest a few changes and areas to consider, and she rigorously recorded these items. She would then call for a second meeting, begin by reviewing the person's suggestions from the first meeting, and then show him or her how those suggestions were now accommodated in the strategy. If they could not be included, she gave a very thorough explanation of why not, and offered a "next-best" option.

TABLE 10-5 Example of a Targeted Communications Plan

| A Communication Plan Example Focused on Four Individuals | | | | | | |
|---|---|---|---|---|---|---|
| Audience | Message | Media | Frequency | Timing | Responsibility | Feedback |
| VP marketing | Revenue margins | Face-to-face | Monthly | Dates | SC director | Report at weekly team meetings |
| Director sales | Revenue market share | Face-to-face | Monthly | Dates | SC director | Report at weekly team meetings |
| VP supply chain | Cost and inventory | Face-to-face | Biweekly | Dates | SC director | Report at weekly team meetings |
| Manager supply chain | What's different | Face-to-face | Weekly | Dates | SC director | Report at weekly team meetings |

Often she would ask for third and fourth reviews, and even more for some people, until they felt real ownership of the strategy. She met with them until they literally would not meet with her anymore; this required a huge time commitment on her part. By the time the final strategy review occurred, the critical players truly felt that they had co-developed the strategy. She believed that people always support things that they helped create. It would have been easier to avoid all of this specialized communication and instead have all the key people as members of the core strategy team. That was possible for some, but impractical for all.

Targeted communications work; group communications do not work nearly as well. In an example we uncovered in a supply chain assessment, a project manager leading a major supply chain strategic initiative thought that he had designed the perfect change management plan. He introduced the topic with a well-crafted 30-minute presentation to everyone affected. He followed that with a one-hour review with everyone directly involved to go deeper into the coming change. About a month after the project began, he issued a newsletter that clearly showed the progress that was underway and the benefits that would be achieved. Finally, as the project neared completion, he managed to get a 600-word article in the company newsletter. This project manager seemingly did many things right, but he failed to target his communication properly. Although it might seem that he did a lot of communicating, the barrage of information that comes at business professionals every day dwarfed the amount of exposure that his project received. His communication effort did not include focused messages delivered to key stakeholders. As a result, major figures in the company were surprised when they found out about the project in its later stages. These key stakeholders had had no opportunity to offer midcourse feedback. When they finally understood what was about to happen, they actively resisted his initiative, causing the implementation to fail.

### Step 3: Continue Communicating as the Business Case and the Project Plan Are Finalized

The communication process must be ongoing and consistent over the entire development of the strategy. In the communication model followed by the executive in this case, she took several actions early in the process that helped to facilitate this third step of ongoing communication. Namely, she had a number of cross-functional representatives on the strategy team, which helped her facilitate communication with the broader organization. She found that having core strategy team representatives from functions like sales, manufacturing, and finance helped in communicating with their respective departments as the elements of the supply chain strategy progressed. Cross-functional representation is not sufficient, of course, but it is helpful.

At the root of her success was the fact that she executed all three steps of her plan extremely well—she identified the key influencers, engaged them and sought their input, and maintained ongoing communication throughout the process. From all of the interviews we conducted, it was clear that she was rewarded with complete organizational buy-in. All of the key players seemed to truly feel that the strategy was their strategy. In fact, they actually seemed to take ownership. She told us, "I truly think they own it now, and I hope I'm right. If they do feel ownership, there is no doubt they will make it work. But to be on the safe side, I'll have to keep monitoring, and communicating the progress as it occurs."

### Recommended Communication Process for Your Supply Chain Strategy

The process for communicating your supply chain strategy should begin early, in the first week of the strategy development process. It should follow the example just given fairly closely and should include the following steps:

1. Identify the key influential people who will determine the acceptance of your strategy at all organization levels. Unless the communication process precisely targets those key players, it will fail to rise above the normal noise level in a large enterprise. For nearly every project in every company, there are people who will make or break it. These people may be anyone from senior executives to critical subject-matter experts embedded in the organization. If you are to manage change effectively, these key people must be identified and exposed to a customized communication plan.

2. Develop a tailored communication message for each key person.

3. Have a solid business case and project plan to use in all communications. The more believable the business case, the easier the sell. A good business case will show how the company and each department benefit from the supply chain strategy. Also,

a solid project plan gives the organization confidence that the strategy is real and will be successfully executed.

4. Set up a disciplined communication schedule, showing when communications will take place, who will do them, and when feedback from the session will be passed along to the strategy team.

5. Incorporate feedback. The feedback mechanism needs to be more than an afterthought. Feedback operates on two dimensions. On the one hand, feedback to the strategy team should drive reasonable changes within the project scope. But more important, feedback to the original audience is the catalyst that creates buy-in.

6. Do group communications to the larger organization, such as large group meetings, e-mails, or newsletters, but don't rely on these too much in getting buy-in for your strategy.

7. Continue communicating with the key influencers throughout the strategy development and well after its completion.

## Failure to Sustain the Momentum

A final barrier to implementing the projects that roll out of the supply chain strategy occurs when the strategy implementation team fails to develop a plan to *sustain* the initial energy and excitement that often exist when the supply chain strategy and its initiatives are first unveiled and initially implemented. In a major durable goods company, we saw an interesting scenario play out. The strategy called for a project to improve forecast accuracy, and that initiative was turbocharged after someone accidentally sent the CEO a report that documented a 60 percent forecast error at the SKU location level. Based on this report, the CEO decided that forecast error had to be the source of many of the company's operational inefficiencies, so he usurped the strategy project plan and assigned responsibility for solving the problem to a young marketing VP who was rising rapidly in the firm. When given the assignment, the VP realized that he needed help in a major way, since he knew nothing about forecasting technology, or about the forecasting approach used in the firm. So he called us, and we came in, did an assessment, and found deficiencies in both the process and the systems used.

We then helped him design a world-class process and persuaded management to bring in state-of-the-art software. We also convinced the VP to initiate a forecast collaboration process with the company's three largest customers. The plan worked quite well. Forecast error fell by one-fourth, from 60 percent error to 45 percent error. There was still room for improvement, of course, but the CEO was fine with the process. Our work done, we left the company and didn't check back until a year later. When we did, we heard a very unfortunate story. The VP went on to other assignments on the assumption that the forecasting process was back on track. Around midyear, he checked in and found that something was very wrong. All of the accuracy improvement had been reversed! By the time the situation stabilized, it was too late; and the results for the year came at a higher level of error than the year before.

What went wrong? The early results were promising, but a key piece was missing, namely, a plan to *sustain* the change. Our experience shows that sustaining change, especially on complex cross-functional supply chain projects, is often more difficult than implementing it in the first place. Yet, project managers rarely develop a well-designed plan to sustain change. We strongly recommend that you include in any project plan a set of tasks focused on sustaining improvements after the initial implementation. When you implement or "go live" with your new initiative, you are not finished. You need to execute an ongoing plan to sustain the change through a focus on continuous improvement, postproject audits, midcourse corrections, training people who come on board after the project is implemented, and continuous communication of progress.

## CHAPTER 10 ACTION STEPS

1. Business case action steps:
   a. Involve the finance function and enlist it as an ally in the strategy development.
   b. Be conservative with benefits and liberal with project costs.
   c. Make sure you quantify all benefits, even those that are difficult to quantify.
   d. Involve sales and marketing in the strategy development from the beginning, and work to get buy-in for the customer satisfaction, revenue, and market share benefits to be generated by the supply chain strategy.

2. Change management action steps:
   a. Develop and execute a change management plan beginning on day one of the supply chain strategy development work.
   b. Focus on the key individuals who have the most influence with a targeted, individually tailored communication plan.
   c. Continue to refine the business case and project plan, and use it in an ongoing communication plan.
   d. Incorporate feedback from the communication sessions into the strategy development.
   e. Don't rely heavily on group communications to get your message across.
   f. Make sure that there is a plan to sustain the supply chain change going forward.

CHAPTER 11

# Case Study: Developing a Supply Chain Strategy

As I mentioned in Chapter 1, my colleagues and I worked with two companies that used a process very similar to the nine steps described in this book. One of those companies followed the process almost exactly, with excellent results. As with any complex process, this firm experienced a few bumps in the road, but nothing that seriously derailed the process. The story is told here as it unfolded, and shows how one company successfully used the method I've outlined to develop a supply chain strategy.

## DEVELOPING A SUPPLY CHAIN STRATEGY AT A DURABLE GOODS COMPANY

Durable Industries is a $6 billion maker of durable goods sold through a wide range of retail outlets, as well as to independent contractors that act as small distributors to the residential construction industry. The company has more than 10,000 customers. Some of these customers are very large national retailers, several are large regional players, many are small mom-and-pop operations, and some are home or apartment builders. This case tells the story of the development of a supply chain strategy at this firm.

Durable Industries' supply chain begins with several thousand suppliers of parts used to manufacture various products in 12 large factories located in the Midwest. Finished product moves into a warehouse located near each factory. Part of the factory output then goes directly to large retail customers' distribution centers (DCs).

The rest of the product flows through a set of eight regional warehouses owned by Durable. At the Durable regional warehouses, orders are processed, and the product moves through a series of 60 staging locations, set up in the 60 major metropolitan areas in the United States. At these locations, the full loads from the regional warehouse are broken into smaller quantities bound for delivery to individual customer locations.

## DURABLE INDUSTRIES NEEDED A NEW SUPPLY CHAIN STRATEGY

Durable Industries began receiving more, and more consistent, complaints from customers about product availability. Customers said that Durable's competitors delivered faster, and that they delivered complete orders. Durable often had to make several shipments to fill an order.

These complaints eventually reached the office of Jay Tyler, who had been the company's CEO for three years at that time. Jay came from the sales side of the company and had deep ties and friendships with executives at many retail customers. These friends did not hesitate to pick up the phone and call him directly. They let him know that his company had major availability problems. One past associate said, "Deliveries of product from your company are late and have multiple missing items. I spoke with someone whom I won't name on your order desk, and he admitted that things were broken there, and that people were blindly following the rules, even when they clearly don't make sense. Sounds like people don't even care at your company any more. As much as I value our past relationship, I'm sorry to tell you that I am immediately shifting 50 percent of my purchases to your competitor, and the rest will follow if things don't improve, and soon."

Jay had a sick feeling after he hung up the phone. He had heard about supply problems before, and he had been assured by the supply chain chief that things would improve. But that phone call made it clear that something had to be done, and fast. Durable's CFO, Leo Bennett, sat next door. Jay walked over, sat down, and said, "We have a problem. We are seriously missing deliveries to our customers, and our competitors are kicking our butts." Leo's eyes got wide. "That's hard to believe. I was just looking at our inventory levels versus our competitors, and we have more inventory than they do. Our turns are 7.6, and their inventory turnover averages are more than 8!" "Our average inventory is higher, but our availability is much worse; that's just great!" Jay exclaimed.

# WHO'S RESPONSIBLE FOR PRODUCT AVAILABILITY?

Coincidentally, Jay's weekly staff meeting was scheduled just after his conversations with the customer and Leo. Jay walked into the executive conference room and saw the executive team already assembled. He paused for a few moments, looked slowly around the room, and then stunned the group by slamming his hand on the table. "Who in this room is responsible for product availability?" he asked. Hank, the SVP of supply chain, had logistics and inventory planning in his organization. Hank looked over at his boss, Mark, the COO, and with some trepidation raised his hand. To Hank's shock and dismay, he was the only one in the room with his hand up! If there was an availability problem, weren't sales and manufacturing partially responsible? After all, the sales forecast was inaccurate, and manufacturing had missed its schedule in a major way last week. But that shared responsibility seemed lost on the CEO. "Hank, I want to meet with you and Mark today."

## Is There Really a Problem?

Hank quickly conferred with Mark as they walked back to their offices. Mark calmly told him to collect all the data he had on availability. Hank called his admin on his cell as he was walking, and asked her to assemble his staff immediately. Hank's supply chain staff members were all in town, an unusual circumstance, and they all met at 11:30 a.m. They quickly gathered all of the availability and on-time delivery metrics and looked them over. The numbers looked normal. The overall availability percentage stood at 92 percent, and the on-time delivery stats were at 97 percent. Hank's staff told him that these numbers were actually slightly better than last year, and consistent with the company's in-house goals.

Hank asked his team what they had heard from customers. Cathy, the VP of inventory management, quickly said, "It's about normal. There are some complaints, but there always are." Hank felt a growing uneasiness. Could their data be bad? He had not talked directly with a customer in months.

## Yep, We Have a Problem

Just before 1:00 p.m., Hank nervously made the long, lonely walk down the hall of the executive suite toward the CEO's office. His boss, Mark, was already there, standing outside. Together they walked into Jay's office. The CEO looked up without any pleasantries. "You own the supply chain function, and it's not performing. We need to get it fixed, and fixed fast." Jay then reviewed his recent conversations with customers. Hank was truly surprised and a bit flummoxed. He sputtered, "I was just looking at our availability numbers, and they look good. We're as high as we have ever been. We're at least 92 percent, which is right on goal. Maybe you just heard about a few isolated situations that hopefully aren't representative?" Jay responded, "My instincts tell me differently. I think your availability numbers are wrong. We need to find out the truth, and you and your team need to tell me how we will fix this."

Hank and Mark left the office, and after a short conversation, Hank made a beeline to his VP of inventory management, Cathy. He asked Cathy to get into the details and make sure that the availability numbers were right. "Cathy, you know that sometimes these numbers get manipulated. We absolutely need to know."

Cathy conducted a thorough investigation. She found to her dismay that over the past three years, certain data had been excluded from the availability numbers. For example, about two years earlier, someone had decided to exclude any data on new stock-keeping units (SKUs) until they had been in the system for one year, so as to not bias the data as a new model ramped up. She also found that data for a few midsized customers were also excluded because of their sporadic and unpredictable order patterns. These customers routinely went through big inventory swings as a result of corporate mandates. The team felt that it was unfair to penalize the availability metric with such random order patterns. Cathy's apprehension grew as she uncovered other data exclusions. Eventually, Cathy found that 20 to 25 percent of the data were being excluded in calculating the metric.

Cathy was not looking forward to sharing her findings with Hank, but she decided that the only possible approach was to lay it all out. Too much was at stake. Simple honesty wouldn't fix the problem, though. She also needed a solution to the availability problem that she now knew existed. Cathy huddled with her team. No one could come up with a quick fix. In fact, each member of

Cathy's team offered different reasons for the problem they faced. By the time they finished, 12 hours later, the whiteboard and multiple flipcharts were covered with a long list of possible causes, with no consensus on the best approach to take. A "ready-fire-aim" approach seemed to be the only option they had, and that wouldn't satisfy Hank, Mark, or Jay.

Cathy and her team decided that they had to bite the bullet, step back, and develop a strategy—the right way, or at least close to the right way, given Jay's demand for a fast fix. Over the next 36 hours, they put together a proposal to develop a supply chain strategy with the objective of moving Durable Industries to the best availability position in the industry. Cathy called me for advice, and I detailed for her the nine-step process, which strongly influenced her proposal. Her plan consisted of the people resources her team would need to complete the strategy, the deliverables, and a development schedule. It would take three to four months. With the proposal in hand, Cathy called Hank and asked to meet with him.

Cathy began by admitting that the availability numbers were wrong. Hank's face took on a look of increasing concern. Cathy said, "Look, I know we have egg on our face, but this problem has been going on since well before you and I came into our current jobs." Cathy then said that she had a solution. She reviewed the proposal to do a comprehensive supply chain strategy. Hank liked the idea and had a few suggestions involving setting up a cross-functional committee to get buy-in. In general, he was quite impressed with Cathy's work, although he was still concerned about how they were going to explain the errors in the availability numbers.

Hank discussed the proposal with Mark, and mentioned in passing that there were some errors in the availability data. Mark's focus was on the strategy proposal, saying that he thought a comprehensive strategy might be overkill. But then Hank reminded him, "You know, the boss hinted at this a few weeks ago. We can fix our availability problem permanently and produce the supply chain strategy that Jay probably wants." Mark was convinced. He reached for the phone and scheduled a time early the next morning to meet with the CEO.

Cathy, Hank, and Mark were in the CEO's suite at 6:30 a.m. the next morning. Cathy began by admitting that their availability data had some problems, which they were addressing. Then she quickly laid out the plan for developing the strategy not only to fix the current availability problem, but also to become the best in the industry. Additionally, she proposed that a major goal of the strategy would be to lower both cost and inventory by 20 percent from current levels. Jay liked the sound of that, since the stock analysts had been increasingly vocal about the company's working capital and cash flow picture. In fact, the company's quarterly conference call had taken place two days earlier, and the participating stock analysts had pointedly told Jay and Leo Bennett that the company's stock price was depressed because of poor cash flow, resulting from inventory being too high. With this backdrop, Cathy had a receptive audience. She then gave a Jay the highlights of the plan to develop the supply chain strategy.

## STOPPING THE BLEEDING

Jay was fairly impressed. "I want you to give me the details, but before you do, how are we going to stop the bleeding right now? I like your ideas, but we can't wait three or four months for the plan, with results even later."

Cathy had considered this question with her team and had an answer. As a stopgap measure, they would fix the current problem by putting an expeditor in place to monitor the large core customers daily and take whatever action was needed to get them their product, including premium transportation. (Cathy knew which customers had a direct line to Jay's office, since Jay talked about them constantly. She would make sure that they received white-glove service until the strategic improvement was implemented.) Cathy had earlier told Hank and Mark that she estimated the cost for this to be $1.2 million, and she now told Jay the cost of applying the tourniquet. Jay grimaced, but agreed. "OK, put the stopgap in place. Now I want to hear your detailed plan. How are you going to develop a strategy to fix this permanently?"

## THE PLAN TO DEVELOP THE STRATEGY

Cathy tried to show confidence as she explained the comprehensive plan to develop the supply chain strategy. "First, we need to know where we really stand in relation to our direct competitors and to the best in the world. They only way to do that is to bring in a company that assesses supply chains." She continued, "Once we have their report, the heavy lifting will begin." She told Jay that she would personally devote 90 percent of her time to the strategy development for the next three months. Jay said, "Well, then who's going to do your job?" Mark jumped in, "We have been developing Bob for some time for a more senior role in the company. This will give us a good chance to see him in action, with Cathy there to mentor him in the background. So, it should be a win/win." Cathy was actually beginning to feel a little insecure until Jay said, "Watch over him, Cathy, but no more than 10 percent of your time. The strategy is your priority." (In spite of the problems, Jay still had confidence in Cathy, and he was swayed by her confidence and her passion for this effort.)

Cathy then said that she needed a couple of her people full time to help with the project, and that she had a plan to backfill them for three months. Seeing Jay nod, she pressed on. "We will be successful with this effort only if we also involve other key functions. I strongly believe we need a part-time representative from sales, finance, and manufacturing." Jay had two questions, "What do you mean by 'part time'? And have you spoken to the SVPs of those areas?" Cathy responded, "I think it will amount to about 30 percent of their time, but we'll define it exactly over the next couple of days. It's a significant time commitment, but it's doable. I'll review it with their management after I flesh out the details. In addition, I strongly feel that we need to set up shop for our team in that vacant area in Building D. When we schedule team time, everyone needs to get out of his or her office and come to the team room." "Good," said Jay. "Let me know if you have any problems."

Mark and Hank, knowing when to shut up and savor the victory, rose and said that they appreciated Jay's support, and would not let him down. Jay, with his usual intense glare, said, "I know you won't. Let's do it, folks. I want weekly updates on your progress." As Mark, Hank, and Cathy walked back up the long hallway, they felt decidedly more relaxed, even euphoric. But then an element of anxiety swept over Cathy. Now she had to deliver!

## THE FIRST STEPS

Over the next two days, Cathy caucused with her team and fleshed out more of the details, and then she called the SVPs of sales/marketing, manufacturing, and finance. Jay apparently had gotten to them first;

so they quickly expressed their full support. Cathy assured them that she would keep them in the loop each step of the way. She was reasonably pleased with the names she was given. She received the people she asked for, with one exception. The SVP of finance felt that 30 percent was too much of a time commitment for the person she had requested, and he wanted to substitute another person in his organization. Cathy reluctantly agreed.

She next made arrangements for team facilities to be set up in some open space in Building D, with a team meeting room and some office space for each team member. Cathy hoped that this physical relocation would prove to be a major factor in molding the group into a true team.

Cathy then developed a request for proposals (RFP) for the outside supply chain assessment. After getting some advice from a friend in another company, she sent it to a large consulting company, to a small boutique consulting firm, and to us at the University of Tennessee. She felt that all three responded well in their proposals. The costs, of course, were dramatically different. Cathy liked the lead consultant from the boutique company, and she was intrigued by our university proposal. She asked us if we could work together with the boutique firm on a blended team, using the most experienced people from each. After some discussion, we all agreed to create a combined team of two outside consultants, Ted and Sue, and two university faculty members, Paul and Rod. All of us felt that this would be a good approach; together, the four possessed a lot of experience and had contacts with hundreds of companies.

## THE ASSESSMENT

The four consultants worked well together and developed an approach to do the assessment. First, they asked for and reviewed all the information they could get on organization structure, metrics, and process descriptions. In parallel, they asked Cathy to identify 30 people from all functions and all organizational levels to interview. Cathy and her team identified the people to interview, including:

- Senior executives: 6
- Supply chain: 20

- IT: 1
- Human resources: 1
- Finance: 1
- Marketing: 6
- Sales/business lead: 3

The consultants created an interview guide and followed an assessment process very similar to the one described in detail in Chapter 3.

The consultants found the interviews to be candid and extremely informative. In addition, they heard a lot about cultural issues and cross-functional problems as the one thing people wished would change. One executive lamented the command-and-control culture. "We seem to be like sheep, or maybe just good soldiers. We just shrug and follow the boss's direction, even if we know it will turn out badly, and some do it just for spite. I call it 'vindictive obedience.'"

The team found the interviews with suppliers and customers interesting, but of limited value. In spite of the confidentiality assurance, the suppliers seemed to be less than candid; nonetheless, the interviews were worth the time. Customers, on the other hand, had no problems with honest responses. For example, one typical customer said, "The people at Durable just do not understand *our* customer, the end consumer. They need a much better understanding of the last leg of the supply chain."

The consultants eventually interviewed 37 people inside the company, reviewed all of the internal data mentioned previously, and talked with four suppliers and three customers. They then compared what they had found through these interviews with their collective data on companies across all of industry that had implemented supply chain processes and achieved good results. They focused especially on the following six areas:

1. New product development
2. Product complexity
3. Inventory management practices
4. Supplier management
5. Warehousing
6. Transportation

The final report followed the format shown in Figure 11-1.

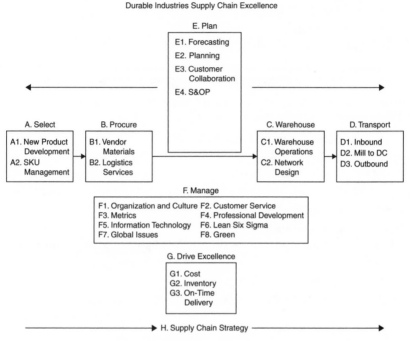

FIGURE 11-1  Supply Chain Audit Framework

## MOLDING THE TEAM

While the assessment was still in process, Cathy assembled her strategy team. It consisted of two people from her inventory management function, one from logistics operations, and representatives from manufacturing, finance, and sales. This group had never worked together on anything like this, and some of them barely knew one another.

She thought it was important that the team get more comfortable with one another, so she devoted a day to team building. During that time, she asked an expert from HR to facilitate a Myers-Briggs exercise, which assessed each team member on personality traits, putting each of them in one of sixteen personality categories. One finding proved very important. Jim, the sales representative on the team, had a totally different personality type from the other five members. The expert cautioned the team that there might be a herd mentality among the other five similar members. He said, "You need to be sure to ask Jim's opinion. He will probably have a different perspective to offer that will prove very important to hear." Ron from operations thought to himself, "That figures; sales is the only function where you have to run a contest to get people to do their jobs." But actually, the team took the advice to heart, and tacked a sign on the wall of the team meeting room that said: "Ask Jim What He Thinks!"

## ASSESSING CUSTOMER NEEDS

The consultants interviewed three customers, all retailers. This was a start, but the team members felt that they needed to go deeper and include other customers. In fact, Paul told Cathy that they really should have started the whole strategy process with customer interviews. They quickly worked through Jim to schedule those interviews.

The team members paired up and hit the road for an intense week. Without exception, they heard about significant problems from each customer they visited. They returned and put together 43 pages of typed notes. They grouped the comments into 14 categories, summarized on the wall of the team room. They felt humbled after this work. They had thought the company was better than this, but they had to admit that they had never actually talked in depth with customers in this manner. A few examples of customer comments are listed here:

1. Ship each PO complete. ("You aren't able to deliver the order complete, and then we have to follow up on the next one to three shipments to complete the total order.")
2. Reduce replenishment lead time. ("The average time from submission of an order to delivery seems like a week. We need this to be 48 hours so that we can reduce the inventory we carry and stay in business.")
3. Meet tight delivery windows at our DCs. ("We expect you to hit 30-minute delivery windows at our DCs.")
4. Provide real-time order tracking. ("It often takes more than 24 hours to get an accurate order status when we ask, so we don't bother to ask anymore.")
5. Provide a home delivery service for our dot-com orders if our customers want to pay for it.

## DOING A SWOT

Following the template that it had laid out for the strategy development, the team next turned to an analysis of the company's strengths, weaknesses, opportunities, and threats (SWOT). To do this, Cathy asked the team members to create their own SWOTs in advance and then come together for half a day to discuss and reconcile their thoughts.

The team had a lively discussion, especially on the company's weaknesses and the threats that it faced. The threats centered on competition. After about 90 minutes of discussion on competition, Cathy suggested that they needed to go deeper than they could as part of the SWOT analysis: "It's clear that we need to do a complete competitive analysis. We need to focus not just on our competition today, but also on the newly emerging competitors in China and Korea. Let's resolve to do a complete analysis of competition." She asked one of her best young managers, Nikhil, to lead that effort.

They next discussed weaknesses and began filling page after page on the flipchart. The list on the flipchart was very similar to the 14 customer needs, now already taped to the wall. The team members began to feel overwhelmed, and Cathy felt the energy in the group begin to ebb. She suggested that they vote on the top five challenges that the company faced. When they tabulated the votes, they listed the top five issues as:

1. Delivery date integrity
2. Long internal lead times causing long replenishment lead times for customers
3. Collaborative forecasting capability for customers
4. A vendor-managed inventory capability
5. A single point of contact for each customer

At that point, Jim from sales spoke up. "You know, our corporate culture is a negative culture. We love to wallow in our problems. We have this pathological fear of inducing complacency. We never hear pure compliments. When we have a good month, we hear, 'That was a great month, but.' There is always the 'but.' But, we need to do even better next month. But, we have the benefit of a good economy. I think we need to spend just as much time discussing our strengths." The group nodded in unison, and the discussion turned to strengths.

The team found listing the company's strengths more difficult, but finally came to consensus on four clear strengths:

1. A good, experienced team of dedicated people
2. A high market share, giving the company the economies of scale to compete effectively
3. A strong process supported by a good IT system to do forecasting and production planning
4. Good partnerships with its third-party logistics providers

# EXTERNAL ENVIRONMENT— MEGATRENDS AND COMPETITION

The team next felt that it should delegate the analysis of external megatrends to the consulting team. After a couple of weeks of work, Paul and Rod produced a concise document analyzing the megatrend elements and showing how they were relevant to Durable's supply chain strategy. The first summary page of that document is reproduced in Table 11-1.

# COMPETITION

While the external assessment of best practices was underway, Ted and Sue, along with Nikhil from Cathy's team, focused on the competition. For time and cost reasons, Ted and Sue suggested a scaled-back version of a full competitive analysis. Ted told Cathy, "I think we can use sources of information that are in the public domain, as well as some input from your suppliers and customers, to do an acceptable job."

Cathy responded, "I am worried about our two big competitors today, but also about those that might emerge in the future." The team members had already learned about new competition during their prior interviews with customers. Ted suggested that they begin by surveying some of Durable's senior executives regarding emerging competition. After all, some of those executives had been following competitive trends for decades. They next focused on information in the public domain, using basically the same sources described in Chapter 5: 10-K reports of competitors, electronic databases, and Google searches. Finally, they spoke with a few of Durable's suppliers about their perception of industry best practices, which indirectly

TABLE 11-1 Megatrend Analysis

| Trend | Summary |
|---|---|
| External collaboration | Our collaboration with suppliers and customers should occur in a win/win environment of trust, with full sharing of information to make joint improvements. We need to find a way to share benefits from improvement projects 50/50 with our partners. |
| Internal collaboration | Internal collaboration involves working smoothly across the functional silos inherent in every firm. We need to implement a world-class sales and operations planning (S&OP) process. |
| Lean and Six Sigma | Lean drives out waste by eliminating non-value-added activities and compressing supply chain cycle times. Six Sigma is an important tool that includes a set of analytical and quantitative techniques to take variation out of processes and achieve better, consistent, repeatable, quality performance. We have pilots using both of these tools, but we need to move faster. |
| Complexity management | Complexity management refers to a focus on reducing product complexity by eliminating unnecessary component parts and SKUs. We have too many SKUs, and we need a disciplined process to control them. |
| Network optimization | Network optimization involves establishing the right network of suppliers, factories, and warehouses to optimize cost, inventory, and customer service simultaneously. We have never done a formal network optimization, and in this era of volatile fuel prices, we need a plan to optimize our network. |
| Global supply chain | Global supply chain excellence creates a global supply chain flow that optimizes cost, inventory, and customer service, while managing risk. We need to develop more expertise in how to move goods internationally in a much more efficient way. |
| Sustainable supply chain | A sustainable supply chain minimizes the carbon footprint, and also includes a world-class process for managing returns to optimize both customer satisfaction and asset recovery. We only give this lip service today, and we need a real strategy in this area. |
| Focus on working capital | World-class supply chains reduce working capital significantly, which enhances the firm's cash flow and return on net assets (RONA). Such supply chains not only minimize inventory, but also help reduce the receivables and payables components of working capital. They do this by reducing supply chain cycle times, which should be correlated with payment terms. We can use our supply chain as a tool to greatly improve the company's working capital and cash flow position. |

gave the team insights into the competition. Finally, they spoke with six Durable Industries employees who had worked for a competitor in the past five years. After completing all that work, they felt they had a good understanding of the company's top two competitors, and reviewed that with the strategy team.

At this point, the team members were getting restless. They had been working on the strategy development effort for a month, and they still seemed far from creating anything resembling a plan. Ted said, "Look, I have worked on a lot of these things. It's important to build the foundation before we leap to the answer. Just two more weeks, and we'll be ready to get into the actual strategy development. And when we do, it will be exciting and will go very fast from there." Another step was necessary before starting the strategy development process, he suggested: "If you don't spend time identifying risks, the whole project could easily go off the rails."

## RISK ASSESSMENT

Ted explained that very few companies ever do a risk assessment. "Haven't we already done that with our analysis of the external environment and the competition?" asked Nikhil. Ted said that was true to some extent, but that they needed to take a day and put all of the information together in a cohesive package. "Right now," Ted explained, "we have total flexibility to deal with any risks. But once we identify the projects, and especially when they near completion, our degrees of freedom to deal with risk disappear." The team was a bit confused, but agreed.

The brainstorming session identified 19 possible risks to implementing the strategy. Guided by Paul, the team members then completed a modified failure mode and effects analysis (FMEA) to prioritize the risks, very much like the process described in Chapter 7. This process required that the team estimate the severity of the following three items on a scale of 1 to 10:

1. The level of negative consequences that could occur
2. The chance of the event's actually happening
3. The chance of discovering the problem early, before much damage occurred

They laid everything out in a table like Table 11-2, which shows the four highest-priority risks and how they were determined.

TABLE 11-2 Risk Prioritization

| Risk | How Negative Will the Consequences Be? Scale of 1–10 | What Are the Chances of This Happening? Scale of 1–10 | What Are Our Chances of Early Detection? Scale of 1–10 | Risk Priority Multiplication of Value in Each Column |
|---|---|---|---|---|
| The plan will not permanently resolve the customer availability problem. | 10 | 3 | 7 | 210 |
| The software we will implement will miss budget and schedule significantly. | 7 | 8 | 5 | 280 |
| We will select a third-party logistics provider (3PL) that does not meet our expectations. | 8 | 3 | 8 | 192 |
| Our competitors are working on plans that will leapfrog our strategy. | 9 | 7 | 6 | 378 |

This process led the team to focus on four key risks that required a risk mitigation plan (see Table 11-3).

TABLE 11-3  Risk Mitigation Plan

| Risk | Mitigation Plan |
| --- | --- |
| The plan will not permanently resolve the customer availability problem. | We will review our strategy with our top three customers, ask for their input, and make modifications as appropriate. We will strive to get their full buy-in before implementation. |
| The software we will implement will miss budget and schedule significantly. | We will use a disciplined project management approach, with a project management office (PMO) to oversee the implementation. We will hold weekly reviews and take action early if problems arise. |
| We will select a 3PL that does not meet our expectations. | We will vet the 3PL thoroughly, and we will especially check all references. We will hold in-depth planning sessions with the 3PL to ensure that there are no misunderstandings. |
| Our competitors are working on a plan that will leapfrog our strategy. | We will identify the most likely two competitors to worry about, and make sure that we track their activities closely, using suppliers, past employees, and all publicly available documents. |

Cathy noticed that the energy level of the team members was again flagging considerably at this point. They were itching to get to the actual strategy work. However, they had one more task to complete first. She gathered the team members and told them, "We're almost ready, folks. I can't express how much I appreciate your dedication thus far. We have one last step to take before we dive into the actual strategy development. We have to review the state of our technology. Are you up for it?" (Note that the nine-step process described in this book advocates doing the risk assessment after [not before] the technology review. However, the fact that this company did a risk assessment at all sets it apart.)

## TECHNOLOGY REVIEW

The team spent the next two days cloistered with the consultants. Cathy and her team explained in detail the current state of the company's technology. The consultants then huddled and agreed on the gaps that they felt existed. At the end of this marathon two-day event, the team produced a summary chart, the highlights of which are shown in Table 11-4.

The team members were shocked and somewhat dismayed at the range of technology gaps identified. They hadn't realized how much the company's lagging supply chain technology was hurting it. But Cathy was concerned that technology might begin to drive the strategy, rather than the other way around. "We need to identify the new supply chain capabilities and processes that we need *before* we do more in this technical area," she said. "The new capability should be paramount, and then we'll look for a technical solution to help support it. This strategy will be about changing our processes, and especially changing the way people across the company look at our supply chain and do their jobs. Technology will be important, but it cannot be the driver." The team agreed, after some reflection on past sins in letting technology drive processes rather than having the right processes drive technology.

## PREPARING FOR THE FINAL PHASE

At this point, the supply chain strategy team had been hard at it, with very long days for just over 60 days. Cathy thought that the team was more than ready to dive into the real strategy work, and so was she. At the team meeting the next day, Cathy congratulated the team on its progress. "It's been a long process, but we're finally ready to get to the exciting part—developing our strategy. Tomorrow, let's get together for a high-level review of all the work we have done so far so that it will be fresh in our minds." She assigned each member of the team to take one of the areas studied and prepare a short review of the highlights.

## DETERMINING THE NEW SUPPLY CHAIN CAPABILITIES NEEDED

To begin the strategy work, the tam members first used the walls of the conference room to post the 14 requirements they had identified as being critical to the customers. These customer requirements

TABLE 11-4 Technology Assessment

| Technology Category | Examples in Industry | Durable's Status |
|---|---|---|
| Software | Forecasting systems | Durable has an excellent in-house forecasting package. |
| | Transportation management systems (TMS) | The TMS system is from SAP and is considered a good system as long as Durable keeps up with the newer releases. |
| | Warehouse management systems (WMS) | The WMS is home-grown. It is considered antiquated and needs to be replaced. |
| | Distribution requirements planning (DRP) | |
| | Inventory optimization software | JDA-Manugistics is used for DRP and replenishment planning. It is good, but it needs to be updated with the newest release. |
| | Network optimization and simulation software | |
| | Production optimization software | |
| | Collaboration software | Collaborative forecasting occurs for the top three suppliers. This is a weekly call supported by spreadsheets, which is perfectly acceptable. |
| | Enterprise resource planning (ERP) systems | |
| | Customer relationship management (CRM) systems | |
| E-business technologies | Automatic shipment notices (ASNs) | ASNs are received from most vendors. They are not always complete. |
| | Electronic data interchange (EDI) | EDI is used with all customers and suppliers where appropriate. A web portal is used with some. Both appear to be well designed. |
| | Electronic requisitioning | |
| | Web-based data interchange and communication | Other e-business tools are lacking. |
| | Electronic invoicing and payment, linked to shipments and receipts | |
| | Exchanges/auctions | |
| | Early warning and visibility systems | |
| | Web 2.0 for collaboration | |

*(continued)*

TABLE 11-4 Technology Assessment *continued*

| Technology Category | Examples in Industry | Durable's Status |
|---|---|---|
| Visibility and productivity | Bar code<br>Radio-frequency data transmission<br>Radio-frequency identification (RFID)<br>Pick to light<br>Voice picking<br>Automated picking<br>Cellular/satellite tracking<br>Carousel and conveyor systems<br>Automated storage and retrieval systems (ASRS)<br>Event management: visibility with real-time alerts | Durable has automated conveyor systems in its largest DCs, but they are dated and need to be upgraded.<br>A voice picking system exists in only two of the warehouses. The remainder of the warehouses rely on paper task lists.<br>The company uses bar codes and does RF scans. It has no RFID. |
| Process advances | Lean<br>Six Sigma<br>Vendor-managed replenishment (VMR)<br>Collaborative planning, forecasting, and replenishment (CPFR)<br>Activity-based costing<br>Carbon footprint management | Durable is doing Lean training as a prelude to a more serious Lean implementation in the future.<br>Durable is not using Six Sigma tools. |

pointed to 14 new supply chain capabilities that Durable would need to develop. The team next reviewed the SWOT analysis and the supply chain assessment results and again noted the striking consistency. With the customer requirements in mind, the internal gap assessment took on a much sharper edge. Next came the supply chain trends. The team decided to map the trends to the supply chain capability list that had been developed so far (see Table 11-5).

The team then stood back, looked at this confusing maze of arrows, and initially had no idea what it meant. However, after a period of reflection, something jumped out at Cathy: The capabilities were lining up well with some megatrends and not at all with others. After a lengthy discussion, the team members felt that they needed to deal especially with the global supply chain area and the management of complexity.

Regarding global supply chain capabilities, the team saw a major gap in its thinking. The company currently wasn't very global. It dabbled in exporting, but that activity involved only 2 percent of sales. The company also imported some raw materials, but that amounted to only 9 percent of procurement spending. Durable clearly wasn't global today. But that was likely to change over the next three years, as the corporate strategic plan called for major increases in exports and global sourcing. To support that change, the supply chain strategy would need to support the development of a global supply chain capability.

Nikhil raised another issue at this point. "What about metrics?" he asked. "Shouldn't we review our metrics as part of this effort, especially given the embarrassing problem we had with our availability metric?" The team members knew that they had some problems with many of the metrics. Cathy observed, "Let not get bogged down right now. Let's complete the strategy work, and then we'll loop back and clean up our metrics. In fact, we shouldn't complete that until we decide what we want to do in the future. Then our metrics should help drive us to that destination and reinforce the new behaviors we need to create." (Note: This is exactly in line with the recommended sequence in the nine-step process. Metrics should be addressed after the strategy is complete, with new capabilities identified.)

The team members next rated the two competitors they were most concerned about on each of these 16 capabilities. They did the rating as shown in Table 11-6, using 3 of the 16 capabilities as examples.

TABLE 11-5 Customer Requirements Mapped to Supply Chain Megatrends

| Supply Chain Capability List | Supply Chain Megatrends |
|---|---|
| **1.** Ship each PO complete. | |
| **2.** Reduce replenishment lead time. | |
| **3.** Date integrity—when you give a date, hit the date. | |
| **4.** Meet tight delivery windows at customer's DCs. | |
| **5.** Provide expedited deliveries when customers need them. | |
| **6.** Provide a reverse logistics service to pick up returns. | |
| **7.** Provide real-time order tracking. | Trend 1: Collaboration |
| **8.** Do VMI (vendor-managed inventory) for some selected items. | Trend 2: Lean/Six Sigma applied to the supply chain |
| **9.** Provide customized packaging and labeling when needed. | Trend 3: Aggressive management of complexity |
| **10.** Provide a home delivery service for our dot-com orders if our customers want to pay for it. | Trend 4: Network optimization |
| **11.** Offer direct-to-store deliveries (DSD) for our high-volume stores. | Trend 5: The global supply chain |
| **12.** Participate seriously with us in a collaborative forecasting process. | Trend 6: The sustainable supply chain |
| **13.** Put in place a single point of contact for all availability and delivery issues. Today, different product lines have different points of contact, a big hassle for us. | Trend 7: Working capital and cash flow management |
| **14.** Deliver damage-free. | |

TABLE 11-6 Competitive Analysis

| Supply Chain Strategic Capability | Better, Worse, or Even with the Competitor | Better, Worse, or Even with the Competitor at the End of the Three-Year Planning Horizon |
|---|---|---|
| Global supply chain expertise | Worse | Even |
| Ship each PO complete. | Even | Better |
| Reduce replenishment lead time. | Even | Better |

Cathy looked at the result, smiled, and said, "This strategy will be a major advance for us versus our competition." She praised her team members for the good work they had done. She felt confident, and she told them so, that they had collectively set the foundation by surveying the firm's customers, doing an assessment relative to best in class, and completing an internal evaluation, followed by excellent work analyzing megatrends, competition, and technology. "I feel good, and I hope you do as well. I think we have accurately identified the right supply chain capabilities for our supply chain strategy."

# WE'VE DETERMINED THE NEW CAPABILITIES—NOW WHAT?

Next came some very difficult work. Cathy assigned subteams of two people to work on the initiatives. She told them, "We have to know how much each of these initiatives will cost in terms of person-years of people's time and any IT cost. Also, I want you to define exactly how much capital investment, such as computer software or new hardware, we'll need. Then I need you to determine the benefits that we will deliver. How much will each project improve availability, and why? How much cost and inventory will it take out?

"Once you get an estimate of benefits, think about how you are going to sell those benefits to the organization. Remember, we will have to live with these estimates, so make them realistic and a bit conservative. But also remember that together they will have to deliver our overall goals for cost reduction, inventory, and fill rate improvements."

This effort involved intense 10- to 12-hour days for the next month for Cathy, the consultants, and the supply chain team members. Cathy really needed the help and support of finance at this stage, and she found it lacking. She needed the A team, that is, people who were willing to commit to the long hours necessary to meet the deadline, and who had enough organizational credibility to help in gaining buy-in. She regretted that she had not fought for the finance person she really needed when she formed the team at the beginning. This part of the process was probably more difficult than it needed to be, but it got done. As the team defined each project in great detail, the cost and the required investment took shape. The team had to do a lot of work to identify the benefits. Each group needed to show how the plan would deliver cost, inventory, and customer service savings. At the end, Ted and Cathy summarized the results (Table 11-7 shows an example for three of the capabilities).

## NO CHERRY PICKING ALLOWED!

One of Cathy's team members, Joe, asked to talk with her in confidence. "Cathy, I've been around this company a lot of years, and there's one thing that's guaranteed to happen when we present our results: the bosses are going to start cherry picking. We need a plan to counter that and show how these projects are synergistic. You can't take out one of the blocks without risking toppling the whole house." Cathy couldn't believe that she hadn't thought of it. "Joe, we need an anti-cherry-picking strategy, and you're just the man to develop it," she said. "I thought you'd never ask," he replied. Joe put together a story showing how all of the projects were interrelated, and he focused especially on those projects with lower returns, showing their strategic importance to the entire project.

## GETTING BUY-IN

At the very beginning of the strategy process, Cathy had assigned each member of the team a communication responsibility. Then every Monday throughout the months of work, the team quickly discussed the meetings they had conducted and the feedback they had received.

TABLE 11-7 Cost-Benefit Analysis

| Capability | Expense of Implementation | Capital Investment | Availability Improvement Expected | Inventory Reduction Expected | Cost Reduction Expected | ROI |
|---|---|---|---|---|---|---|
| Global supply chain expertise | $1.2 million | $3.2 million | Small | $5.0 million | $6.7 million | 97% |
| Ship each PO complete | $2.1 million | $1.5 million | Large from the customer perspective: from 91% to 94% | $3.4 million | $1.1 million | Negligible, but demanded by the customers |
| Reduce replenishment lead time | $0.8 million | $4.3 million | Additional two-percentage-point improvement | $22.9 million | $5.5 million | 157% |

Cathy asked each team member to try to develop a communications package that would resonate with the person he or she was assigned.

Paul told Cathy that although group communications were worth doing, the change management process would succeed or fail because of a small number of people. He pointed to extensive change management research in this area done at the university. Cathy saw the logic in that, and she identified eight individuals that she thought were critical. These included the CEO, the COO, the CFO, the VP of manufacturing, and the SVP of sales and marketing. In addition, there were three directors in the organization that she felt could make or break the effort, since they carried so much respect in the organization. Two of them were from the sales regions, and one was the corporate planning director. The change management communication plan looked like the example shown in Table 11-8.

In these review meetings, the executive invariably suggested changes in the strategy. Cathy made sure that those suggestions were captured, and for the most part resolved. However, in one instance, Donald, the SVP of sales and marketing, strongly argued that the company needed to deliver product to several key retailers daily, not weekly as was the practice. Cathy explained the major cost and inventory implications of daily deliveries. She also pointed out that those customers had not highlighted delivery frequency as a priority in the customer interviews. Donald disagreed. After going back and forth on this point for several weeks, Cathy and Donald compromised on two deliveries per week for these retail customers.

## THE PREAPPROVAL BY THE CEO

When the team totaled the money required for the strategy implementation, it came to $52 million in software that could be capitalized and $26 million in expense. Cathy and her boss, Hank, scheduled time with the CEO, Jay, and the COO, Mark. Jay was cautiously optimistic given what he had seen so far in the weekly reviews of the strategy work, but he was not fully aware of the cost to implement it. Cathy knew going into the meeting that the high level of investment was going to be a problem, but she rationalized that she needed to quantify all of the benefits and have an ROI before she communicated the full cost. In this final review, Cathy unveiled the numbers, and immediately told Jay that it would have an 18-month payback

TABLE 11-8 Change Management Communication Plan

| Person or Group That Needs Communication | Strategy Team Member to Do Communication | Frequency | Message |
|---|---|---|---|
| CEO | Cathy | Every two to three weeks | Overall impact on the business, including the impact on cost, working capital, and especially product availability. She further translated those expected improvements into an improvement in RONA, economic value added (EVA), and shareholder value. |
| COO | Cathy | Weekly in his staff meeting | Same as for the CEO, but with special emphasis on cost and inventory reduction. |
| CFO | Doug, the team member from finance | Every two weeks | Improvements translated into working capital, cash flow, and RONA terms, as well as shareholder value. |
| SVP of sales and marketing | Cathy and Jim from sales | Every two weeks | Emphasis on the major expected improvements in product availability. |
| Director of sales—eastern U.S. | Jim from sales | Monthly | Same as for the SVP, but with a specific emphasis on the eastern region. |
| Director of sales—western U.S. | Jim from sales | Monthly | Same as for the SVP, but with a specific emphasis on the western region. |
| Director of corporate planning | The four consultants | Every two weeks | Full discussion on how the strategy was developed and justified, along with the expected results. |
| VP of manufacturing | Joe from supply chain | Every three weeks | Emphasis on the cost and inventory reductions expected. |

with a 67 percent internal rate of return (IRR). Jay was surprised at the cost. "I'm not sure where we will find that kind of money, and by the way, you should have told me this much earlier. We've been cutting back in a major way during the past four months." Jay asked multiple questions over the next 30 minutes, then he finally shrugged and said, "I suppose this is what we really need to do, but I'm still not sure where we will find the money. Come to my staff meeting on May 4 and we'll discuss it with the executive team." As Cathy got up to leave, Jay asked her, "Are you willing to stake your career on those numbers?" Cathy forced a smile and said, "Yes!"

## THE FINAL APPROVAL

With the strategy finally complete, Cathy and the consultants turned their attention to preparing for the final approval meeting on May 4. When the big day arrived, Cathy was tense. As she told one of the consultants, "This is my baby. I will be devastated if we don't get approval."

All of the company's senior executives gathered. Jay began the meeting. "As you probably know, Cathy and her team have just completed the long-awaited supply chain strategy, and she is here to present it for a go–no-go decision. The decision will be yours. I will withhold my comments until I hear all of yours. You will see that they propose spending $52 million on software and $26 million on other expense. As you know, we don't have that budget available. In fact, I have recently asked you for cutbacks. So, if we go ahead, this will have to come out of your collective budgets."

When Cathy heard that introduction, her heart pounded. She had been hoping for something more supportive, but she stood up, brought up the first slide, and launched into her presentation. At the conclusion, Jay turned to Donald, the SVP of sales and marketing, and asked, "OK, what do you think?" Donald responded with a smile, and with a record short response, for him: "I've had my debates with Cathy and her team, and we've reached some reasonable compromises. So, I support it and will do my part to help fund it." The responses of the other senior executives mirrored this one. Cathy felt vindicated for all of the communication time she had put in and had motivated the team to put in. It had clearly paid off. Jay smiled and said, "Well, let's do it. Good job, Cathy. Please pass along my thanks to your team for a job well done." Cathy was floating on air as she left the boardroom. But then almost immediately a wave of anxiety swept over her. "Good grief," she thought. "Now we actually have to implement this!"

## PROJECT MANAGEMENT PROCESS

The projects were rolled out over the next three years. Cathy hired Frank to run the Project Management Office (PMO). Frank held weekly meetings where the project managers came in at assigned times and reviewed their progress. They were expected to answer three questions honestly:

1. What did you do last week?
2. What will you do next week?
3. What barriers are you facing?

Frank cautioned Cathy on how important this discipline is. "It's easy to do this for a while," he said. "But in the past we've let things slip, especially on a big project that unfolds over a long period of time. Missing a week or two doesn't seem like a big deal in a project that you know is going to take two years, but in that short period of time, a metric can start showing an early warning sign, and you miss it." Cathy vowed that they would demand weekly checkpoint meetings and expect people to come prepared every week during the three-year implementation.

Frank published a report each week showing the project status, with each subeffort characterized by a stoplight indicator—green projects were on or ahead of schedule; yellow projects were on schedule, but at risk of falling behind; and red projects were behind schedule or stalled. Cathy focused her attention on the red projects, those that were falling behind schedule. She made sure that her help did not disrupt the ownership felt by each project team. "This is your project," she would stress, "but I want to help with any of the barriers. So don't hesitate to ask." Frank would also periodically conduct a "pulse" survey. This anonymous survey asked just a couple of questions, the most important being: "Do you think we will meet the schedule for this project, on a scale of 1 to 5?" Not all projects had 5s, indicating that the troops knew something that the leaders did not. This allowed Cathy and her staff to focus even more attention on those projects.

Cathy knew that the PMO meetings were critical, and she attended almost every time. In addition, Cathy asked Mark, the COO, to attend periodically and to rotate his direct reports as meeting attendees. This added a positive sense of tension and urgency to the meetings. Frank, Cathy, and the project managers split each project into an average of three business releases (BRs). As each BR was completed, Cathy's finely honed communication machine fired up and let the organization know of another significant accomplishment, giving the company a sense of great progress and momentum.

## FAST FORWARD—THREE YEARS LATER

Three years later, Cathy looked back on this effort with great pride. They had actually exceeded all goals for availability improvement, inventory reduction, and cost reduction. More important, the major customers were extremely pleased. Jay called Cathy and said, "Hey, I just got off the phone with Reuben, the guy who runs the big buying group out of New York. He told me that not only are we good, but we are consistently good. It's been a long road, Cathy, and you delivered. Congratulations! Now, let's talk about an even greater challenge that I have in mind for you."

# Notes

## Chapter 1

1. R. E. Slone, J. P. Dittmann, and J. T. Mentzer, *The New Supply Chain Agenda: The Five Steps That Drive Real Value* (Boston: Harvard Business School Publishing, 2010).

2. G. B. Stewart, *The Quest for Value: A Guide for Senior Managers* (New York: HarperCollins, 1999).

3. K. O'Reilly, "Global Chief Supply Chain Officer Strategy," *Eyefortransport*; retrieved January 20, 2012, from http://www.eft.com.

## Chapter 3

1. A. Gardella, "A Company Grows, and Builds a Plant Back in the U.S.A.," *New York Times*, October 12, 2011; retrieved January 21, 2012, from http://www.nytimes.com.

2. R. E. Slone, J. P. Dittmann, and J. T. Mentzer, *The New Supply Chain Agenda: The Five Steps That Drive Real Value* (Boston: Harvard Business School Publishing, 2010).

3. J. Collins, *Good to Great* (New York: HarperCollins, 2001).

## Chapter 4

1. R. E. Slone, J. P. Dittmann, and J. T. Mentzer, *The New Supply Chain Agenda: The Five Steps That Drive Real Value* (Boston: Harvard Business School Publishing, 2010).

2. "Keeping Ahead of Supply Chain Risk and Uncertainty (2008); retrieved January 20, 2012, from http://www.oracle.com/us/products/applications/accenture-oracle-risk-pov-bwp–069959.pdf.

3. Voluntary Interindustry Commerce Solutions, *CPFR White Paper*, May 2008.

4. *Product Lifecycle Collaboration Benchmark Report* (2006); retrieved January 20, 2012, from http://www.oracle.com/partners/en/058849.pdf.

5. Key facts about the Coca-Cola Company; retrieved January 23, 2012, from http://www.europeancareers.coca-cola.com/en/home/our-company/key-facts/.

6. S. Tibken, "Intel Cuts Its Outlook," *Wall Street Journal*, December 13, 2011; retrieved January 20, 2012, from http://online.wsj.com.

7. T. Aeppel, "Stung by Soaring Transport Costs, Factories Bring Jobs Home Again," *Wall Street Journal*, June 13, 2008.

8. R. Murphy, "Strategic Trends Influencing Warehousing," WERC Annual Conference, May 5, 2008.

9. E. Durkalski Hertzfeld, "Details Emerge About Wal-Mart's Packaging Scorecard, May 5, 2007; retrieved January 20, 2012, from http://www.packaging-online.com/state-industry/industry-report/details-emerge-about-wal-marts-packaging-scorecard.

10. "2016: Future Supply Chain Appendix, (2008); retrieved January 20, 2012, from http://supplychainmagazine.fr/TOUTE-INFO/ETUDES/GCI_Capgemini-SC2016.pdf.

11. *State of Logistics Report*, Council of Supply Chain Management Professionals, June 2008.

## Chapter 6

1. R. E. Slone, J. P. Dittmann, and J. T. Mentzer, *The New Supply Chain Agenda: The Five Steps That Drive Real Value* (Boston: Harvard Business School Publishing, 2010).

2. A role-play simulation developed at MIT in the 1960s to illustrate an integrated approach to managing the supply chain. Detailed information can be found at http://Beergame.mit.edu.

## Chapter 7

1. Singhal, Vinod, "Supply Chain Disruptions and Corporate Performance," College of Management, Georgia Institute of Technology, April, 2011.

2. B. Powell, "The Global Supply Chain: So Very Fragile," *CNN Money*, December 12, 2011; retrieved January 23, 2011, from http://tech.fortune.cnn.com/2011/12/12/supply-chain-distasters-disruptions/.

3. A. Latous, "Trial by Fire: A Blaze in Albuquerque Sets Off Major Crisis for Cell Phone Giants," *Wall Street Journal*, January 29, 2001.

4. J. P. Dittmann, "WT-100 and the University of Tennessee: Supply Chain Survey," *World Trade Magazine*, July 20, 2011.

5. D. Gilmore, "Worst Supply Chain Disasters," *Supply Chain Digest,* January 26, 2006; retrieved January 23, 2011, from http://www.scdigest.com/assets/FirstThoughts/06–01–26.cfm.

6. I. Manuj and J. T. Mentzer, "Global Risk Management Strategies," *International Journal of Physical Distribution and Logistics Management*, 38(3), 2008, 192–233.

## Chapter 9

1. Eliyahu Goldratt, *The Haystack Syndrome* (Croton-on-Hudson, NY: North River Press, 1990).

2. R. E. Slone, J. P. Dittmann, and J. T. Mentzer, *The New Supply Chain Agenda: The Five Steps That Drive Real Value* (Boston: Harvard Business School Publishing, 2010).

## Chapter 10

1. R. E. Slone, J. P. Dittmann, and J. T. Mentzer, "Are You the Weakest Link in Your Company's Supply Chain?," *Harvard Business Review* 85(9), 2007, 116–127.

# Index

## A

Action steps:
  business case development, 207
  competitive analysis, 107
  customer focus approach, 41
  global risk management, 143
  internal supply chain assessment, 60
  megatrends, 88
  new capabilities and project plan, 167
  organizational buy-in, 207
  supply chain organization and people, 190
  technology survey, 123
Advanced planning, technology survey, 117–118
Aging customers, customer focus approach, 33
Assessment of external factors:
  competitive analysis, 89–108, 221–223
  megatrends, 65–88
Assessment of global risk (*see* Global risk management)
Assessment of internal supply chain, 43–64
  about, 17–18, 43–44
  action steps, 60
  common supply chain problems, 49–52
  company culture, 56–57
  compare results against best practices, 49–50
  conduct interviews, 47–49, 60–63, 216–218
  consumer packaged goods (CPG), 46
  continual change process, 44–45
  customer focus approach, 59
  customer needs assessment/ reassessment, 31–33, 219
  data gathering, 46

durable goods company example, 216–221
economic challenges, recession, 57–59
five pillar analysis, 53–55
internal environment assessment, 52–55
scope, 46
SWOT analysis, 52–53, 103, 220–221
Avoidance strategy, global risk management, 139–141

## B

Benchmark:
  competitive analysis, 105–106
  metrics, 188
Best practices, compare results against, 49–50
Business case development, 191–199
  about, 19–20, 191–192
  action steps, 207
  cost-benefits analysis, 194–198, 233
  estimating product availability benefits, 196–197
  finance function, 192, 198
  organizational buy-in, 199–208
  political resistance, 192–193
  sales and marketing function, 198–199
Buy-in, organizational, 199–208
  about, 19–20
  action steps, 207
  business case development, 199–208
  communication barriers, 199, 201–206, 235
  durable goods company example, 232–237
  functional resistance, 199–201
  political resistance, 199–200
  sustained momentum challenges, 199, 206–207

# C

Capabilities and project plan
    development, 145–174
    about, 19
    action steps, 167
    automotive supplier example,
        155–160
    capabilities checklist, 168–174
    capability determination, 147, 226,
        229–231
    capital and expense constraints,
        160–163
    vs. competitor capability, 164–165
    consumer packaged goods (CPG),
        152–155
    durable goods company example,
        214–216
    multiyear plan, 145–146
    prioritization, 148–149, 160
    project plan changes, 166–167
    project plan development, 165–166
    recommended approach, 160
    retailer example, 149–151
    team assignments, 147, 218–219
Capital:
    cost focus and working capital, 84–87,
        222
    expense constraints, 160–163
Case studies and examples:
    auto manufacturers, 176–181
    automotive suppliers, 155–160
    competitive analysis, 100–104
    consumer packaged goods (CPG),
        30–31, 46, 152–155
    development case study, 20, 209–238
    durable goods manufacturer, 20,
        134–136, 209–238
    food manufacturer, 133–134
    order allocation capability case study,
        122–123
    retail companies, 149–151, 181–183
    technology survey, 122–123
Cherry-picking, avoiding, 163, 232
Collaboration:
    five pillar analysis, 55
    megatrends, 65–70, 87
Collins, Jim, 56
Communication, organizational buy-in,
    199, 201–206, 235

Company culture:
    assessment, 56–57
    supply chain strategy, 13–14
    technology survey, 112
Competitive analysis, 89–108
    about, 18, 89–90
    action steps, 107
    benchmark, 105–106
    case study, 100–104
    conduct a study, 96–100
    consultants for competitive
        intelligence, 95–96
    cross-docking, 93–94
    durable goods company example,
        221–223
    global issues, 106
    identify competitors, 90–91
    new capabilities and project plan,
        164–165
    process comparisons, 91–95
    public information (SEC Form 10-K),
        90, 96–97
    scenario planning, 103–104
    transportation, 94–95
    warehousing operations, 92–93
Competitor identification, competitive
    analysis, 90–91
Computing power, technology survey,
    115–116
Conduct a study, competitive analysis,
    96–100
Conduct interviews, internal supply
    chain assessment, 47–49, 60–63
Consultants for competitive intelligence,
    95–96
Consumer direct, 37
Consumer direct through retailer, 37
Consumer trends awareness, 33–35
Continual change process, 44–45
Control/share/transfer strategy, global
    risk management, 139, 142
Cost focus:
    business case development, 194–196,
        198
    cost-benefits analysis, 194–198, 233
    green initiatives, 82–83
    megatrends, 84–87, 222
CPFR (Collaborative Planning,
    Forecasting, and Replenishment),
    65, 66– 68

Cross-docking, competitive analysis,
    93–94
Cross-functional accountability, metrics,
    186
Cross-training, technology survey,
    121–122
Customer focus approach, 25–42
    about, 17, 26
    action steps, 41
    aging customers, 33
    benefits, 28–29
    consumer direct, 37
    consumer direct through retailer, 37
    consumer packaged goods (CDG)
        example, 30–31
    consumer trends awareness, 33–35
    customer needs assessment/
        reassessment, 31–33
    customer segmentation, 38–40
    durable goods company example,
        210–211
    emerging shopper marketing, 33,
        40–41
    enhanced customer-first approach,
        29–30
    future operating models needed, 36–38
    green sensitivity, 33, 35
    internal supply chain assessment, 59
    Internet shopping, 33
    shared supply chain model, 37
    social networking, 33–34
    supplier forward approach *vs.,* 25–28
    supply chain management, 35–36
    technology trends, 33–35
    time pressures, 33
Customer needs assessment/
    reassessment, 31–33, 219

**D**

Data gathering, internal supply chain
    assessment, 46
Demand:
    creation *vs.* fulfillment, 175–176
    risks of, global risk management,
        136–138
    supply and demand mismatch, 51
Development:
    of business case, 191–199
    of model, 2–4
    of new project plan, 145–174

Disruption impact, global risk
    management, 126–128
Documentation, technology survey,
    121–122
Durable goods manufacturer case study,
    20, 134–136, 209–238

**E**

E-business, technology survey, 111
Economic challenges, recession, 57–59
Economic value added (EVA), 2, 85, 193,
    235
Effectiveness, productivity, five pillar
    analysis, 55
Efficient perfect order metric, 187
Elderly customers, customer focus
    approach, 33
Emerging shopper marketing, 33, 40–41
Enhanced customer-first approach,
    29–30
EVA (economic value added), 2, 85,
    193, 235
Expense constraints, 160–163
External collaboration, 55, 67, 222
External factors, assessment:
    competitive analysis, 89–108, 221–223
    megatrends, 65–88

**F**

Failure mode and effects analysis
    (FMEA), 133–134, 223
Finance function:
    business case development, 192, 198
    capital and expense constraints,
        160–163
Five pillar analysis, 53–55
    effectiveness, productivity, 55
    external collaboration, 55, 222
    internal collaboration, 55, 67, 222
    internal supply chain assessment,
        53–55
    talent, 53–54
    technology, 54
FMEA (failure mode and effects analysis),
    133–134, 223
Forecasting:
    capabilities checklist, 171–172
    collaboration, 65–66
Form 10-K, SEC, 90, 96–97

Functional integration, organizational, 179–181
Functional resistance, organizational buy-in, 199–201
Future advances, technology, 113–118
Future operating models, 36–38

## G

Gaming metrics, 188–190
Global issues:
    competitive analysis, 106
    megatrends, 77–79, 87, 222
    network optimization, 76
    risk management, 125–144
    supply chain problems, 51–52
Global risk management, 125–144
    about, 19, 125–126, 142
    action steps, 143
    avoidance strategy, 139–141
    control/share/transfer strategy, 139, 142
    demand risks, 136–138
    disruption impact, 126–128
    durable goods company example, 223–225
    at durable goods manufacturer, 134–136
    FMEA approach, 133–134, 223
    at food manufacturer, 133–134
    hedging strategy, 139–140
    local considerations, 132
    operational risks, 136–138
    outsourcing trends, 129–131
    postponement strategy, 139
    risk consideration, 128–129
    risk identification and prioritization, 132–136, 225
    risk management strategies, 138–142
    risk mitigation plans, 225
    security risks, 137
    security strategy, 139, 141–142
    speculation strategy, 139–140
    supply risks, 136–137
Goal setting, metrics, 188
*Good to Great* (Collins), 56
Green sensitivities:
    customer focus approach, 33, 35
    as megatrend, 80–84, 87

## H

Hedging strategy, global risk management, 139–140
Hidden agenda, interview, 47–48
Human resource limitations, technology survey, 118–119

## I

Identify competitors, competitive analysis, 90–91
Implementing new technology, 112–113
Influence grid, communication, 201–202
Insourcing, globalization, 78–79
Internal collaboration, 55, 67, 222
Internal supply chain assessment, 43–64
    about, 17–18, 43–44
    action steps, 60
    common supply chain problems, 49–52
    company culture, 56–57
    compare results against best practices, 49–50
    conduct interviews, 47–49, 60–63, 216–218
    consumer packaged goods (CPG), 46
    continual change process, 44–45
    customer focus approach, 59
    customer needs assessment/ reassessment, 31–33, 219
    data gathering, 46
    durable goods company example, 216–221
    economic challenges, recession, 57–59
    five pillar analysis, 53–55
    internal environment assessment, 52–55
    scope, 46
    SWOT analysis, 52–53, 103, 220–221
Internet:
    shopping, 33
    speed, 115–116
Interviews:
    durable goods company example, 216–218
    guide and questions, 60–63
    hidden agenda, 47–48
    internal supply chain assessment, 47–49, 60–63

sample interview guide and questions, 60–63
two experienced interviewers needed, 49
wish list, 49
Inventory:
  management capabilities checklist, 169–170
  obsolete, 50

# K

Key performance indicators (KPIs), 185, 187–188

# L

Lean:
  capabilities checklist, 173–174
  megatrends, 70–72, 87, 222
  technology survey, 111
Local issues, global risk management, 132

# M

Managers and management (*see* Supply chain organization and people)
Manuj, Ila, 136, 139
Marketing function, business case development, 198–199
Materials requirements planning (MRP), 117–118
Megatrends, 65–88
  about, 18
  action steps, 88
  collaboration, 65–70, 87
  cost focus and working capital, 84–87, 222
  durable goods company example, 221–223
  global supply chain, 77–79, 87, 222
  green initiatives, 80–84, 87
  Lean and Six Sigma, 70–72, 87, 222
  list of, 87
  network optimization, 74–77, 87, 222
  product complexity management, 72–74, 87, 222
  sustainable supply chain, 80–84, 87, 222
Mentzer, Tom, 136, 139

Metrics, 184–190
  benchmarking, 188
  capabilities checklist, 172–173
  cross-functional accountability, 186
  efficient perfect order metric, 187
  gaming metrics, 188–190
  goal setting, 188
  key performance indicators (KPIs), 185, 187–188
  perfect order metric, 186
Momentum challenges, organizational buy-in, 199, 206–207
Moore's Law, 115–117
MRP (materials requirements planning), 117–118
Multiyear plan, project plan, 145–146

# N

Network optimization:
  capabilities checklist, 169
  megatrends, 74–77, 87, 222
New products, capabilities checklist, 171
*The New Supply Chain Agenda* (Dittmann), 2, 53, 65, 112, 184

# O

Operational risks, global management, 136–138
Opportunities, SWOT analysis, 53, 103
Optimization, technology survey, 116–117
Order allocation capability case study, 122–123
Order management, capabilities checklist, 171
Organization (*see* Supply chain organization)
Organizational buy-in, 199–208
  about, 19–20
  action steps, 207
  business case development, 199–208
  communication barriers, 199, 201–206, 235
  durable goods company example, 232–237
  functional resistance, 199–201
  political resistance, 199–200
  sustained momentum challenges, 199, 206–207

Outsourcing:
  global risk management, 129–131
  supply chain problems, 51–52

**P**

Packaging, 30–31, 84
People issues:
  network optimization, 74–77, 87, 222
  technical skills, 183–184
Physical network problems, 51
Political issues:
  business case development, 192–193
  IT, technology survey, 119–121
  organizational buy-in, 199–200
Ports, globalization, 78
Postponement strategy, global risk
  management, 139
Prioritization:
  project plan, 148–149, 160
  risk prioritization, global, 132–136,
    224
Processes:
  competitive analysis comparison,
    91–95
  technology survey, 111–112
Procurement, capabilities checklist,
  172
Product availability:
  business case development, 196–197
  durable goods company example,
    211–214
Product complexity management:
  capabilities checklist, 170
  as megatrend, 72–74, 87, 222
  supply chain problems, 50, 58
Product design problems, 51
Productivity, technology survey, 111
Project benefits:
  business case development, 194–196,
    198
  calculating, 194–198
Project plan:
  changes in, 166–167
  development, 165–166 (*See also*
    Business case development)
  (*See also* Capabilities and project plan
    development)
Public information, competitive analysis,
  90, 96–97

**Q**

Questions:
  interview question, 60–63
  in technology survey, 113

**R**

Radio-frequency identification (RFID),
  114–115
Recession as a challenge, 57–59
Replenishment, 65–66
Report documentation, technology
  survey, 121–122
Reporting relationships, supply chain
  organization, 177–178
RFID (radio-frequency identification),
  114–115
Risk identification and prioritization,
  global, 132–136, 224
  (*See also* Global risk management)
ROI (return on investment), 55, 135,
  160, 162, 193

**S**

Sales and operations planning (S&OP),
  67–69
Sales function, business case
  development, 198–199
Sample interview guide and questions,
  60–63
Scenario planning, competitive analysis,
  103–104
Scheduling systems, technology survey,
  117–118
Scope, internal supply chain assessment,
  46
Security, global risk management, 137,
  139, 141–142
Security and Exchange Commission
  (SEC) Form 10-K, 90, 96–97
Segmentation, customer focus approach,
  38–40
Shared supply chain model, 37
Six Sigma:
  capabilities checklist, 173–174
  megatrends, 70–72, 87, 222
  technology survey, 111
Skills, supply chain organization,
  183–184

SKU management:
  capabilities checklist, 170
  as megatrend, 72–74, 87, 222
  supply chain problems, 50, 58
Social networking, 33–34
Software, technology survey, 111
S&OP (sales and operations planning),
  67–69
Speculation strategy, global risk
  management, 139–140
Stockdale, Jim, 56
Strategy (*see* Supply chain strategy)
Strengths, SWOT analysis, 52–53
Supplier forward *vs.* customer focus
  approach, 25–28
Supply and demand mismatch, 51
Supply chain management, customer
  focus approach, 35–36
Supply chain organization and people,
  175–184
  action steps, 190
  auto manufacturer example, 176–181
  demand creation *vs.* demand
    fulfillment, 175–176
  design, capabilities checklist, 172–173
  functional integration, 179–181
  people and skills, 183–184
  reporting relationships, 177–178
  retail company example, 181–183
  technical skills, 183–184
Supply chain problems, 49–52
  global issues, 51–52
  inventory, obsolete, 50
  outsourcing, 51–52
  physical network problems, 51
  product complexity, 50, 58
  product design problems, 51
  supply and demand mismatch, 51
Supply chain strategy:
  about, 1–24
  approval to begin, 15
  benefits, 15
  business case development and buy-in,
    19–20, 191–208
  company culture, 13–14
  competitive analysis, 18, 89–108
  consultant pros and cons, 12–13
  customer focus approach, 17, 25–42
  durable goods case study, 20, 209–238

  elements of, 16–20
  global risk management, 19, 125–144
  internal supply chain assessment,
    17–18, 43–64
  megatrends, 18, 65–88
  misconceptions, 8–9
  model development, 2–4
  need for, 9–14
  new capabilities and project plan, 19,
    145–174
  organizational, persons and metrics,
    19, 175–190
  political concerns, 14
  process *vs.* organizational function, 7–8
  reasons for, 2
  reasons for company lack of, 10–14
  resources needed for planning, 10–12
  self-test, 20–22
  supply chain, defined, 5–8
  survey, 4–5, 22–23
  technology survey, 18, 109–124
Supply risks, global management,
  136–137
Surveys:
  supply chain strategy, 4–5, 22–23
  technology survey, 18, 109–124
Sustainability:
  customer focus approach, 33, 35
  as megatrend, 80–84, 87, 222
Sustained momentum challenges,
  organizational buy-in, 199, 206–207
SWOT analysis, 52–53, 103, 220–221

**T**

Talent, five pillar analysis, 53–54
Targeted communications, 202–204
Team assignments, project plan, 147,
  218–219
Technical skills, people, 183–184
Technology:
  five pillar analysis, 54
  Internet, 33, 115–116
  network optimization, 76–77
  social networking, 33–34
Technology survey, 109–124
  about, 18
  action steps, 123
  advanced planning and scheduling
    systems, 117–118

Technology survey (*Cont.*):
  computing power, 115–116
  culture, 112
  customer focus approach, 33–35
  documentation and cross-raining,
    121–122
  durable goods company example,
    225–229
  e-business technology, 111
  future advances, 113–118
  human resource limitations, 118–119
  implementing new technology,
    112–113
  Internet speed, 115–116
  Lean and Six Sigma, 111
  materials requirements planning
    (MRP), 117–118
  Moore's Law, 115–117
  optimization, 116–117
  order allocation capability case study,
    122–123
  political issues and IT, 119–121
  processes, 111–112
  questions to ask, 113
  RFID (radio-frequency identification),
    114–115
  role of technology, 109–112
  software, 111
  tools, 112
  visibility and productivity, 111
Threats, SWOT analysis, 53, 103
Time pressures, customer focus
    approach, 33
Tools, technology survey, 112
Transportation:
  capabilities checklist, 168
  competitive analysis, 94–95
  globalization, 78
Trends (*see* Megatrends)

**V**

Vendor management, capabilities
    checklist, 172
Visibility, technology survey, 111

**W**

Warehousing operations:
  capabilities checklist, 168–169
  competitive analysis, 92–93
Weaknesses, SWOT analysis, 53
Wish list in interview, 49
Working capital:
  improvement strategies, 85–86
  managing, 85
  megatrends, 84–87, 222
  steps to manage, 86–87

# About the Author

**J. Paul Dittmann** is Executive Director of the Global Supply Chain Institute at the University of Tennessee, where he teaches and is responsible for integrating all supply chain programs at the university. He is also responsible for the Supply Chain Forum. He consults extensively with many firms on a wide range of supply chain issues. Prior to this, he had a long industry career and served as Vice President of Logistics, Vice President of Global Logistics, and Vice President of Supply Chain Strategy for Whirlpool Corporation. He holds a PhD from the University of Missouri and is a member of their Industrial Engineering Hall of Fame. He is coauthor of the 2010 book *The New Supply Chain Agenda*.